Urban Parent Education
Dilemmas and Resolutions

Qualitative Studies on Schools and Schooling
John K. Smith, series editor

Urban Parent Education
Dilemmas and Resolutions

Louis M. Smith
Washington University

Wilma M. Wells
The Danforth Foundation
St. Louis Public Schools (1968-1993)

HAMPTON PRESS, INC.
CRESSKILL, NEW JERSEY

Printed in the United States of America

Library of Congress Cataloging-in-Publication Data

Smith, Louis M. (Louis Milde)
    Urban parent education : dilemmas and resolutions / Louis M.
Smith, Wilma Wells.
        p. cm.
    Includes bibliographic references and index.
    ISBN 1-57273-165-6. -- ISBN 1-57273-166-4 (pbk.)
    1. Child rearing--Study and teaching--United States.
2. Parenting--Study and teaching--United States. 3. Education,
Primary--Parent participation--United States. 4. Parents as
Teachers National Center (U.S.) I. Wells, Wilma. II. Title.
HQ769.S57155 1997
649'.1'071--dc21   97-14141
                                                            CIP

Hampton Press, Inc.
23 Broadway
Cresskill, NJ 07626

CONTENTS

SERIES PREFACE

This series of studies is designed to offer educators and other interested people the results of qualitative/interpretive inquiries on schools, schooling, and the education of children in general. There are two main considerations that frame the nature of the volumes in this series.

First, the unifying theme for the individual contributions in this series is not that they all address a specific subject matter, as is the case with many other series, but rather that they are qualitative studies that contextualize schools, schooling, and the education of children in broad societal perspectives. This series is founded on the proposition that educational events and processes are deeply shaped by social, cultural, and political factors. To seriously understand these events and processes requires that we study them in light of these broader factors.

Second, the series includes work by not only established scholars, but also by people in the early stages of their careers. In addition to the well-crafted and substantively interesting work being undertaken by more practiced researchers, a number of high quality studies, often using innovative approaches, are being produced by beginning researchers. This series is intended to provide a publication outlet for innovative work by people who have recently entered the field of educational inquiry.

ABOUT THE AUTHORS

Louis M. Smith is Emeritus Professor of Education and Washington University in St. Louis. He holds the Ph.D. degree in Psychology from the University of Minnesota. Over the course of his distinguished career he has authored numerous articles and a half dozen books. Among the latter are the well-known Complexities of an Urban Classroom (with W. Geoffrey) and Innovation and Change in Schooling. In addition to other activities, he is presently working on a biography of Nora Barlow.

Wilma M. Wells earned her doctorate in early childhood education and individual and family studies from Pennsylvania State University in 1987. Over the course of a 25-year career with the St. Louis Public Schools she has taught developmentally disabled adolescents, served as coordinator for the infant/parent center, and held the position of Director of Early Childhood Education for the district. She also is a nationally recognized consultant on early childhood education and family support issues. At present, she is associated with the Danforth Foundation.

ABOUT THE BOOK

This volume, the first in the series, is an interpretive/qualitative study of the Parents as Teachers (PAT) program in the St. Louis Public Schools. The PAT program is designed to provide parents with more effective child rearing practices. Primarily through visits by trained parent educators, parents are given information on patterns of child development up to age three, on how to encourage language and thinking abilities in their children, on how to foster the social development of their children, and so on. The program is based on the idea that the first years in the lives of children are the crucial ones for their intellectual, social, and emotional development.

In the late 1980s, it was clear to many people involved with the program that a study had to be undertaken of PAT adaptation for disadvantaged urban families—families that are difficult to reach and then to maintain in the program. During his initial discussions with the PAT staff in St. Louis, he realized that Wells was a significant figure in the project. He raised the possibility that she become a co-investigator of the project. She eventually accepted and, as such, the study is much enriched because of this important "outsider-insider" combination.

With this agreement to collaborate, Smith and Wells began their ethnographic journey through urban St. Louis with a focus on how the

PAT program operates with those parents who are difficult to contact, difficult to enroll in the program, and then difficult to maintain in the program. They later added another, most disturbing, category of parents to the list—those who are difficult to help. These are parents who are the most problematic for the PAT staff because, in short, they often do not want to be parents.

From beginning to end of this text, Smith and Wells vividly portray for us not only how important it is to reach and assist these parents, but also how very much of a struggle it can be for those who attempt to educate parents in order that they may better education their children. Smith and Wells supply important insights on the problems facing programs such as PAT. These insights are important not only for practitioners, from school administrators to teachers, but also for all of us who are vitally concerned with the future of American society and the role of education and human services in our society. It is only through insightful, well-crafted qualitative studies like this one that we can come to better understand how we must deal with poverty and the problems it presents to all of us.

John K. Smith
University of Northern Iowa
Series Editor

Lous Heshusius
York University
Associate Series Editor

Thomas Schwandt
Indiana University
Associate Series Editor

section
one

*An Introductory Overview**

By intent, this section provides readers with a quick introduction to several key issues and ideas, the topography of the program, and the research project. The first of these might be called the philosophy and goals, or the formal or official doctrine, of the overall Parents as Teachers (PAT) program. This refers to the representation of the program in the documents and presentations from the PAT National Center. Mostly, we draw briefly on material presented in the revised *Program Planning and Implementation Guide* (PAT National Center, 1989). This is a perspective important for readers who eventually will be taken into the special world of the parent educator working with the hard to reach, maintain, and help urban family.

Vivid images of episodes in the lives of parent educators working with difficult urban families is the second key idea presented. We have a strong commitment to giving the reader scenes of "people in action." We build these views from our intensive and detailed interviews, field notes of observations, and interpretive memos. Practical thinking improves with the use of concrete images as well as general abstractions.

A third major idea is reflected in a "finding," the heterogeneity of urban communities and families. The city of St. Louis, and we would

---

*Although a few parent educators are male, almost 100% are female. We use the female pronoun throughout.

1

argue most if not all cities in recent decades, has been stereotyped by many citizens. Probing conscious and unconscious assumptions is a major part of our agenda. We depict neighborhoods in which parent educators work. Furthermore we delve into the varieties and complexities of nuclear and extended families, the clients of the parent educators. In a very preliminary fashion, our descriptions flow into interpretations, which, in turn, flow into recommendations for working with such diverse communities and families.

But mostly we hope readers, regardless of their major occupational or reference group (from legislators to administrators to parent educators to citizens), will have images, grist for their later thinking and acting, about the PAT program, in an urban community with families living in difficult circumstances.

chapter
one

The Typography of the Parents as Teachers Program

PROLOGUE

Final report of a research project and *manual* for practitioners of an educational program, and now *book* in an educational ethnography series are words that seldom come together in close juxtaposition. But that merging of ideas defines precisely our hope for this chapter. We worked in and studied carefully for several years, the Parents as Teachers (PAT) program in the St. Louis Public Schools.

Program

PAT is an educational program for families with young children. The fundamental goal is the facilitation of the child's growth and development through helping parents with their childrearing. The intended format is relatively simple. Essentially, a parent educator meets once a month with parents to discuss issues in child development and problems parents perceive in raising their children. Topics range across intellectual, motor, social, and emotional development for infants and toddlers in the first 3 years of their life. "Stages of development" is an important aspect of the content. These meetings typically occur in the family's home, hence the name, *home visits*. Guidelines and lesson plans for the

3

content procedures of the meetings have been collated into a "program planning and implementation guide" developed by the PAT National Center. Individualization of content and instruction is encouraged.

Additionally, group meetings of parents are held once a month to present further information of interest regarding child development and parental practices and to provide a forum where parents can meet each other and engage in informal discussion. These meetings are led by parent educators, supervisors, or visiting experts from the local community. Typically, they occur in PAT centers in the local school or local community center settings.

The third strand of the program is an annual screening, an assessment of the child's development, which provides a further basis for planning and action.

The program is open to all parents with young children in the community. It is not a "targeted program" aimed at a specific subpopulation. Administratively it operates through the local public school system. In Missouri, the funding is from the Missouri Department of Elementary and Secondary Education (DESE), a division of the state government, to the local school district. As with many innovative educational programs, the implementation often involves variations depending on the nature of the local school situation. *Mutual adaptation* is a label often given to this kind of shifting of goals and procedures. As our story and analysis unfolds, we find that this is an important idea regarding events in the program.

Our Research Project

Our research procedures were essentially those that carry the labels of *qualitative field methods, action research, school ethnography*, or *educational case study*.

We focused most directly on a group of families that we labeled initially, *difficult to reach and maintain* in the PAT program. Such a focus means that our findings are not representative of the entire St. Louis program, nor, obviously, of the PAT program in the state of Missouri. *Difficult* families, by definition, suggest problems, more problems than one would expect in a random sample of families. We, and our sponsors as well, assumed that such families exist in every community and public school system, and that they are problematic for educational programs like PAT, and that close study would yield interesting and important information and ideas for improving the program and extending it to other communities.

Our "story and interpretation" of this part of the PAT program contains a series of "suggestions" or "recommendations" for individuals in other communities who might want to adopt or adapt a program like the one in St. Louis. By intention, our audiences are practitioners and scholars of several kinds. First, but not exclusively, are urban school administrators who are thinking of installing a PAT program in their schools. We hope they will see the "realities" of a program in action, one that has been functioning for about 4 years. Second, we have suggestions for an audience of parent educators, the individuals who will be working directly with service to parents and children. For those who have never worked in an urban community we hope they will see the possibilities, the excitement, and the frustrations in such a position. Furthermore, for those who have been a part of an urban community, we believe they too could read with benefit our account of other urban parent educators. Third, we believe that we have created materials that will be of use to educators at the PAT National Center and elsewhere who train parent educators. We have episodes and events that will be provocative for discussions that have a flavor of "How would you handle this situation if you had this kind of client?" Principles-in-contexts and principles-in-action might be another way of saying what our intent is.

Less focused, but still on our minds are audiences of citizens, of professionals interested in the world of early childhood education, and of legislators, both state and national. Increasingly in the mid-1990s debates have been rekindled regarding the nature of U.S. society and the place of education and human services within the society. Poverty, families of many forms, and children are part of those discussions, debates, and national and state legislation. All of this is what we mean when we say that we have what we think is a "research report" and a "manual," a document that might supplement the National Center's *Program Planning and Implementation Guide* for the Missouri PAT program. Moving our account to a "book" broadens the relevance to scholars, teachers in university education and child development programs, and social policymakers.

Thesis

"Dilemmas and Resolutions" in the title of this volume is a shortened version of an earlier title, "issues, dilemmas, strategies, and resolutions," from the earlier research report. For us, these represent carefully chosen labels. Although we do not want to raise a large discussion in this prologue, we do want to accent for our more theoretically oriented audience the idea that concepts like these place us within a "normatively oriented kind of educational and social symbolic interactionist theory." More concretely, over the last several years we pursued the situations that the men and women, and mostly they were women, in the program found themselves. We were concerned with their perceptions of those situations, the beliefs they began with and those they modified, the real and frequently conflicting dilemmas they saw, the varied options they perceived, the choices they made, the actions they took and the reflections they then made. We feel that our views are grounded in real people going about, doing, and partaking in the many day-to-day aspects of the program. And we believe that this is an important level of observation, thought, and experience. Furthermore, in our view, this kind of social interaction of the individuals in the program provides the substance from which larger educational and organizational structures and processes arise. Still further, such concrete data also provide the kind of reality that makes lists of simple "dos" and "don'ts" open to question. Our position in knowing the immediate social context suggests a phrase that runs through our teaching and administering, "It depends on . . . " Along the way we raise a number of items to clarify the particulars of what the "It depends on . . ." depends on. In summary, we believe we have a practical manual that surmounts the too easy recommendation, although our last chapter does attempt to be quite specific regarding a number of important recommendations.

We are not so naive that we do not appreciate the problems of criteria and values that underlie concepts of *success* and *recommendations*. Statements of these kinds clearly go beyond any traditional concept of science, social or natural, as well as beyond most "descriptive and analytical" qualitative field studies, which have much in common with ours. We hope we present enough data for readers to see their own situations and their own values in conjunction with the situations and values of the PAT program. Some of our own perspectives and values appear as well. We perceive ourselves to be social idealists, but as we have joked between ourselves, neither "missionaries" nor "true believers." In this context, readers can judge whether the program and the "successful resolutions" of the dilemmas fit their situations and meet some of the educational needs of the citizens in their communities. Continuing such dialogue among educators remains a high value of ours.

Each of us as coresearchers and authors, one external and one internal to the PAT program, remains positive about the program in action in St. Louis and the possibilities of adaptation and adoption in other communities.

Teaching from Our Book

In format, style, and content we believe we have a special kind of book. Furthermore, we believe that its use as a teaching document or text takes on some special characteristics as well. Although every teacher will make his or her own decisions, we have our own preferred set of theory and practices. And that is the nature of the argument we present here.

Most fundamentally, we believe that being a parent educator is an instance of being a reflective practitioner, that is, no technical rules exist that can be applied in a rote or routine fashion to the problems of working with parents in a program such as "parents as teachers." One is faced with problematic situations, dilemmas on top of dilemmas. To paraphrase Schon (1983) ambiguity, complexity, instability, value conflicts, and uncertainty vie with one another in unique and unending combinations. One must think one's way through practical situations. Choices of "what to do" appear constantly. And one uses one's best judgment. As actions are taken one must reassess the situation and go through ("iterate" is the big word for the activity) the process again and again.

As two individuals who have worked in and studied the PAT program, we have questioned continually, how we can best help individuals work and educate in the special setting of an urban community. Our essential response has been to select particular events of people working and talking together, build them into detailed but interesting stories and vignettes, and present them to the reader. These stories enable you to think about the situation and the people and to begin to ask: "What would I do in that situation with that problem?" "How would I go about my business in my school district and community that is similar and different in this or that regard?" We hope that we will have started you thinking about yourself, your families, and the program possibilities. Furthermore, and usually, the stories contain a moral, concept, or idea that we believe is important and that we offer to you as reader for your perusal and thinking. These ideas are patterned into larger themes that hold chapters and sections together. These syntheses present further curriculum and teaching possibilities. In this way, with our book, we want to move along the conversation between you as reader and practitioner and us as practitioners, observers, and authors.

In an important sense, we have an educational perspective—curriculum, teaching, and learning with a special group of students in a special organizational context usually called a school. We believe that this is an important perspective and that it pervades everything we have to say and how we would hope our textual materials might be perceived and used.

AN HISTORICAL PERSPECTIVE

Even in a sketch, history can be written from a number of perspectives. In our view, the most provocative approach for the kind of research report, manual, and now book we want to produce is through a combination of ideas, people, and events. A chronology or timeline gives a processual view of what has happened. We believe this is important for citizens and school administrators who might want to implement a similar program for "difficult to reach, maintain, and help families" in their communities and schools.

By ideas, we mean the interrelated set of beliefs about children's development, parenting, and helping parents become better at the task of being parents. Ideas become codified into conventional wisdom, philosophy, formal doctrine, and ideology as they are presented in authoritative manuals such as the *Program Planning and Implementation Guide* and as they are taught in workshops and other training programs (Selznick, 1949/1966; Smith & Keith, 1971). Part of our task has been to see the ideas as they are implemented and put into practice in one urban community with a focus on what we initially have called *difficult families*. As one might expect, this has been a fascinating and exciting charge.

By *people* we have reference to three individuals in particular. Burton White of Harvard University did the groundbreaking research and development in Brookline, Massachusetts and provided the initial model for what has become the Missouri PAT Program. Early on, White trained and worked with the Missouri personnel. Along the way, sharp differences in point of view arose over the nature and rapidity of development of the program. Now he is quite critical of aspects of the Missouri program. Mildred Winter, originally of the Ferguson-Florissant School District in suburban St. Louis began, with a small group of colleagues, a series of early childhood educational innovations in her district. Later as a Missouri DESE administrator, she studied the Brookline program and began to adapt it to the Missouri context. With four school districts, her original one and three additional districts across the state, she initiated a Parents as First Teachers pilot project (Pfannensteil & Seltzer, 1985). This educational effort, with its attendant outside evaluation, became a crucial turning point in early education in Missouri. The third individual important for our story is Audrey Gooch of the St. Louis Public Schools. She initiated several programs in early childhood for the city schools. She also was influential in the beginnings of Headstart in the St. Louis community. One of the city school programs, The Parent/Early Infant Center was a replication of the PAT program and funded through a court ordered desegregation program. When the Missouri Early Childhood Development Act (ECDA) was passed with funding included for a statewide implementation program, the city public schools incorporated the PAT program into the already established Parent/Early Infant Centers. Mrs. Gooch continued as the key administrator.

In their own ways, each of these individuals has been a major educational figure, worthy of far more intensive biographies than we are able to present here. The important recommendation for those instituting a PAT program in urban schools elsewhere is intellectually simple, story find and nurture able, proactive, and yes, charismatic, incumbents for key leadership positions. Doing the finding and nurturing is another, and not so simple, story.

Key events refers to items in the chronology we have already begun to present—Harvard University's Brookline experience, the Brookline Early Education Program (BEEP), the PAT pilot project, the complex political process in the extension of the project into a statewide program, and the flow of children and administrators (such as Mrs. Gooch) from community-instituted Headstart projects and preschools into the city public school programs, one of which is the PAT program in St. Louis. The events can be painted with both broad and narrow brush-strokes. Once again, detail must be compromised with the restricted length of our report. We tend to err on the side of microanalysis and overdetailed reporting, for we believe that the specific actions of individuals is one major place to anchor recommendations for improvements.

We believe that an appeal to this kind of history is necessary for anyone's understanding the PAT program and is consonant with the kind of deliberation and practical reasoning that underlies our efforts in this report.

THE NATIONAL STORY

The national story is really two stories, or a story with two major episodes. First it is the Burton White story of an idea, the idea's development and transformation into a workable practical program, and its extension across the country. Part of that extension involved the coming of the idea and the program to Missouri. Early on, White was a major consultant with the Missouri program, "a comparatively rare example of a full-fledged service of that sort" (White, 1985, p. 12), an adoption and adaptation of his ideas.

The second part of the national story occurred over several years. The first of the extended trial in four districts in the state of Missouri, with both national foundation and state funds, the extension to all school districts in the state, and finally the creation of the PAT National Center, with a National Advisory Board, with continuing sup-

port from several national foundations, and with national training, evaluation, and dissemination efforts.

In this section we concentrate on the set of beliefs originated by
White and published in several places, but most extensively in his book,
The First Three Years of Life (White, 1985). He recounted some 30 years of
research, development, teaching, and consulting regarding child development and parent education. For our purposes, just a comment or two
seem essential. First White believes that "not more than one child in ten
gets off to as good a start as he could" (p. v). He follows that with another two sentences: "This book will also concentrate on the normal, near
normal, and well developing child. It will have little to say about seriously handicapped or underdeveloped children" (p. vi). Taken together,
those two quotes raise potentially serious questions about the available
knowledge base for the specially targeted families in our study, the difficult to reach and maintain. It is just this lack of knowledge within the
PAT program that gave rise to the present research effort.

White dealt primarily with two-parent families. He argued
strongly that mothers should be home with their children during the
first 3 years of life. Our hard to reach and maintain families are often
headed by single parents, many of whom work and many of whom live
in extended families with their own siblings and mothers. The "realities"
of our situation contrast with his "ideal" situation.

White also argued the importance of beginning with the first-
time parent when the mother is in the third trimester of her pregnancy.
The current Missouri program is much broader than this and takes any
family with a child less than 3 years of age. Some of the families have
older children, who may be 5 or 10 years old, siblings of the child in the
program. One of the best recruiting techniques is enrolling infants of
parents with a child already in the program. We believe these are fundamental and important differences in clients and in clients' childrearing
needs in our study and White's early work.

Much of our report becomes an extended description and analysis of these differences and how parent educators cope with these differences. Many of our recommendations flow from some of these differences. We believe this makes an important argument for continuing historical research on the origins and transformation of PAT, and other programs as well (e.g., those reviewed in *Fair Start for Children*, Larner,
Halpern, & Harkavey, 1992).

One of the most powerful aspects of White's perspective, as it
impinges on our special group of parents and children, is that it is an
educational point of view. The accent is on teaching and learning, on
what it is that parent educators can do with parents to help them learn,
and then what the parents can do as the child's first teacher to help their

children learn. We see that perspective tapping and focusing the social idealism found in most public school educators, and also appealing to the kind of practical realism of most teachers in dealing with the concrete and particular actions and interactions in day-to-day working, "doing," with parents and children. The here and now of parents, children, and their immediate situations is irrevocably present. Many psychologists, sociologists, and other academics often do not speak at that level of discourse.

Finally, we note the wide applicability of the general child development goals White holds for us as parent educators. The rough rubrics of physical and sensory development, the complex of perceptual, linguistic, and cognitive abilities, and the personal and social competencies are useful and helpful categories of objectives, congruent with those held by most teachers and parents. Expectations of parents for their children can be clarified. Much less discussion occurs about conflicts in priorities among these well-accepted developmental goals. Many parents and parent educators we observed and talked to often phrased their needs around specific difficulties and big problems faced by the child. Suggestions become less clear-cut under those circumstances. Another kind of thinking seems necessary, more of a kind of deliberation. Some of these issues were discussed elsewhere (Smith & Klass, 1989).

All this is to say that the Missouri program is hugely indebted to White and his continuing efforts. His ideas form a major starting point in our thinking about difficult to reach and maintain families, but as we continuously emphasize, it remains a starting point. Although the focus of the Missouri program remains educational, over the years since 1985, the philosophical and empirical base of the program has broadened to include the work of researchers such as Brazelton (1981), with his emphasis on affective development, and Zigler (1987–1991), with his concern for the development of children from economically disadvantaged families. Thus the PAT curriculum has already begun to build on White's intellectual efforts in ways useful in making the program directly applicable to more diverse family structures. We hope our study continues to build on their combined efforts for those working in other urban communities.

PAT IN MISSOURI

PAT in Missouri is the tale of an individual, Mildred Winter. And she is a complex story of energy, creativity, missionary zeal, and educational and political charisma. Although this may seem adulatory, the important point (a recommendation if you like) for other states and other school administrators is the need to find unusual individuals to lead the initial local and statewide efforts in the establishment of the program. As a consequence of Winter's efforts, "Missouri is in the vanguard with its policy initiative for families with young children. In 1984, it became the first state in the nation to mandate parent education and family support services, beginning at the child's birth, in every school district" (Parents as Teachers, 1989, p. 1). The roots run deeper than Winter with a number of state bodies meeting and conferring regarding policies of early childhood education. But she and the Ferguson-Florissant school district, where she taught, have a history of innovative programs.

In 1981, Winter's earlier experience, the ideas and the help of White, multiple sources of funding (the Department of Education, the Danforth Foundation) and four local Missouri school districts (Farmington, Ferguson-Florissant, Francis Howell, and Independence) who had won the bidding competition with their proposals joined together to carry out the state pilot project. The independent evaluation by Research and Training Associates (Pfannensteil & Seltzer, 1985) indicated that the children of the families involved showed significant developmental gains over children not participating in the program.

In 1983 and 1984, the governor, the heads of relevant state agencies, and the legislature developed, wrote, and passed the ECDA, which mandated services for children from every school district in the state. Since then the program has been expanded to allow 30% of eligible families to be supported by state funds. Some districts, with local funds, have expanded the services to include more families. It should be noted that the PAT program, as legislated in the ECDA, differed in two substantial ways from the original New Parents as Teachers pilot study. First, as mentioned previously, the new program was not limited to first time parents, but was open to any family with a child less than 3 years of age. Second, although school districts were encouraged to provide families with monthly home visits and monthly group meetings, a total possibility of 20 contacts per program year, under ECDA full reimbursable program services were defined as a prescribed combination of personal visits and/or group meetings to equal a total of 5 contacts (3 of which must be personal visits) per program year. In our view, these are major changes in general, and changes with particular importance for the difficult to reach and maintain families.

The *Program Planning and Implementation Guide* (1985/ 1989/1993), written and produced by the PAT National Center in conjunction with the University of Missouri/St. Louis and the Missouri DESE is a 500 page document. In the first two chapters it contains a brief history of the program and a model for implementation in communities across the state and "eight steps to successful program implementation."

The two longest chapters are those giving detailed "Personal Visit Lesson Plans" and "Your Child Materials." The former organizes ideas chronologically to fit developmental stages of the child, and, within that, lessons related to physical, linguistic, intellectual, and social growth. The lessons have a "textbook/recitational" flavor with statements of objectives, handouts and reference material, and activities. The "Your Child Materials" chapter presents a wealth of back-up material and reading for the parent and parent educator to help with the content of the personal visits.

A short chapter exists on "Group Meetings" and another on "Other Resources for Parent Educators." The discussion and the models have a "Madeline Hunter" quality, that is, they have a deductive, recitational lesson format, rather than, for instance, an open-ended Brunerian inductive lesson quality. The final chapters include "Resources for Developmental Screening," "Recordkeeping Forms," and "Evaluation Forms." An index completes the guide.

Our current research flows from several general considerations raised in the guide:

> Statewide expansion has challenged the program to demonstrate its effectiveness in the inner cities, with the rural poor, with adolescent parents and other special populations. The Missouri experience has shown that need for support and assistance in the parenting role crosses all socio-economic and educational levels. High-risk families are attracted into a non-targeted program because it does not imply inadequacy on their part or view them as bad parents. Their special needs are met through intensified service. (Parents as Teachers, 1989, p. 5)

Our research might be seen as an effort to look carefully at one piece of that "Missouri experience" and see what seems to be working well, what problems exist, what innovative resolutions are available, and what might be of help to other urban school districts across the country. Explicitly the guide notes: "An 18-month case study of PAT adaptations for the disadvantaged urban families in St. Louis was initiated in January, 1988. It is anticipated that this report, scheduled for September 1989, will provide valuable information on program operations in the inner city" (p. 6). In effect, our project is a very small piece of research on a specific problem, difficult to reach, maintain, and help urban families nested within a large ongoing public school program. Phrased alternatively, our research is a study of "an adaptation of an adaptation." We construe our effort as a kind of action research (Elliott, 1978, 1991) with an involved and detached, inside and outside, perspective. As conceptions of program evaluation broaden, for example, "illuminative evaluation" (Hamilton, Jenkins, King, MacDonald, & Parlett, 1977), to include studies other than pre-and posttest control group experiments, our efforts can be phrased as part of program evaluation.

EARLY CHILDHOOD PROGRAMS IN ST. LOUIS

In perhaps less dramatic fashion than White's initial research and development efforts in New England and Winter's presence at the state level, the St. Louis early childhood programs reflect the important and continuing presence of Audrey Gooch. Now retired, at the time of the project research she was director of several early childhood programs, of which PAT is one. Kindergartens as part of the public school programs began in St. Louis more than 100 years ago with the work of Susan Blow. Tax-supported educational extensions to the earlier preschool years, even though community-centered rather than school-centered, awaited the arrival of Headstart in the 1960s. Gooch moved from classroom teaching and administration in the city public schools to the initiation and administration of those community-based programs in St. Louis. Along the way, she was involved with Title I programs, the Right to Read program, Family Support Services, and the St. Louis Reading Clinic programs and Early Childhood Education. Through all this she was continuously and equally concerned for breaking cycles of poverty and racial discrimination through increased opportunities for young children and parents.

Before the state passed the ECDA and instituted the statewide plan, Gooch had taken the White PAT training and had begun an early childhood parent education program. In addition, she helped write an early proposal for the PAT pilot project for the St. Louis Public Schools, which languished because of lack of local resources and funding and lack of faith in its importance. When the state funding became available, the St. Louis program was folded eventually into the overall PAT program. In the future, according to Gooch, lurked possibilities such as the Even Start program and daycare centers in the high schools, as well as homebased day care for infants and toddlers. Much of this has now come to pass. As Gooch commented in an interview: "The key again there is education. Getting those parents educated and helping them to have better parenting skills, so that they'll be aware of their education and the child's education and together they'll keep growing."

The PAT program in the city of St. Louis has several important facets. Gooch, as the key administrator of the program during the duration of our project, is located both physically and organizationally within the division of state and federal programs. This is important for several reasons. Although most of the funds for PAT come through ECDA, not all of the funds do. In St. Louis, all of the fulltime salaries are funded through the court-ordered desegregation program. That is a major financial contribution, and links PAT with another important St. Louis program. And it is not just the desegregation program's financial contribution to the PAT program that is significant. Equally important, the district operates 30 preschool centers/academies, some of which are funded through the desegregation program. As is developed later, one of the parental incentives for the PAT program is that a percentage of places in the preschool program are reserved for PAT families. Waiting lists for those preschool positions are in the hundreds as needs far outrun resources. This is no small item to parents in general, and especially not so for parents whose resources are too limited to afford private day care or preschool. Although this relationship of PAT and desegregation programs is particular to St. Louis, each urban community will have its own idiosyncratic but important context for a PAT program. Knowing the local "lay of the land" and being able to see this context as possibilities and opportunities seems important at all levels of program implementation. A liability exists however, as the other programs change (e.g., financial cutbacks or elimination) the consequences will ripple through one's early childhood program. Risktaking stories run through our observations and interviews of the program in action. "Winning some and losing some" is a part of this world's reality.

Two committees help with the implementation of the PAT program. The Internal Coordinating Committee and the Community Advisory Committee are described in one district memo: "The two committees function with two way communication. Coordination of resources and surveying the urban community continues as an ongoing operation."

The realities of difficult service dilemmas and choices occur in the following statement from a district document:

> According to the census of 1980, there were 12,816 children ages one and two in the St. Louis City School District. The Missouri Department of Elementary and Secondary Education has indicated that 15% [now 40%] of this age group can be served for purposes of reimbursement. Priority was given to those children between the ages of one and two and a half in order that there be enough time to provide screening and eight opportunities to the family for parent education before the child's third birthday.

This context is probably not much different from what other communities might expect, although accented and exacerbated in the urban areas. We note only that it is a far cry from White's early "teachable moment" and the conditions surrounding the early pilot project. These policy decisions influenced the program as presented—and as observed by us.

With a little hesitancy and speculation, we raise several longer term issues about which no experience or data exist with the St. Louis program as yet. With the intertwining of PAT and desegregation programs a question arises of the later choices of parents regarding the education of their children. Do more of the "difficult to reach and maintain families" elect to send their children to county schools as part of the desegregation program or do more elect to send their children to the local public schools, or is PAT irrelevant to this? If the children attend one place or the other, is there differential success within the programs and with children without the PAT service? And how will these events be influenced by the plans for Magnet Preschools operating as "campuses" of early childhood education, with children age 3 through second grade, in conjunction with a department of education from a local university? Continuing questions such as these arise in regard to PAT, the metropolitan desegregation program, and the role of the courts in preschool, elementary, and secondary education in metropolitan St. Louis. We find this fertile ground for inquiry and action in the improvement of urban schooling and the enhancing of children's development, and especially the development of children from difficult families. Our long-term research and evaluation perspective and agenda, the bringing of intelligence and empirical data to program decisions, runs through our analysis and recommendations.

Part of our concern here lies in the relationship of administrative risk taking, the continuing evolution and change of the context of the PAT program, and the importance of these changes on the day-to-day life of a particular parent educator working with a particular family. Among these families are those that are difficult to reach, maintain, and help. For instance, during the year of our study, the four St. Louis PAT centers were reconstituted into eight centers, in anticipation of the expansion of the program. The four new centers were located within the high schools, in contrast to the earlier ones being in the elementary schools. However, later decisions within the larger desegregation program indicated that this expansion was not going to happen. The eight were folded back into the original four. The physical locations of the four centers changed to the locations of three of the new centers and the fourth went to a totally different location. Changing school populations and numbers of pupils and class sizes were a part of this. Now that the centers are in the high schools, the chances for increased stress and priority with teenage mothers is an easier possibility. This kind of "evolution" or perhaps "instability" ripples throughout the organizational structure of PAT and then eventually into the program of services. Such changes are part of the urban scene and the difficult to reach and maintain sample of families. Working creatively within such a context is exciting, difficult, and sometimes stressful.

Although this is a St. Louis "example," and one arising during the years we studied the program, we believe each city, and each year, will have its own kind of legislative and judicial context for its districtwide organization and program of educational services. When we speak of the realities of program implementation we find this to be a not atypical kind of illustration. The developers and implementors of a PAT program in other communities must build such concerns into their resources, planning, and activities. Continuing research and evaluation into these events, and similar ones elsewhere, and the consequences of such events on staff, parents, and children seems both difficult and necessary if programs are to continue to be relevant, improved, and successful. The mixture of courts, state legislatures and departments of education, and innovative and risk-taking administrators is not atypical of our experience in evolution and development of other urban school programs. One might conclude that opportunities and headaches are everywhere.

THE SMITH–WELLS INQUIRY PROJECT:
A GLANCE AT METHODS AND PROCEDURES

The story of our research has an idiosyncratic flavor, and one worth telling in brief for the effects ripple throughout the substantive report itself. Here, we report mostly on the early informal negotiations that had several critical elements.

Winter and the advisory board of the PAT National Center recognized the need for more information about the nature of the program with urban families. The DESE, part of the state of Missouri's formal educational organization, was also interested in such information. The Smith–Richardson Foundation agreed in principle to support the effort. Gooch, then director of the city program, supported the idea from the beginning. Among the coordinators, Wilma Wells was one of the strongest voices for such an effort. The initial phrasing of the problem focused on "difficult to reach families."

About this time, in Smith's recounting, The Department of Education and the chair, Alan Tom, at Washington University became a part of the discussions that included a larger role of possibly housing the PAT program and developing a much larger research and training effort, all at the university. Eventually, these discussions led to the possibilities of Smith's involvement as principal investigator of a smaller effort. In the course of those discussions, he met with the PAT staff of the St. Louis Public Schools. Their concerns and his initial phrasing of what might be done resulted in a vigorous discussion, in the course of which the problem received its first reconstrual. "Difficult to reach families" became "difficult to reach and maintain families" in the program. The most vigorous and outspoken member of the city group was Wells. Beyond a raised eyebrow, Smith's question to himself was "Who is this person who is so articulate, analytical, and sensible?"

Out of these discussions, a proposal was drafted, reviewed, and critiqued, and redrafted in a form acceptable to all parties and eventually to the Smith–Richardson Foundation. At no time in these discussions did Smith meet with members of the Missouri DESE. That part of the negotiation was handled by the staff of the PAT National Center. In retrospect, that was a mistake on Smith's part. The state was a bigger "player," then and continuously, than he had realized at the time, and later, as he would come to find out at the end of the project (Smith,in press).

In the early weeks of the project, Smith perceived Wells as a significant figure in the St. Louis PAT program. Also, he continued to find that she was both stimulating and thoughtful on the one hand and, on the other hand, an individual he thought he could work with. In his view, the research would benefit if she became a formal collaborator in the project. So he raised the possibilities with her. No immediate decision was needed, for in his view she had a number of things to consider—most importantly of which was the fact that she would remain in the St. Louis program after the research project and after Smith had gone back to the university. After several months of consideration Wells elected to join in as co-investigator. From Smith's perspective this had major consequences for the carrying out of the project and the kind of data—principally long interviews that turned into important analytical discussions—that ultimately figured strongly in the form and substance of the final report. And now the relationship continues into the revision of the final report into this book.

Wells, from her earlier insider's perspective, phrased the evolving project and research relationships this way.

Following the rapid state-wide expansion of how the Parents as Teachers program, frequently asked questions focused on how the project was doing in reaching non middle class families. Mildred Winter approached Wells about documenting successful recruitment and retention strategies employed in the St. Louis City Program.

After discussion with the St. Louis PAT staff—other coordinators, parent educators, and her immediate supervisors—Wells drafted a proposal to document effective strategies using a mix of qualitative and quantitative methods. The agreed upon final product of this effort was to be a manual which could be shared with others. Upon reviewing the proposal, staff of the Smith–Richardson Foundation suggested that the study be conducted by an outside evaluator.

Wells backed out, not without some small relief, since concerns about balancing the demands of the research project with her day to day responsibilities had lurked somewhere below the surface as she prepared the proposal. Mildred Winter began the search for an outside evaluator.

It was against this background that Wells approached the initial meeting between Smith and the St. Louis PAT staff. Smith's presentation was low key and informal as he discussed his interest in the project, shared his ethnographic research methods, and clarified the specific focus of the study. From Wells' perspective two significant reconstruals emerged from this discussion. As Smith has observed, "difficult to reach" families became "difficult to reach and maintain" families. Of equal importance, the goal of "developing a manual" became "capturing the program in action." This shift in focus had ramifications for the entire project. At the conclusion of the discussion, everyone agreed that Smith should develop a full proposal.

During the first weeks of the project, Smith quickly became a fixture in the St. Louis program. This was due in part to his low-key, easy going demeanor, and his sincere interest in and respect for the staff and parents. He pitched in to help with childcare during group meetings and seemed to genuinely enjoy himself.

Smith's proposal for a formal collaboration was appealing but presented several dilemmas for Wells, not the least of which were possible changes in her relationship with him (which had quickly evolved into a collegial, mutually respectful, intellectually stimulating one) and her co-workers. The other big set of issues related to life in the District after the final report. After several months of discussions with her supervisors and other co-workers, Wells decided to join Smith as co-investigator. The relationship thrived, has continued over nearly a decade, and now is focused on revisions of the final report into a book.

Our views accent different items, yet reflect a significant common perception of the project and its possibilities. The potency of the "inside–outside" relationship seemed latent from the very beginning of the effort. That kind of relationship we feel is one that merits extension and application to a wide range of educational problems (Smith & Geoffrey, 1968).

THE LONGER AND WIDER REACH OF PARENT EDUCATION

What is usually called a *literature review* in a research project is broken apart and scattered throughout this volume. In qualitative inquiry, at least as we practice it, we find ourselves wanting only a broad initial view of the topography of the area. Our intent is to observe closely events in a setting and gradually come to a point of view about what we have seen and heard. Increasingly, we then hope to dialogue with the literature—asking the sort of questions that are encompassed by "What do others know that we don't know?" and "What do we know that others don't know?" Finally, the array of "Whys?" and "How do these integrate?" become part of our agenda. Within education, Atkin (1973) referred to approaches like ours as "practice based inquiry." In sociology, Glaser and Strauss (1967) raised similar ideas in their groundbreaking "discovery of grounded theory." Inquiry is driven less by a disciplinary position and more by the problems of practice within a complex naturalistic setting. Our more abstract and general statements tend toward a kind of "reasoned eclecticism."

In the more recent child development, parent education, and urban studies literature we have been highly influenced by a number of major statements. White's (1985) *The First Three Years of Life* was a substantial part of the original rationale of the PAT program. Bronfenbrenner's (1979) *The Ecology of Human Development* is very close to the systemic position we have been developing in education (e.g., our "longitudinal nested systems model of educational innovation and change"; Smith, Dwyer, Prunty, & Kleine, 1988). Schorr's (1988) *Within Our Reach: Breaking the Cycle of Disadvantage* is a broad policy statement drawn from a wide primary literature on the problems of a society producing children afflicted with what she called "rotten outcomes." Zigler and Lang's (1991) *Child Care Choices: Balancing the Needs of Children, Families, and Society* takes the ecological and systemic case into the broader reach of our social policy and institutions. Garbarino (1992) *Children and Families in the Social Environment* is a further attempt to locate child development in the broad sociocultural setting. From a very different political position, Magnet's (1993) *The Dream and the Nightmare* has helped us integrate our thinking into the current political policy debates associated with what is being called the Republican Party's "contract with America." The resolution of those congressional debates will have much to do with programs such as PAT.

In the more general urban literature, Wilson's (1987) *The Truly Disadvantaged: The Inner City, the Underclass, and Public Policy* is a major statement of the nature of race and class in the urban ghettos of the United States. Schoenberg and Rosenbaum's (1980) *Neighborhoods That Work: Sources for Viability in the Inner City* takes up five of the multiple communities of St. Louis and argues the case for making neighborhoods viable. We worked in several of those neighborhoods as they continued in transition. Jacobs' (1961) *The Death and Life of Great American Cities* presents a perceptive journalist's view of cities, focusing mostly on New

York, and a strong critique of much urban social policy. Lewis' (1961) *The Children of Sanchez: Autobiography of a Mexican Family* raises his "culture of poverty" concept, mostly from Mexican data but with a much more general worldwide reference.

But the book we found most helpful in the later stages of our analysis, as we focused our efforts into its present form, was Larner et al.'s (1992) *Fair Start for Children: Lessons Learned From Seven Demonstration Projects*. In this edited volume, they and their coworkers present a three-part discussion: a one-chapter introduction, a seven-chapter set of case studies, and a four-chapter set of cross-site generalizations, lessons learned. Their book is similar yet different from ours. The comparison helped clarify our audience, focus, format, and intellectual perspective.

They did a series of evaluative case studies. We did an ethnography of a single project. Their contexts and settings varied from rural to urban and from one ethnic group to another and from one part of the United States to another. We, in contrast, stayed with one program in one community, St. Louis. Their projects and research were all part of the Ford Foundation's Child Survival/Fair Start program of research. We were a smaller stand-alone project. They had multiple teams of research specialists. We had a unique ethnographic blend we called the "insider–outsider" pair of individuals and roles. They had a more general public policy orientation. We focused more on problems at the coalface of service delivery. They had more of a summative evaluation stance. We focused more on the processes of helping improve the program; that moved us toward a more formative evaluation stance. Their language tended toward macro concepts. We emphasized a more micro focus, experience near reports, and a concrete symbolic interactionist type interpreting and reporting. They tried to gather quantitative data in an attempt toward a more pre-set design for experimental and quasi-experimental analysis. We stayed with a more qualitative responsive design for data collection with the analysis organized into vignettes, interpretations, and eventually recommendations. They had an implicit falsification or hypothesis-testing framework. We tended toward a more hypothesis-creating, discovery-oriented, model-building, and reconstruing approach. Their disciplinary conceptual structure tended toward a political science kind of policy orientation. We were grounded in a more educational language. Finally, the references they cited to locate and establish their position are mostly quite contemporary and focused. We tended to cite alternative sources, those from a wider range of disciplines and with a longer historical perspective.

Ultimately, we see the orientations as neither competing nor being mutually exclusive. Rather, we believe they can be blended toward a larger framework for thinking about parent education and child development at multiple levels of abstraction and generality, for multiple audiences, and for multiple purposes. Larner and associates helped us mightily in our final discovery of what it was that we were about. And that is no small accolade. Aspects of the ideas and data from this set of references appear throughout our reporting and interpreting.

SUMMARY

In our view, the PAT program is a rapidly growing political and educational success story. In a very short period of time, the ideas and practices of White's research and development project on parent education have been adopted, adapted, and expanded in scope to a statewide program. In a decade, what began as a small pilot project in four school districts led by Winter, has grown to every school district in the state and now receives funding of the order of 10 million dollars a year. Under her impetus and direction, a National Center now exists in St. Louis. A detailed curriculum of personal visits, group meetings, and screening of children is implemented by a cadre of parent educators, all trained by the National Center. Inquiries from almost every state in the country and from a number of other countries have appeared. This kind of national dissemination and the program expansion in the state of Missouri has provoked a number of questions. One of these questions concerned the program's functioning with "difficult to reach, hard to maintain, and difficult to help urban families." Our qualitative case study research of the urban "St. Louis experience" attempts to speak to part of that concern. What has been learned that might be of use to other urban educators phrases our hope for this book.

chapter
two

An Urban Parent Education Program: Preliminary Sketches

INTRODUCTORY CONTEXT

Most educational innovations suffer because the innovators do not have concrete images of the proposed program in action in other settings, some similar to and some different from the new site. Ethnographic research brings a strength to the resolution of this need. In particular, as we pursued the "difficult to reach and maintain families" as well as a number of "contrasting cases" we had an array of experiences which we found stimulating and important. With sketches, that is, stories, anecdotes, and preliminary interpretive asides we try for these concrete images of life in the PAT program. Drawing on our interviews and observations we present several multifaceted views of people and events in this one urban community and school district. We cluster the sketches into four rough groupings: initial view of two PAT centers, heterogeneity of urban neighborhoods and communities, extended and nuclear families, and episodes in the lives of urban parent educators.

TWO PAT CENTERS: INITIAL VIEWS

Often one's first perceptions contain a vividness and clarity that dulls through later visits, furthermore there is an acceptance of the settings and scenes as another instance of the way things are. In February 1988, Smith made his first round of getting acquainted visits with coordinators and parent educators. He went to the Branch Center and the Hawthorne Center. As recorded in the summary observation and interpretation notes, his impressions were both particular and wide ranging. The project was underway—even more than he realized at the time.

> I've just been to the Branch Center and had an hour's talk with Sheila [the PAT coordinator]. I phrased the meeting as a "get-acquainted meeting" and beginning to sketch out what is it that I'm doing and how, etc. From my point of view, and I think hers, too, it went along very well. She strikes me as an attractive, intelligent, articulate, concerned, organized individual. She has a delightful easy way and manner about her in talking about the program and about how she goes about doing what she does as coordinator. (2/10/88)

Without engaging in formal interviews and explicit reading of credentials, the initial perception of talented school people staffing the program at the supervisory level became a part of one of the significant emerging patterns.

Another view of what would become a pattern appeared regarding the physical facilities housing the PAT program in the city, and, indirectly, a small but an important aspect of the program also appeared.

> The facilities are very jammed and cramped. Sheila, the coordinator, has a little desk cubicle kind of area at the back of what used to be a long thin classroom. Her parent educators were all around the room filling out their forms and keeping their records up to date. There must have been 6 or 8 in this morning. She has a secretary whose desk is up close to the door at the front of the room. Sheila actually was there when I came in typing some materials that were confidential that she had to do herself. She has an office or has another room which is about the size of a half of a classroom or less, across the hall and down a little way. This room is the play area and they have a rug on the floor and all kinds of toys and books and shelves of materials. There was an aide working there and there was also a volunteer mother whose little boy Joey is just 2 and who was playing on the carpet with some objects that he'd made into a train. He's starting to talk up a storm and we had a big conversation about what was going on. He later come in for a half stick of gum at noon just before I left. (2/10/88)

The mixed image of jammed space, busy parent educators keeping up with their records, volunteer mothers and small children playing and engaged happily would appear and reappear throughout the inquiry. Joey and his mother became a symbol of play as an important and enjoyable learning activity and volunteering as a commitment to the program and its possibilities.

The notes continued about the observations and the conversations that occurred that morning with Sheila. Initial speculations would eventually become confirmed and elaborated with further interpretations.

> *In the course of all that, one of the things that came out was the issue—that their group meetings went from 5 or 10 people per meeting down to one person over the last three meetings when the taxi cab service was cut out. Apparently it was very difficult for some of the mothers to get to the program and the free cab service was a major help in that. With that money now gone, it came from some other school funds out of the desegregation program or somewhere, the program just evaporates underneath one. That's as insightful a particular about some aspects of the program as I suppose one can get this quick into the program. Poverty and limited resources are everywhere: in the neighborhood, in the school buildings themselves which are very tacky and in need of painting, cleaning up, and all kinds of the usual things, in the resources that parents have to bring to the situation, and in the administration, coordination, and running of the program itself. There's a huge big issue around cost-effectiveness and providing social services. That one we'll need to highlight at some point. (2/10/88)*

The St. Louis Public Schools have since completed a multimillion dollar renovation of all its schools.

When hard to reach families are brought into the program, further problems are created in maintaining them and providing "standard" program activities such as group meetings. Cab service solves that problem to a degree. But that takes extra resources. At this point, improvisation takes place, the PAT program merges simply but creatively with the desegregation program. Larger goals become specified in particular ways as these improvisations take place.

Other aspects of these larger organizational or systemic contexts kept appearing in the conversation: research and evaluation, bureaucratic structures, program design, and ongoing discussions and negotiations. If all this be true, and our later data suggest that it is, then multiple levels of politics are occurring in the development and diffusion of the PAT program.

One such item concerns investigations such as this one, the one that inquires into urban families and underlies this book. A note appeared on that as well.

> *Another item that came up very early as we were talking back and forth and kind of getting acquainted was that Sheila talked to her staff and indicated that she wants them to be honest and to talk as freely as they can about the program. She's very much sold on the program and thinks they're doing a good job. If they ferret out problems, then they work on those and the program continues to work, in spite of problems of one kind or another. This seems very close to the same stance that Wilma has suggested or argued for. To me it's somewhat in contrast to the stance it seems that some others are indicating. (2/10/88)*

Although it did not come up in the conversation, the point of view was reminiscent of one advocated by Campbell (1969) under the general title, "reforms as experiments." Campbell argued that administrators needed to take on an experimental attitude and stance, collecting data on problems and their proposed solutions, reflecting upon the results, and then modifying once again. Images of Lewin's (1948) conception of "action research" and Schon's (1987) "reflective practitioner" also come to mind. Inadvertently, we are suggesting possible alternative stances in the administration and coordination of parent education programs, as we try to build on particular concrete ideas and practices currently underway. The beginnings of our perspective appeared early, continued to evolve throughout, and now finds itself taking a stable form in writing the final draft of this book.

When one makes even a bare nod toward life history and biography of participants in a program, details appear that lead to broader issues. When Smith spoke with Sheila he had no idea that he was moving into issues of staffing from indigenous local populations versus staffing from populations from the larger metropolitan community. Unwittingly, the complexities of this and the multiple pros and cons appeared.

> *Some other odds and ends of personal information. Sheila indicated that she's taught elementary school for 18 years or so and has been employed by the city schools for 24–5 years. This makes her older than she really looks. I would have guessed more in her 30s than in her 40s. She has a 15-year-old son who she's been raising as a single parent. Apparently he's beginning to give her a bit of a time of it. She's been a single parent*

for 10 years she said. She grew up in St. Louis, went to elementary, high school, and Harris-Stowe college. I don't know what her advanced work has been or where. Presumably its interrelated with early childhood and elementary education.

Later we found that she has a master's degree in early childhood special education. Those more historical background items wove importantly into discussions of her current personal and professional activities.

She's also very much a member of some part of the local community. I don't know for sure where she lives, but she talked about meeting a nurse in a supermarket line and from that came the connection with something called the WIC Center. It's the women, infants, and children's nutrition program. There are several around town and they are referral agencies for physicians who think young children need better nutrition. There's money from the federal government that provides vouchers for milk, bread, vitamins, and whatever. Sheila was able to get from this woman the names of women who were involved, and then with a telephone number and address went out looking for them. The recruiting is a continuous problem. (2/10/88)

The recruiting issue got generalized with another particular. Conjectures for strategies and tactics for working in the urban community continued to unfold in this early get acquainted conversation.

Similarly, she has connections with someone over at the Regional Health Center, the old St. Lukes East Hospital. She gets names from them and now is permitted to make a presentation once or twice a week to the mothers who are in the program and having their babies. In this way they keep getting families to add to the rolls. She has now 10 parent educators, down from the 12 she is supposed to have. She lost one recently and she's due to pick up another one shortly. Everybody helps in the recruiting and they carry a load of 60 to 65 families.

The recruiting comments and conjectures moved into issues of organization and administration of the program. Other metaphors arose.

When some case loads run over, they give other families to other parent educators and share them in some way. Apparently she runs the unit as a "family."

> *The family metaphor may be one that runs all through the project from its explicit focus, to Mildred, to people like Sheila, and to the Black culture generally. We'll have to look into that one more explicitly. Running the office as a family was her verbatim label. (2/10/88)*

The intellectual world of schooling is full of metaphors—business, social agencies, military, prisons—and now "family." Our interpretations both implicitly and explicitly flow in and out of the family metaphor.

But the ideas growing out of this initial meeting still would not end. They moved more broadly once again.

> *A couple more reflections on this morning. In an area where there's so much poverty in the city the development of a program like this is in effect bringing a small industry to the community. I don't know where the women, the one man Patrick, come from but if they're from the neighborhood, as I guess many of them are, hiring 10 or 12 people plus a secretary plus an aide plus the coordinator herself and doing this in four spots in the city brings a huge amount of payroll into the community. At some point, I need to work out the economics of all that and what it means to the community. It also supports a social service both at the parent level and at the kid level which it seems to me you can make a very strong case for. Having people more involved with their kids and doing it with the best evidence and support and ideas that are currently available has got to, in some level, be helpful or useful to the parents per se. Sketching that all out seems to me to be part of the problem. (2/10/88)*

At the time we didn't know Jane Jacobs' (1961) fascinating book, *The Death and Life of Great American Cities*, a volume raising contestable issues regarding public policies in the redevelopment of urban areas. We did know Whyte's (1955) earlier *Street Corner Society*, a study of an Italian community in Boston. Both raise issues in involvement and hiring of indigenous citizens for community action programs. Without realizing it, we were moving toward a stance on a major political issue of our times.

The notes continued in an almost free association style rather than what a memo or more logically organized essay might contain. Smith's thoughts wandered back to Joey and the specifics of the PAT program.

Similarly with the kids [sketching out the dimensions of the issues] I think of Joey who was the little boy in the playroom today with his mother as a volunteer. She was doing some kind of artwork on posters and helping the aide while Joe was playing with the variety of toys available. In and out were people including Sheila and myself who interacted with him, talked to him, talked to him about what he was doing and he in turn would talk back about his train and about Big Bird that was posted on the wall and the photograph of himself posted in a larger collection. All of this seems to me to be of the essence of what the program is about. Introducing this child probably more than he would be able to be introduced to it with the program of ideas and colors and objects and toys and games and language, it seems to me is again an objective one can't quarrel with in and of itself. (2/10/88)

But always in this kind of reflection and theory generation, a disclaimer appears. This time in two short sentences.

The tougher issue by way of objectives is what the trade-offs are and what the alternatives are for spending this kind of money and effort doing some other kinds of things. We'll need to sketch that one out at some length also. (2/10/88)

But that provocative day was not over, for Smith then drove to the Hawthorne Center which was located across town in South St. Louis, generally in that part of the city in which he had grown up and gone to elementary school. His reminiscences mixed with his observations and interpretations as he dictated summary notes while driving.

It's sort of strange going down South Kingshighway through some of the old haunts. It's been a long time. It's a few minutes til 2 and I'm here, at the Hawthorne Center.

The meeting occurred and the notes picked back up.

It's now a little after three and I've had an hour's discussion with Helene. It went along very well also and as far as I could detect there are no problems with going ahead with the project.
I cut west on Eichelberger to Brannon and now I'm going north on Brannon. I've gone by the Hope Lutheran School and the Hope Lutheran Church. Deja vu everywhere. Southwest St. Louis is still basically very neat and tidy. Lots of duplexes, lots of two-family flats, and lots of small little houses. Most of them seem very well kept up.

Comparisons began to arise with the Branch Center and with Sheila the coordinator. Helene, who had only recently been hired, was new to the project and new to the neighborhood. The notes picked up on some of the comparisons and broader issues in the PAT program.

> It is a very different neighborhood and community from the Branch northside area. In a sense, the whole shop seems to be different down here. Helene lives way out in South County, a good distance away. Her husband is a lawyer. She commutes 15 or 20 miles into work every day. She says that most of her parent educators are also not locals. They come from outside somewhere, half from the county and the others scattered around the city. We need to look at some of that a little more carefully. (2/10/88)

The indigenous staff issue was in the air at that time. The notes, although a bit rambling, toyed with the implications of that issue and others as well, as Smith drove through the neighborhood he had lived in for 10 years as a young child and dictated on his way back to the university.

> I drove down Brannon to Miami Street and then west on Miami to Sublette and then back around. Strange feeling.
>   The physical facilities and the spatial aspects of the program at Hawthorne are much much better than the ones I've seen at the other centers. She's got two large classrooms, one is the playroom–meeting room, and the other is the office space. The Hawthorne Center building is a former elementary school building and now is very heavily a community center at this point. You could get everything from Kung Fu to Bingo and as we saw today a number of elderly couples doing ballroom dancing. It's quite the affair.
>   As I drive along and free associate, one of the things that seemed to come to mind as I thought about the Hawthorne Center is that Helene, new to the program, doesn't really know the neighborhood in the same way it seems as though Sheila knows her neighborhood. She couldn't click off names of streets and addresses and institutions that she worked with to feed the program. It seemed like a major contrast to the click-click-clicking that Sheila had in terms of the WIC Center, and this hospital, and that person at the hospital, etc. Helene seems much less connected in some fundamental way with all of this.
>   I'm back at the university. It's 3:40 p.m. (2/10/88)

Our intent in this chapter is the creation of concrete images of the program. Our thought and hope is that the images will contribute to the reader's thinking with us about the nature of parent education in an urban setting. The very nature of qualitative inquiry, at least as we practice it, is to use the images for creative and critical thought about the nature of the program. Eventually, we raise the intellectual activity we call reconstruals, thinking through new ways of conceiving and implementing the program. The summary observations and interpretations, are long dictated accounts that blend the particular with the general, the concrete with the abstract, and the realities with the ideal or the normative. These initial views and conjectures will return both fleetingly and systematically as our descriptions and interpretations continue. That seems appropriate and enough for now.

HETEROGENEITY OF URBAN COMMUNITIES

Cities have been eulogized for their diversity for countless centuries. In his summary observation notes and memos, written along the way, Smith caught some of that variety. In only slightly edited form we present several of those images: a high-rise project, other high rises, a rapidly changing neighborhood, and a rehabbed city neighborhood.

A High Rise Housing Project

One of the stereotypes of the city these days concerns, "the projects," the large federally supported low-income housing projects. In the course of our research we flowed in and out of settings such as these. The observer saw some continuity in other experiences he had had. At the risk of over personalizing the interpretation, we leave some of these asides in the memo, for they help indicate how we thought about the project as we were carrying it out and because the asides help convey the sights and sounds—and the odors—of the images we had. They should make the images transfer more easily and more fully to other communities and other settings.

> *Earlier in the semester, at a staff meeting, I had heard expressed, by new parent educators, a feeling of some concern about meeting with parents in the high rise project apartments. "The projects," as they are called, elicited all kinds of reactions from the one extreme of fear to the other extreme, "What's the problem, I grew up in one." Most experienced parent educators had routines and a cautious concern for safety as they went about their task.*

So, the other day I went along with one of the parent educators to call on a parent on the seventh floor of one of the projects. Even though the meeting had been set up well in advance (and clearance for me to come along had been arranged), the parent educator called just before we left the office. The mother and infant met us in the lobby. The outer door was locked and was opened by a security guard. The lobby, which was clean, well swept and mopped, had several women, varying in age from one young woman who looked pregnant to an older woman who looked to be in her 60s, coming in and going to the mailboxes, checking the mail, for it was just 1 o'clock. We had to wait several minutes for the one elevator. The second one was not working. Both elevators being out of commission is rare according to the mother who has lived in the apartments for several months. The elevator itself was clean and fairly recently painted a chocolate brown and had graffiti scratched through the paint or written on with felt pens. Nothing special. The elevator shook, rattled, and wheezed through several stops to the seventh floor. The two women got out on their floors. The man pushing the buttons had on a blue "Catholic security services" uniform. I thought initially that he worked for the project, but he left the elevator on the seventh floor also, and walked down the hall ahead of us.

As we walked down the long hallway, I was reminded of my mother-in-law's apartment in Flushing, New York, but the cooking odors were different, not as pungent as the Jewish cooking in New York. Perhaps it was the midday visit. The apartment had a deadbolt lock, although not the three that my mother-in-law's had.

The inside reminded me, strangely, of "the barracks," the university veterans housing we had lived in for three of our five graduate school years, when we had our two young children. I think it was a feeling of temporariness or newness. There were few pictures or hangings on the wall, a bare caramel color, which had been ours too at that time. The project apartment had a main room which was kind of kitchen, dining room, and living room combination, as our barracks had. But this was more modern, with a large refrigerator and a gas stove. The cupboards were painted metal, a kind popular several decades ago, in my experience, and perhaps still. A few groceries were on painted wooden shelves with a cotton curtain as a screen, sort of a pantry. The only furniture was a new Formica top kitchen table and chairs, an old molded wooden chair with plastic cushion, a small TV, and VCR and tape deck player. A new baby's swing with a musical sound box and a baby's car seat were along one wall. The telephone, with a very long extension cord, rested on the kitchen counter near the table. (Memo 16)

That image of the "neighborhood" flows into the personal visit per se. In response to the parent educator's query, the mother, Sarah, reported that her 3-year-old, Livie, was doing well in preschool. Preparing a 3-year-old child for the imminent arrival of her new sibling was one of the several topics that fell under the general category of a prenatal visit. The mother was somewhat uncomfortable physically, but she obviously found the visits enjoyable and helpful, because she was interested in going through the program a second time. In contrast to this time, she originally enrolled in the PAT program when she was in her third trimester with now 3-year-old Livie. Sarah will reappear in our discussion, for she is a complex instance of the success of the program with a teenage mother who had dropped out of school and who was trying to put some kind of long-term order in her life.

High Rises and High Rises: Parenting and Parenting

Contrasts exist everywhere. Part of the research strategy into "difficult to reach, maintain, and help families" involved going on personal visits with parent educators with other kinds of families. These contrasts illuminated the central issues in unexpected ways, as in the discussion of "high rises and high rises."

> This past week I went into another high rise apartment. But it was different from the one mentioned in Memo 16. And the point I want to make is again on the variability among families in an urban population. The seventh floor of this "high-rise" is an elegant apartment of spacious rooms, Berber rugs, grand piano, and a sunny room of his own for Michael, the young child in the program. Interestingly, this apartment building is also locked and has a uniformed security guard who inquires about your destination and whether you are expected. The elevator works better. No graffiti exists. The hallways are carpeted and the walls are covered with wallpaper and beautiful pastel paintings and prints. Michael's parents are well-educated professionals. The grandparents are attentive, interested, and available, although they live elsewhere. Paid babysitters are part of the child's world a couple of days a week.
>
> But being a first time parent has its own kind of overriding imperative. Safety proofing was one of the major items under discussion. Michael's mother raised the various kinds of holders for cutlery, and particularly a magnetized one that they had received as a gift, one that left the blade exposed. The parent educator countered with several kinds available, and in particular one that she had bought for her own kitchen. A glass

and metal coffee table with sharp edges and corners became a focus of humor as well. The mother jokingly asking for a letter for her husband so that she could refurnish the entire living room. The multitude of exposed wires for audio, TV, and other electronic equipment also became part of the discussion. It wasn't as though the parent was unaware of all this, but rather that she had not gotten to the point of thinking about it and doing something about it. The parent educator was part of the focusing and part of the more outside, detached world with whom the mother could talk and plan. The mother's spontaneous comment that she enjoyed the friendliness and the good humor of the parent educator in their visits spoke to the quality of rapport.

For the moment, I am struck with what is perhaps an obvious set of interrelated points, there are high rises and high rises, and first parenting has its own kind of imperative. The urban world is interestingly varied yet similar. (Memo 26)

Rehabbed City Neighborhoods

A kind of excitement prevails in those communities in which rehabilitation of older houses is under way. St. Louis has a number of those neighborhoods. A visit to one of these provoked another image or two.

St. Louis, as with many American cities, has a long history of diverse neighborhoods. Currently they are being celebrated with banners of identity one sees as one visits the areas. A recent parent-child visit took me into another of these, the Soulard area in the near south side. Named after an open air market that continues to thrive after some 200 years on the same location, the area has been the site of considerable redevelopment of homes, restaurants, and smaller commercial establishments.

One of the PAT families lives in an older house that they had begun rehabilitating some dozen years ago. The street contains single-family dwellings, duplexes, and an occasional four-family apartment. In this instance, the house is turn of the century, front door on the left front, opening into a small hallway, with steps to the upstairs directly ahead. A small living room with fireplace is in the front and opens into a large dining room, which in turn leads into a kitchen in the back. A spacious quality exists. The furnishings are a mixture of traditional and modern. Comfortable might be the watch word. Original paintings, both oils and water colors, brighten the walls and offset the hardwood floors and the area carpets. Occasional objects, for example LLardro statues, are scattered about the room. The mother indicated that her daughter through training or their own "dumb luck" had never really bothered them and the objects had not needed to be put up nor away.

Planners who might want to import a PAT program into their urban communities, and those who develop models for the exporting, need to realize and work with this community diversity. Those of us who live and work in St. Louis have an advantage for Sandy Schoenberg and her colleagues have published brief historical accounts of four of these neighborhoods —Soulard, Carondelet, The Ville, and The Hill. Further they have a book, Neighborhoods That Work (Schoenberg & Rosenbaum, 1980), that generalizes some of this. (Memo 31)

Later, we find in the setting from Memo 31 a single parent, a woman divorced shortly after the birth of her child. It had been a very difficult time for the young and inexperienced mother. Crises of this kind appear in and out of our records, regardless of socioeconomic status (SES). The parent educator had been working with her since this time, shortly after the birth of the child. "Working with her" seems an expanded conception of the conventional parent educator role.

Rapidly Changing Neighborhoods

The instability of some urban neighborhoods is a reality for city government, urban planners, and service personnel. It is a reality for PAT parent educators as well. Excerpts from one of our long interviews clarifies our perceptions.

LS: *We were just talking about the hard to reach and some of the situational factors around housing and parts of town or "geographical factors" to use Wilma's word for it.*

WW: *Well, I think one of the things that contributed so much to the Laclede Towne success was that it was a mix of subsidized and non-subsidized housing. It truly ran the gamut in terms of socioeconomic status and educational level. What has happened now is that everyone and everything has moved out except the low SES families. With the financial base moving out, problems of upkeep have become a major issue. And so people who don't have a lot of money but are really concerned about the surroundings in which they live have also left Laclede Towne in large numbers. The result has been that all of the problems that are frequently associated with high rise low income housing are now synonymous with Laclede*

> *Towne, only laid out on a low rise plane. Now even the way*
> *the community is laid out is a source of concern for some*
> *parent educators. There are several short lanes that are*
> *closed in on three sides, so you can't really see or be seen*
> *from different angles. If somebody is about suspicious busi-*
> *ness it's a wonderful place in which to be about it.*
> LS: *So what would be cozy in another set of circumstances is a*
>   *haven for trouble?*
> WW: *Yes.*

A discussion of neighborhood change and diversity in urban communities raises several issues that are particularly germane to our focus on families who live in circumstances that make them hard to reach, maintain, and help through the PAT program. At the most elementary level, questions of parent educator safety arise. Do parent educators use different strategies in scheduling visits? What are the implications for scheduling evening visits for working parents or young in-school parents? At a more complex level, questions of program philosophy arise. And what of personal crises, regardless of economic levels? Is there an explicit or implicit policy position on neighborhoods and their contribution to the child's development? How is that policy translated into practices in the personal visit and group meeting? Foreshadowed questions such as these are discussed in detail in later chapters.

FAMILIES: SINGLE, EXTENDED, AND NUCLEAR

Multiple kinds of family structures and organization are another of the realities in an urban PAT program. Our notes are full of these variations. Of these ways of living, the most complex in terms of parent educator intervention is the extended family. Households with several generations, a mix of siblings of the mother, and cousins, the children of the siblings, present the parent educator with a series of fascinating dilemmas. Extended families are not synonymous with difficult and hard to reach families, but the overlap makes a large enough subgroup that it requires some discussion. We present a memo extract and a conversation or two from our interviews with parent educators with headings such as "Poignant Moments," "Negotiating With Grandmothers," and "Having It All Together." Lurking behind these sketches, if not directly in them, lies the parent educator who must perceive what exists, assess its importance, and then devise strategies and actions for coping and getting on with the program. Our intent here is mostly images of kinds of urban realities.

Poignant Moments

In a memo, we captured the poignancy of a young couple whose lives had grown apart but who shared a young daughter.

> *It is a truism that direct service to people, whether of an educational or social service form, brings one in close contact with fragile and poignant moments of individual lives. On a recent home visit, the parent educator had scheduled for early in the morning, 8:30, before the mother went to work. We arrived just before that time on a lovely spring morning. The neighborhood was one of St. Louis' older near downtown areas which is being redeveloped. The Johnsons were one of the early "rehabbers," beginning over a decade ago, part of that young professional's dream of urban revitalization. The house was a lovely two-story brick home with new doors, thermal windows, paint and roof, and a sign indicating it to be a part of a preservation neighborhood.*
>
> *The mother greeted us almost before we had knocked. She was dressed and ready to leave for work, but most importantly she was waiting the arrival of her daughter, Jennifer. Shortly thereafter, the father arrived with Jenny and we were part of a scene of a young couple, now divorced for over 2 years, since Jenny was 6 or 8 months old. At this point the relationship seemed relatively easy but awkward as the mother welcomed the child who wanted a long hug in her mother's arms, introduced us briefly (the parent educator had not met the father previously), and checked on how the daughter had been over the weekend. Jenny stays with her father and stepmother from late Saturday afternoon until Tuesday morning.*
>
> *The activity of the morning was the final screening for the child had recently turned 3 and the program was ending. A "happy go sorry" quality, to use an old vanished-from-usage expression, existed. The mother had come into the program shortly after the separation and the parent educator had been with her the entire time, almost 2 1/2 years. They recounted briefly, almost as old friends, some of the early memories of the mother getting started with the problems of both child rearing and single parenthood.*
>
> *The child's development as reflected in her behavior during the visit and on the Denver Developmental Screening and the Zimmerman Preschool Language Scale that day was well above average. (Memo 30)*

Over the years, changes occur in the relationships between parents and parent educators. That has important implications for case loads, success of the program, and recruiting of new clients.

Negotiating with Grandmothers

When an unmarried young mother lives in her mother's household, that is in the home of the child's grandmother, parent educator intervention takes on another kind of complexity and subtlety. We talked about that in one of our extended interviews.

LS: *Is there any conventional wisdom on working with extended families or any rules or regulations?*

WW: *The conventional wisdom is that when you go into an extended family household, you really have to work with the entire family, if at all possible. It is a delicate situation because generally extended households consist of relatively young moms, and so there's probably some conflict or some ambivalent feelings there already that are natural parts of any household with teenagers. The fact that the teenager is also a mother only exacerbates a traditionally emotionally charged period in a family's development. You want to empower the mom in the parent–child relationship. But you also have to negotiate with the grandmother whose house it is and who really sets the tone for what goes on in her house. The issue then is how to support the mother as the central authority figure in the parent–child relationship without appearing to diminish the authority of the grandmother.*

          One of the other things that arises here is that sometimes the grandmother—the parent's mom—receives the parent educator as a threat. For example, we come in, saying a whole lot of things that contradict conventional wisdom. We come in, and say that children ought to have free choice. You should rearrange things for children. Well, there are several generations of folks to whom that is directly opposite to their belief that children ought to accommodate the adults all the time and not be heard. And so we come in with these notions about moving things out of the way; that sometimes it's OK for your child to say no. It's OK for the child to win an argument. Some grandparents sit and listen and think—or even worse—say, "What is this mess?" [laughs] So in a sense we may sometimes be perceived as not only being involved in the power struggle of who heads the household and by extension the people in it, but also we may be perceived as challenging and calling into question entire belief systems that surround childrearing practices.

          A third issue that frequently arises with extended families is one of simple overcrowding—there are so many people in a limited space that issues such as room to have an uninterrupted visit, providing space for children to explore, etc. become major issues.

Power, adolescence, belief systems, and space are conceptual issues and practical realities. They intermix in fascinating and challenging ways for the parent educator. But it's the "negotiating with the grandmother" in an extended family that is the issue we want to highlight. No simple answers, but be alert to how you as parent educator will try to play it out.

"Having It All Together"

Extended families vary also. Our interviews developed a theme of "having it all together," an account of a supportive extended family. Contrasting cases continue to provide fertile ground for extending our ideas and suggestions, this time about the constellation of individuals and relationships in an extended family.

LS: *On the other end of the continuum, a family where some-how everything clicked and fell into place?*

WW: *When I first met Sharon, there was a mother, uncle, and a sister who also lived in the household along with Sharon and her daughter. Then Sharon had a second child so there were two children in the household. And later on, the kids' father moved into the household.*

LS: *And he's the father of the second child or both kids?*

WW: *Yes. Both kids. Now this is a household where the grandmother is really very receptive to my presence. She doesn't always sit in on the meetings. She perceives my contribution to that family to be quite valuable. She especially likes the activities that I bring in for the kids and Sharon. Grandmother sometimes participates in these also. If I call the household and Sharon's not there, her mom recognizes my voice right away and we talk for a minute or two. This is a grandmother who recognizes that even though her daughter lives in the household, that her daughter is the head of her own family.*

LS: *Sharon the person who's sort of in charge now or is her husband Joe in charge or . . . or whose house is this? The grandmother's house?*

WW: *It's the grandmother's house.*

LS: *It's still her house?*

WW: *It's her house. It is her house. But she . . . she recognizes where her authority ends and where Sharon's picks up. She doesn't try to impose her will over Sharon's when it comes to the way Sharon raises the children or the influence that Sharon has on the children, which sometimes happens in households with a grandma.*

It takes considerable skill to generate significant and supportive relationships with grandmother, mother, and child. On some occasions, each of the parties has her own relationships worked out and are receptive to the parent educators entry into the network. With a skeptical grandmother, the parent educator has her work cut out for her. As we indicated earlier, authority and its spheres of influence become very important. Trust takes time. When the breakthrough comes, its a pleasure to have the grandmothers answer the telephone, talk, and contribute to the child's development. This seems another aspect of "success."

EPISODES IN THE LIVES OF PARENT EDUCATORS

In this chapter we moved from vignettes of diverse communities to the heterogeneity of families, with an accent on the large extended family and the special problems posed in the complex interrelationships. Now we continue the progressive focusing toward the centrality of the parent educator in the vignettes. As this focus increases, the kind of experiences shade into the possible strategies and tactics that have been developed and utilized. Once again we blend interviews, summary observations, and memos as the core data underlying our images.

Millie: A 2 Year Relationship

The buffeting about and the turmoil of episodes in the lives of families are a mix of internal and external events. In some of these events, the families seem to have a chance at some control. Other events seem well beyond the reach of the families' self-determination. These events shift the focus, form, and content of the parent educator's (PE) personal visits.

PE: *Millie was 18 years old and had one child when I first met her.*
        She lived with her mom and her older sister who had two chil-
        dren. Millie dropped out of school in the 11th grade because
        she was pregnant. She didn't know very much about raising
        children. She was a bright young lady. Now she has a sec-
        ond child, a boy. . . . Millie has lived in four different homes in
        the 3 years that I've known her; with either her mother or her
        grandmother. She now lives in the children's father's moth-
        er's household. [laughs]
LS: *Same father of both kids?*
PE: *Yes. He lives in the household, too, along with his sister and*
        invalid grandmother. They are thinking of getting married
        and are looking for their own place, so I am expecting a fifth

household by the end of this school year or early next school year. Millie had gone back to get her GED three or four times but just had not been able to stick with going to the classes at night. She recently went through a period of postpartum depression following a pregnancy that ended in a spontaneous abortion. For a period of about 8 months, it was really difficult to engage Millie in the regular day-to-day activities that mothers typically engage in with their children. I was more concerned for the possible effects on David's development because Dorothy was attending preschool during this period. During the course of our visits, Millie revealed that she was feeling overwhelmed by her childcare responsibilities and the feeling that she wasn't doing enough with her life. At that time the children's father wasn't contributing a whole lot to their instrumental care.

The events and the parent educator's perception of those events have determined much of the thinking, strategies, and tactics of the parent educator. She perceived Millie to be bright. Her talks with her supported Millie's desire to study for and obtain her GED. Keeping track of the mother through five different moves symbolizes the issues in maintaining families in the program. Living with her mother-in-law to be has been successfully negotiated by Millie. It, too, was part of the parent educator's exploration. Dealing with postpartum depression, as it influenced the lives of the children, and especially the youngster who was home full time, requires both common sense and professional skill. Millie's "not doing enough with one's life" suggests a further array of discussions concomitant with, if not prerequisite to, the mother's attention to her child's development. The strength and possibilities arising from the children's father in the picture raises additional alternatives to be considered. Plans of action are developed, tried, revised, and tried and revised continually. And this is part of the St. Louis parent educator role.

On the Edge—And Can't Get Out

One parent educator (Mary) used the phrase, "on the edge," to represent a crisis in the life of a family. Such a categorization became a major element in her definition of the problem and her subsequent strategy and action with the family. The interview went this way.

Mary: *However, I've had a lot of personal referrals where the mom will say, "My sister has kids. And boy, does she need help!"*

LS: *So you may in some sense be getting families who are perceived to have problems of one kind or another?*

Mary: Right. . . You'll have some people that seem to be on the edge, so to speak, in one way or another. And that's really okay with me because I feel better when I have some cases—not cases that I have to literally run Mom down to get her to accept the program—but challenges, like handicaps. I have kids that have handicaps. And I find that real rewarding, to be able to serve those kinds of families.

LS: Tell me a little bit about people on the edge. What does it mean when you use a phrase like that?

Mary: What it means when I say "people on the edge" is that people are having some particular challenges in their life right now. And I don't mean life and death kind of challenges. It could be that Mom's recently been separated from Dad, has no means of support, has three little children, and this whole case has been referred to me by her sister. So when I get in there, the situation is not calm. It's crucial that I help Mom make some—or help her see what her alternatives are. So that may be my first action, to have Mom list her own alternatives. And I don't see that that is something that people are—that people know how to do. I see more and more that people don't know how to list their alternatives.

LS: Now this was a point you were making way back in the beginning when we were talking. Tell me a little bit more about that. Where does all that come from and what does it do in your view?

Mary: Why they can't make—why they can't list their alternatives? I'm not really sure. I don't know if that's—that may be part of the whole isolation issue. You know, families that are isolated within themselves, don't have friendships, don't have education, don't have outside interests that they can pursue, you know, because of maybe poverty or just restrictions on money. There's a whole—there's a whole restrictive kind of thing where depression has to be part of that, when a person's life feels restricted. You know, they have no—they have no ways of getting out. Mom and Dad were like this, Grandma and Grandpa were like this, now this is my lot in life. And that's—that's depressing. I mean people get depressed over that. And depression is a form of mental illness. It's not—it doesn't mean they're crazy. It means they're depressed. And to be able to break that cycle for your own children is a tough nut to crack.

LS: Now do they perceive it that way or is that your perception?

Mary: No, that's what they've told me. I mean that's what I hear from them, is that the cycle is intergenerational. And it's true. It's my perception, too, because it seems to fit. It's an intergenerational kind of problem and no matter what they do, they can't get out. And there could be lots of reasons for that.

The reasoning flows relatively simply: a continuing array of problems that puts the family "on the edge." The scope and frequency of the problems give rise to the feeling of an inability to cope, "can't get out" of their quagmire. Often this was true of parents or grandparents. And the feeling that follows, that one's own children will similarly be caught, leads to depression. The essential strategy of this parent educator is to move toward a consideration of concrete alternatives that address some of the problems and to engender a feeling of support that the problems can be worked out together. On the one hand, that is direct help to the family context and indirect help to the development of the child. As is discussed shortly, one of the options for the parent educator is referral as those problems move beyond the scope of the PAT program.

When one pushes in an interview for the origins of the parent educator's point of view, one quickly finds a kind of causal pattern. The parent educator's own family background is the source of many of the ideas. These are brought to bear on the perceived realities of the mother's plight. The space for creativity and caring is very wide.

A Day in the Life of a Parent Educator

Some days in the life of a naturalistic field researcher are atypical in that they capture so much of what one is seeing, but the perceptions occur in a short period of time. Such days are also atypical in the life of a parent educator, for seldom does the weight of "difficult to reach and maintain families" appear in such concentrated form. In addition, as the days occur late in a school year they tend to have a more overwhelming quality for the parent educators than days at other times. But for illustrative purposes, such days say a lot about the problem at hand. They present one more image of a parent educator at work in an urban community with a difficult to reach, maintain, and help clientele. Smith phrased it as "a day in the life . . ." in one of his memos.

> On occasion an event will occur that is symbolic of the larger pattern of events. Such was a recent Tuesday. I had made arrangements the week before with several parent educators to accompany them on home visits. I was taking sort of pot luck with a group of clients already scheduled, a nonselected sample as it were.
>
> When I arrived at a little after 11, the parent educator, Suzanne, was busy working on her record keeping. She told me that our middle client in the 11:30, 1:00, and 2:30 series had canceled. She indicated that she had another family whom she would try to contact and reconfirm her Friday appoint-

ment during that time period. The family has no telephone. Sometimes she uses these canceled times to stop by and talk with other families who are hard to contact. We talked a bit about her feeling of the difficulties of the parent educator's job. In her view, turnover is high among parent educators. I raised the "teacher type question" of whether the problems were the usual late Spring, end of the year, tired out, stressful time which face all of us in education. I am in the middle of similar problems at the university. Suzanne said no. It was more fundamental than that. The difficulties of meeting quotas, the parttime, no benefits structure of the job, and most of all the problems of the client families.

On the way to the first appointment, she illustrated "the problems" with reference to one of her mothers' cousins who had tried to commit suicide a few days before. The cousin's new baby was just 7 days old. The baby's father had not been around since before she went to the hospital. The cousin had not made any preparations for the baby. Suzanne had collected for her some of her own children's outgrown clothes and accessories. Since the cousin's suicide attempt, the other four children had been put in the care of the two grandmothers, one of whom had told her that both the mother and the father were into drugs. Allegations of sex abuse of one of the children had been made by one of the grandmothers against the boyfriend/father. Our conversation flowed in and out of her client, the client's cousin, and the one's we were to see today.

The first visit was a recent enrollee who was transferred from another parent educator who had quit recently because she was about to have a baby of her own. The late-in-the-year transfer was necessary because the woman had had only four contacts during the year, and one more was necessary if full reimbursement was to be obtained according to the state formula. Suzanne had called the night before to confirm the appointment. We arrived shortly after 11:30 with the appropriate papers and forms, a bag of toys, and a plan for a language lesson. The house was a lovely old brick two-story residence on a well-kept street in the north central side of the city. It took a sharp knock or two on the door, after trying the bell, to bring a sleepy eyed young woman in her early 20s to the door. Yes she was the mother, yes she had just gotten up, and yes she had forgotten that Suzanne was to be here.

She invited us in. Opening the heavy front door was a major struggle for the door hinges were torn partially from the frame. Inside it was very dark. The shades and curtains were drawn. No lights were on. The entry hallway had several chairs. We were told to wait in the small living room which was also dark and filled with heavy overstuffed furniture. We had to go through the kitchen and the dining room to get to the living room. On the kitchen stove a large aluminum pot was boiling and the other three gas burners were lit, presumably to warm the downstairs, for it was a very chilly, more like April than May, morning. Meanwhile the mother went upstairs to change clothes and get 18-month-old Lisa dressed. That took a full 20 to 30 minutes. We could overhear her shouting at another child or two to stay out of the closet on threat of a whipping. We waited and talked. I asked Suzanne about the significance of the darkly kept rooms, which I had run into on other occasions. She didn't know, but guessed that it was that they were afraid of something—neighbors, bill collectors, other people on the street. I wondered to myself whether the dynamic was more fundamental. About the time Suzanne was ready to tell the mother, Mary, that we had better leave, she came down with her tiny daughter, Lisa. Both were dressed now for visitors.

After a brief introduction of herself and the transition, the mother finally got a lamp turned on, and Suzanne turned her attention to the child. Although seemingly both sleepy and shy, Lisa was soon enticed with a simple plastic toy, a set of different sized rings stackable on a conelike plastic cylinder. After letting her play with it for a few minutes while she talked with the mother, Suzanne moved easily and invitingly toward asking the child a series of questions and giving her a series of directions—put the rings on the toy, bring me a ring, etc. Later a "noisy-when-shaken" container also intrigued the child. She played with the blocks, clapped them together when directed, and returned them to the container when asked. The child's receptive language was very good. It contrasted vividly with the inability of the 2 1/2 year old I had played with and tried to teach to roll a ball a few days before. He could not seem to understand. She could and did.

The mother proved to be an interesting young woman as well, a mass of contradictions to me. Part of the time she seemed an attractive, shy, almost girl-like young woman. This image disappeared dramatically when she would call out sharply and loudly to the children upstairs with warnings and threats. "I told you to stay out of the closet." "Where did you get that toy gun?" Mary's behavior with Lisa varied also from intrigued and smiling interaction to angry "no's" and "I won't give you any candy if you don't . . ." Interwoven with this was a discussion of Lisa's casting her eyes downward rather than looking directly at Suzanne. The mother exhibited the same behavior. We talked, perhaps too briefly, of her similar reaction, a longstanding pattern she had had since childhood. Suzanne suggested that the mother should help her daughter to look at her when they talked.

Eventually, Mary's 3 year old son and his cousin came downstairs to meet us. At that time we discovered that the quilt on the floor on the far side of the dining room held another sound asleep cousin. Mary's oldest, a 5-year-old, was at school. I wondered how she had gotten up and out that morning. In spite of the mother's positive report, I wondered too how she was faring in what was probably a very structured and traditional school setting. And I wondered about the 3-year-old beginning preschool this next autumn. Questions and hypotheses appeared at every juncture.

Suzanne was able to maintain the thread of language development throughout the hour as other aspects of child development and family matters arose. Mostly this occurred through the various toys she had and her talking with the child and the mother. In closing the session, Suzanne raised the group meeting to be held the next day. Her phrasing of that had an "if you want to get out" quality. She wrote the center's telephone number on the materials she left with the mother, and she indicated that cab service was provided. She told her she hoped she would be able to attend and that facilities existed for the children. The mother realized this for she had been to an earlier group meeting. With a "bye-bye" to and from Lisa, we departed. Later Suzanne commented in regard to the mother that she felt at times she was talking to the couch.

As we drove across the city to the Laclede Town Housing Project, we talked of Lisa and her mother, the program, and the larger problems facing poor families in the inner city. Laclede Town, once a showplace of middle-class integrated housing, is now half to two thirds abandoned and boarded up. The project is alleged to be a drug hangout. Suzanne showed me the passageway where, the night before, a young man ran, after robbing and beating a young woman in Suzanne's night school class who had been sitting in her car studying for an exam. Suzanne had been parked just behind her, also studying. All she could do was honk her horn and create a ruckus. Today she was looking for the apartment for her Friday appointment. We found it. A tall slim young man came to the door. Suzanne talked from the outside to the woman in the darkened room. She said she would be home on Friday. We checked with a postman who was delivering mail, on the whereabouts of one other street. A few men were the only people about.

We drove next to the Clinton Peabody project. Most of the high-rises were abandoned and closed. Suzanne pointed to one where she had had a scary experience a few weeks before as she walked down the stairs from the eighth floor. She had told me of the experience on an earlier day. We entered the project through a street across from the Peabody

Elementary School. As we got out of the car, two men in their 20s or early 30s walked by, one carried a brown paper bag with an opened pint bottle. They paid us no mind. Suzanne commented to my comment that mostly she was ignored by residents as she went in an out. Occasionally a group of kids would make a comment or two of the order "Where ya goin' mamma?" to her. As we got to the apartment, a young woman and a teenage boy approached us on the walk behind us. She said that her sister, the mother we were to see, was not in. The mother had had to take the baby to the clinic. The woman had gone over to the school to pick up her sister's boy who had been hit with a rock while playing on the playground. Under a handkerchief which had been used to stop the bleeding, his lip showed a nasty quarter to half inch cut which looked like it needed stitching. She was on her way to her apartment to figure out how she would get him to the hospital. Suzanne gave her the information about the group meeting the next day for her sister. As we walked back to the car we saw several other young men going in an out of apartments, talking back and forth to each other, and carrying their own brown paper bags and bottles. It was a new setting for me. I was pleased to be in Suzanne's company and not alone.

As we drove back across town, once again, to the Center it seemed fitting that West Florissant was full of sirens and lights as the police converged on a street from several directions. We continued on. I left Suzanne at the entrance to Northwest High School and returned to the university to grade end of semester papers. Suzanne returned to the office to finish her paper work and get organized for the next day.

One client seen in a long half day's effort seemed minimal results. Suzanne still has her quota to meet, according to the state formula. Something seems drastically wrong to me. But such is "a day in the life of an urban parent educator." (Memo 41)

In writing this memo, the intent was to take an unusual but true day, one that captured dramatically the frustrating side of working in an urban community with parents who are difficult to reach, maintain, and help and to paint in bold colors and strokes a world that the St. Louis parent educators face and respond to with concern, with skill, with perseverance, and with cumulating success. In our view, "the day in the life" of Suzanne shows a reality that coordinators, central office administrators, National Center personnel, and state department staff as well as state legislators need to keep vividly in mind as they make decisions about parent education and child development in promoting the well being of a large group of citizens. These families live in any large city and are potential clients for any parent education program such as PAT.

SUMMARY

Solving professional problems is a subinstance of general problem solving. Clear and vivid images are a requisite of both. In this chapter, in a beginning way, we have sought to help school officials and those interested in early childhood, parent education programs from other urban communities solve the overall problem of initiating their version of a PAT program. This has been a first view of "our" urban community, one noted for its diversity and heterogeneity. Within that kind of diversity another appears. Families can be loosely categorized in overlapping ways as single parent, as extended, and even as nuclear. When one adds a concern for the hard to reach and maintain families another view appears. Finally we wanted to enlarge those images with a gradual concentration on the parent educator interacting within this diverse urban community. Each parent educator brings her own experience, background, skills and strategies as she copes with the fascinating and sometimes frustrating task of helping parents understand and cope with their young children toward the enhanced development of those children. Progressively, we focus on the more particular issues, problems, and successful strategies used in the St. Louis program. For now, images have been our goal.

section
two

Difficult Family Situations: The Interplay of Recruitment and Services

---

In this section, we move to the heart of our project, a description and analysis of the interdependence of successful recruitment practices and the challenge that then places on the delivery of services. In the course of our interpretation, we present in considerable detail the innovative ways of thinking and action that have arisen in the St. Louis community. Our word for this is reconstrual, a rethinking and reordering of a number of the ideas that we raised briefly in the introductory overview. "What we have learned," and "What we believe is useful to other urban programs," are alternative ways of talking about this reconstrual.

Specifically, we have three chapters. Chapter 3 opens a discussion of recruiting the difficult to reach. We believe that the staff in St. Louis has raised a provocative set of alternatives for "reaching the difficult to reach" families. These families then raise issues that stretch and extend the idea suggested in the PAT training materials. In chapter 4 of this section, the original focus of our research project, the conception of the parent educator as teacher of the difficult to reach and maintain families, is modified significantly as we raise another kind of "difficulty." This is the group of parents who are "difficult to help." We now speak of "difficult family situations: reaching, maintaining, and helping." We believe this is a more powerful way to think about program issues and actions than we had at the beginning of our research. These ideas have led us to an extension or reconstruing of the parent educator role and relationship. In this context we present a number of quite specific "gam-bits and techniques" used successfully by St. Louis parent educators with families in difficult situations. Finally, in chapter 5, we look at the program, the home visits and the group meetings, as an issue in curricu-lum. Lessons and lesson topics run the gamut from discipline and toilet training, to language and intellectual development, to nutrition and motor development. We present specific practices and recommendations from our interviews and observations.

Overall, we believe we have a powerful supplement to the National Center's program guide (1986, 1989). We continue with our belief that readers should have a view of the day-to-day excitement in being an urban parent educator. This view can then be adapted and used in their own circumstances.

chapter
three

Recruiting the Hard to Reach

THE PROBLEM

Stated simply, the usual recruiting procedures of announcements in the public media of the availability of these new services for parents of infants and toddlers do not work well in St. Louis' urban community. For multiple reasons, many parents do not respond to such announcements. These nonrespondents, almost by definition, become the hard to reach families. A major related issue arises at this point. Among many school people, the belief exists that many of these families "need" a program like PAT. Insofar as the correlates of poverty—limited prenatal care, teenage motherhood, and low birthweight of the child, prevail, then the child seems at risk of later school difficulties. The PAT program becomes one of the possible interventions to help minimize those risks. The school system's self-interest, and the community's as well, in willing and able children entering school in the kindergarten and first grade arises. The state legislature and the state executive branch, through the governor and the department of elementary and secondary education, also have a legal interest in and responsibility for all citizens.

As these arguments expand, the question arises, "Is the PAT program "up" to these demands, that is, are we asking too much of the program on a problem that is both different and larger, at least in degree, than the one spoken to with Missouri's initial PAT pilot study?" As our

51

view is developed here, we give a qualified "yes" and "no" to these issues. But our initial point is "yes, there are recruiting practices that bring difficult to reach families into the program." And second, once in the program, "these families pose difficulties for the parent educators," and "yes, there are ways of dealing with the difficulties." And finally, the long-term possibilities in parent education, family development, and child development are hopeful. In our view, all those "causal" linkages in the chain of events require considerably more inquiry and evaluation of multiple kinds for the judgments to be made with evidence convincing to all the audiences involved with a program as broadly based as PAT.

In a sense, this kind of introductory argument is a major and very important outcome of observing and talking to people about the issues in "recruiting the hard to reach family." Dilemmas are posed for everyone—the legislature, the National Center, the city school system and, eventually, the coordinators and parent educators who are at the close end of providing services. Resolution of dilemmas always involve trade-offs. Changing a key element in an educational social system creates changes all through the remainder of the system. Recruiting successfully the hard to reach is one of those elements.

Recruiting Strategies and Practices

A single sentence conveys a major result of our inquiry: The recruiting strategies and practices for the hard to reach family must be outreaching, aggressive, imaginative, and personal. In our interviews and observations we explored several implications: the citywide connections that one must have, the kinds of organizational incentives built into the program, and the importance of referrals and recruitment through families and friends.

The Citywide Connections

In retrospect, the principles are simple and well known, but difficult to apply imaginatively and courageously: know your local community, have positive connections with people in responsible positions, and present yourself and your program confidently and vigorously. For PAT, the Women's, Infant and Children's program (WIC), the Division of Family Services (DFS), the local health clinics and maternity hospitals, and the local supermarkets are all recruiting sites. The ideas appeared vividly in one of our interview/discussions.

LS: *Where did you get her first time through?*
WW: *I got Wanda from the WIC Center.*

LS: *Ah . . . tell me if you can recall the specifics on that one, and if not, more generally, how did you come to meet her? . . . I guess I'm curious in getting a detailed account of how Wanda and Kevin came there. What do you do when you get somebody from the WIC Center, I guess, is one way to phrase that?*

WW: *Okay. I can give you the general account. There are two ways that . . . we might get people from the WIC Center. One is that early on in the program, the coordinators make contact with key people in a number of different social ser-vice agencies. . . . Once you've gone through the hierarchy and gotten approval from the Human Development Corporation, who oversees the WIC Center—the person that you deal with at the WIC Center is the WIC technician, the individual who hands out the vouchers and does the paper-work associated with each one of the clients. . . . Each of us made contact with the WIC technicians in our areas. We explained our program. We left flyers with them. If they ran across anyone that they thought would benefit from our pro-gram, we asked the technicians if they would please give the mothers the flyer. We posted posters in the centers. We then check with the WIC technician periodically to see if she has any referrals for us. When you get the referral that way, you follow up with a telephone call to the parent, if they have a phone. If they don't have a phone, you follow up with a letter to the parent. It's always nice to be able to say, "I got your registration from Carolyn, the WIC technician" because the client knows Carolyn and feels a personal bond with you through your mutual acquaintance.*

Another way that we get clients from the WIC office is through direct recruitment on the part of the parent educa-tor. That is, some days I will sit in the WIC outer office, in the waiting room, and as clients come through, Carolyn sends them to me by saying something like "There's a lady out there with a program that I think you'd really be interested in." They come and talk with me right there and I can sign them up and answer any questions that they have, and set an appointment. One of the really nice things about this arrangement is that you can almost, in a little 10 minute peri-od, demonstrate to a parent almost what's going to happen in the private visit. As you talk, you observe things that her child is doing and you can just say, "Oh, I noticed your child is doing such and such and such." That's a very good selling point, if you're in a situation where you can actually talk to the mom about her child and give her a bit of new informa-tion in terms of what she can expect or whatever. And again you can sign the client up right then, set an appointment

and schedule a time to go out to do a visit. And that's basically how we work. We also work that way with the Division
of Family Services, for example.

LS: So there's WIC and the Division of Family Services?

WW: WIC, Division of Family Services, the health clinics, the—actually the same procedure can work at the supermarket. Now
we have done that. We have gone, for example, into
National Supermarket and they've given us permission to set
up tables with our flyers. As parents come through, we hand
them a flyer and tell them about our program a little bit. Um .
. . let me see, and the other—the other really great recruitment strategy seems weird—I didn't believe it would work
when I first started—that is just seeing someone walking down
the street with a baby.

LS: [laughs]

WW: Honestly.

LS: Hey, lady, whoomp!

WW: It is amazing. It is absolutely amazing. You see someone
with—waiting at the bus stop with a baby, standing in the
line at the grocery store, you just say, "Oh, what a delightful
baby." Then you begin to tell people about your program.
The other ways that we get recruits is that we go through—
we've gone and talked to childbirth education classes. We
go to Y infant-toddler classes, the little tadpole classes, you
know, where they're teaching kids to swim. We go to play
groups, we go to PTA meetings. We go to, believe it or not,
during holidays, we'll go to Giuliani's Carnival Supply. What
you have to do is identify places where people who have
children go. And then you have to make yourself visible to
them at those points.

Although the recruiting practices may seem obvious, making
these techniques work is no simple matter. Note for instance, the subtleties in working through the various hierarchies of authority and
administration in the different organizations and still finding and
obtaining the cooperation of the contact person at the day-to-day service
level. And then there is the skill in noting within the child's behavior, at
the moment, a significant item and being able to comment on it to the
parent, almost legitimating the idea that the parent educator has something of importance to say and contribute to the parent's understanding
of helping the child's development.

Finally, the general advice of an outreach program, go to places
where parents and children are—bus stops and sidewalks—where mothers and children are waiting or walking down the street. With imagina-
tion and confidence you take your program to people who might not
have heard about it or who might be reluctant to approach a school or

agency. In this way you reach the hard to reach. Some parent educators find this kind of activity very stimulating and exciting. Others find it very difficult to do. Thus, a new "problem" is created for supervisors and coordinators: How do you select or train parent educators for such a task?

Organizational Incentives

One of the most powerful incentives for reaching and maintaining families in the program is a simple organizational item. The city public schools reserves a significant number of preschool places for the 3-year-olds who have been in the PAT program. In recruiting, the argument of future benefits to the child and the mother can be made as in the following:

> WW: The waiting lists for the preschools I think are months long. Although Josie will not have to wait that long. One of the things that we do to provide continuity is that we reserve slots.

A further question elicited a comment on the special characteristics of the preschool curriculum, a kind of continuity with the PAT program.

> WW: It's 4 days a week. Monday through Thursday. Fridays are devoted to what they call personalized instruction—instruction sessions where preschool teachers go to parents' homes, group meetings, and individual consultation.
> LS: It's like the PAT program?
> WW: Yes, in terms of going into the home.

As with all public services, the state rules and regulations give order to those services but they also make it difficult, as in the birth dates, to provide services in special cases. The intertwining of successful experiences in one program being adapted into another, Fridays for home visits, seems a major point as well. The overall effort toward continuity of the child's experience remains a major goal as well. In short, recruitment becomes a systemic problem, with connections to other aspects of the Program. Working that creatively is a major challenge and source of satisfaction to the program staff.

Referrals and Recruitment Through Friends

When parent educators use words such as recruitment images of formal program announcements as well as planned strategies abound.

The age-old technique of informal contact through friends and acquaintances worked well in the St. Louis PAT program. Laurie was one of these.

WW: *Well, let's see. Laurie first enrolled in the program back in 1984. And she was referred to me by a mutual friend who was also in Parents as Teachers at the time. She let me know that Laurie had just had a baby.*

LS: *So the friend told you that initially. And then did you call Laurie or did she call you?*

WW: *The friend told me that Laurie had the baby, that she had told Laurie about the program. She gave me her number with my knowledge that Laurie had said it was okay for her to give me the number. So that when I called Laurie, she knew who I was, and I knew a little bit about her.*

LS: *How many of your cases would be sort of relatives or friends of other cases?*

WW: *It seems that the longer I'm in the program as people get to know me, they talk to their friends and relatives about the program. I get a lot of referrals that way. I think that's a real good way to get them.*

LS: *Talk about why that's a good way to get them.*

WW: *It's a good way to get them because of—for example, the home visit that I had last night. It's a family where both parents work outside of the home. I've been with them since Mom was pregnant—I mean she got in early. And they feel comfortable with the program. When a family is happy with a parent educator, they can tell, on a very personal level, another person. Otherwise, new clients have to believe me and I'm a stranger. But when a personal friend of theirs or a relative says, "This is of value to me," they're more apt to listen. This kind of recruitment takes more time, of course, because you have to build that kind of relationship before parents are willing to share you.*

The theme of personal contact sometimes mediated by a mutual acquaintance is a major characteristic of the recruitment strategies that parent educators found most successful. In subtle ways this changes the nature of the population being served. Networks of families and friends become salient.

The ideas of mediation and personal contact can even be seen in the more formal mass recruitment efforts. One such effort involved a collaboration between PAT and the Interfaith Partnership—an interdenominational group that is actively involved in community service activities. Not only did Interfaith print flyers and registration forms endorsing the PAT program, but also declared a citywide PAT Sunday on which churches throughout the city were urged to speak to their congregations about PAT. One parent educator recounted a direct result of this effort. A mother in her early 20s who felt that she might abuse her child because she frequently felt herself losing her temper with him called in to join the program. She had heard about the program at church and her minister had also personally counseled her and strongly suggested that she enroll in PAT.

A key difference between this mother and those discussed earlier is that this mother self-initiated the contact. In the following interview, Wells discusses the relationship between recruitment strategies and hard to reach, maintain, and help families.

LS: *How does all of that compare to the kind of formal effort that you put into the Roosevelt School and the Family Affair occasion?*

WW: *I feel this is true for a significant number of people—you hear an advertisement, or you see a flyer, or you see a brochure, and you say, "Oh, that sounds interesting. I'm going to look into that." But somehow you just never quite get around to it. But when you've seen those things and someone comes up to you and says, "Hi, I'm with the Parents as Teachers Program," the response may likely be "Oh yeah, I've been intending to get involved in that program." So I think that with the formal advertisement, we're just now beginning to see some results of that. We're beginning to get more and more and more telephone calls. County school districts tell us that that's how they do their major recruitment. They do a mass media campaign and people call in. That does not seem to be a major characteristic of the group of families we work with.*

LS: *In a sense it's almost as though no matter what technique you use, it takes your group a little longer to—and I don't mean this negatively or pejoratively—but just to learn how that game is played before the sort of voluntary call-in will come.*

Recruitment through friends is now extended to "friendly organizations." The personal contact remains a central part of the recruiting experience.

The Shelter Experience

The subtleties in recruiting appeared in a visit to a shelter for homeless women and children. On the one hand, the story is a tale of an imaginative and aggressive recruiting practice, and is important in this regard. On the other hand, and even more importantly, the story tells of the understandings, attitudes, and skills of a parent educator doing the recruiting task in a particular social setting. That blending of individual talent in action in a complex and difficult situation lies at the heart of our attempt to locate, analyze, and recommend successful procedures. In Smith's view, at one level, "be like Wilma Wells" says it all. At another level, until we can break apart the actions in the setting and relate it to other persons in similar settings in other communities, our project has not helped in the way we would want to. A memo caught our intent very well.

Quid Pro Quo in Recruiting the Hard to Reach: The Shelter Experience

It is not quite "quid pro quo," but it sort of works that way. This morning I attended an hour-long meeting of a group of mothers in the women's shelter of a local church. Some of the mothers arrived about 9:15 and others kept coming for the next 45 minutes. One mother had to leave at 9:25, before the discussion actually started. Others left at varying times, mostly after 10 a.m. Some lingered on until 10:45, a full 15 or 20 minutes after the formal ending of the program. Coffee, pretzels, and some cupcakes, the latter left over from another meeting, were available.

"Before the meeting began," if the initial 15 or 20 minutes, could be so described, the parent educator "worked the room," to borrow and extend a Jerry Berger phrase. "My name is Wilma Wells. We haven't met before, I don't believe. How are you? Do you have children? Where are they in school? I used to teach near there in the public schools." And on and on. It was a virtuoso performance—simple, direct, honest, interested. No parent could or did resist the overtures. To the contrary. When the formal program began and each woman was asked to introduce herself, none refused. Most related personal episodes about themselves, their situations, and their children.

Most of the women were mothers, but not all. Many had young children, but again not all. A few had come to St. Louis from neighboring towns or cities, essentially fleeing from husbands, ex-husbands, or boyfriends who both would not leave them alone and who would beat them or the children, sometimes in spite of court orders to the contrary. From the conversation it seemed that several of the women, and possibly many more, had serious problems of personality disorganization. What seemed like delusions, of having a "mansion" from which they had been turned out, CDs that they didn't want to cash right now because of the penalties for early withdrawal, and the need for $100 to file a court order against the husband occurred in a couple of the women. It provoked images of ambulatory mental patients no longer served by closed mental hospitals. Other images of strength and coping appeared and vied with images of how badly the world beats up on some of its inhabitants. I was reminded of plants and flowers growing in cracks and crevices of the Grand Canyon, a very hostile environment for them. With just a little bit of water and soil among the rocks, they hung on and survived. The world seemed no more hospitable for these women.

The PAT parent educator led the discussion, the topic of which had developed out of a prior meeting the month before, on the stresses in living in shelters and the impact of this stress on the children. Part of her involvement hinged on extending the PAT program to city parents who normally would not be a part of the program. The initial key issue in the discussion focused on the shelter's rule that no one, staff or parent, could use physical punishment to control or discipline the children. For every parent who spoke, and the majority did at one point or another, for it was a superbly run open discussion, "whuppin's" were standard policy and procedures. Reasons for the rule were raised in answer to the leader's question, "Why would they have such a rule?" Implications of the no physical punishment rule centered in the children's awareness and their complete refusal to obey when they realized the parents were not able to whip them in the church. Several mothers told of taking the children outside, "whupping the daylights out of the child," and then returning to the shelter. Alternatives to punishment were raised and the discussion turned to a variety of illustrations of deprivation of privileges, of isolating the child, restraining and insisting because of the parents size and strength, and of rewarding positive behavior. A concluding issue was what could we as individuals do to help solve our problems. Talking among themselves, and working with each other and with staff became part of the possibilities. I was reminded of what N.R.F. Maier (1963) and his colleagues some years ago called "developmental discussions" in their books and articles on human relations and supervisory development.

But in spite of how magnificently run the meeting was, my point is that this contribution to a community agency was part of the outreach of PAT in building awareness in the social work community, positive esteem from the shelter staff members, and a referral system for recruiting parents into the program. Another memo must speak to the problems in actualizing such initial contacts into real clients. And then there are the further problems created for the parent educator both in terms of individual home visits and in terms of attendance at group meetings. That, too, belongs in another memo to those who seek to develop PAT programs for inner-city populations. And then there needs *to be a memo to those who would evaluate programs like PAT when recruitment is so ungodly "irregular," that is, unusual and imaginative. Gordian knots everywhere. (Memo 17)*

As we thought and talked about this memo we began to raise a number of additional questions regarding recruitment and service, questions we will leave mostly for the reader to speculate about. In other contexts and settings, how does one respect the variable arrival and departure times, yet keep moving one's agenda? Or, more generally, how does one tailor one's staff agenda to the clients' agendas? What is the role in providing even simple refreshments to limited income families? What are the personal qualities and skills that succeed in recruiting encounters such as this one? What of the dilemma or dangers in recruiting parents for a program like PAT versus the need for much stronger intervention for some of the women such as those in the center? And what of the parent education program as a validation of current parental beliefs and practices, as in the case here of physical punishment for disciplinary problems, rather than a more critical and judgmental move by the parent educator toward other beliefs and practices? Even a meeting as provocative and powerful as this one raises issues that we as reflective practitioners need to keep re-examining.

The Farther Reaches of Recruitment

One of the strongest conclusions from our study is that the difficult to reach, maintain, and help population scatters along a continuum. The families are not of a single piece in configuration nor in severity of their personal problems and social situations. The "farther reaches" of this continuum vividly presented itself in our visit to the "Beginning Again Center." The observer did a summary memo on this experience. The questions at the end of the memo remain. Are there limits to the degree of hard to reach and maintain families beyond the scope and potency of PAT? If so, what is the community responsibility?

The Farther Reaches of "Hard to Reach" Families

A university colleague, with whom I had talked informally about the PAT project on "hard to reach and difficult to maintain families," indicated that I should talk with Sister Betty Nolan who is the founder and director of "Beginning Again," a center that rehabilitates young women with criminal records. After a series of telephone calls, one of the parent educators and I spent an hour with Sister Betty and two of her staff, a drug counselor and an education coordinator.

Their clientele was mostly remanded from the courts. The women were given a choice—the "Beginning Again" program or incarceration in the city jail. Some had heard of the program from friends and were self referred. Mostly, they were women in their 20s. The majority had children, some of whom were living with relatives while the mothers lived in "halfway houses," other children had been taken from the mothers and were now in foster care, and some remained with the mothers. The center's program involved providing food and clothing, helping with housing arrangements and in some instances employment, sustained counseling for drug and alcohol abuse, and tutoring in the basic skills of reading and writing and arithmetic for some of the women as they prepared to take GED tests. Some of the women were referred for medical help for addiction and physical and sexual abuse. A bi-weekly youth activities program existed for the children.

To the best of the knowledge of the "Beginning Again" staff and the PAT staff none of the mothers was enrolled in the PAT program. It seems a safe inference that most of the children will grow up to have school problems.

I will cut the story off at this point, and leave it as a stimulus for conversations with a number of you in the PAT program. Does PAT have a role or a responsibility here? Are there other similar organizations serving "pockets of difficult to reach families?" What is the role of interorganizational cooperation with such families? Are these women and their children beyond the resources, both programmatically and financially, of PAT? What are the implications for the parent educator who takes on 5 or 10 such mothers and children as clients?

What do you think? What should I put in the final report or Manual about experiences like this one? (Memo 4)

Discussions of recruitment by word of mouth and at agencies set up to serve economically disadvantaged families almost naturally lead to questions of selectivity.

LS: *Does it tilt you to getting a particular slice of either geography on the South Side or does it give you a particular social class slice or does it . . . ? Who does that kind of referring more frequently—your families who are basically doing well economically, socially, etc., or your families who fall along our hard to reach–maintain–help continuum?*

WW: *My experience has been that they refer at about the same rate. Of course most of the families in my caseload would fall into the general category of hard to reach.*

Families of all kinds do enter the program. One of the necessary parent educator skill clusters lies in making a judgment that the parent has bigger problems than the program can handle and then helping make referrals to health clinics and social agencies.

Implications of Aggressive Recruiting

Successful aggressive recruiting that results in enrolling larger numbers of hard to reach, maintain, and help families carries with it both program design and fiscal implications and consequences.

A common characteristic, a major finding if you like, of the recruitment methods that worked best with hard to reach, maintain, and help families is that they take time, are labor intensive, and rely heavily on the personality and skill of the individual parent educator. The first two characteristics suggest that administrators in other communities who seek to set up PAT programs that serve hard to reach, maintain, and help families must build ample time into the program's yearly schedule for recruitment activities and need to have a relatively large recruitment team, both of which require a substantial financial commitment. In the St. Louis program new parent educators spent the better part of the first 2 months of the program year recruiting families. Furthermore, recruitment activities filled a significant portion of the parent educators' work day through December—the amount of time that most parent educators required to reach the caseload goals established by the district. This has obvious implications for delivery of services.

The third characteristic of aggressive recruitment strategies is that they yielded differential results in large part as a result of the personality and skill of the individual parent educator. At one level, some parent educators clearly enjoyed this activity and perceived themselves to be good at it, whereas others clearly felt uncomfortable with more aggressive recruitment activities. This suggests the desirability of some degree of role differentiation—with some parent educators having greater responsibility for more aggressive recruitment than others. At another level, it was clear that there was an intricate relationship between the skill level of individual parent educators and the success of aggressive recruitment strategies—even among parent educators who seemed to enjoy this activity. School districts that wish to implement programs for hard to reach families must build in training opportunities.

As alluded to earlier, the challenges of aggressive recruitment do not end with enrollment. In a very real sense they can be said to have just begun. The following comments from a discussion of recruitment methods foreshadow additional consequences of aggressive recruiting.

WW: *If I could say one more thing on recruitment, I think that it is important for a person from the . . . the superintendent from Naples to know about. Is that the one we're writing this for?*

LS: *Venice. Venice.*

WW: *Venice, okay. The guy from Venice. That's important to know. And it is that when you go to DFS and you go to WIC, when you go to a public health clinic, you can get some marvelous families, people who are really interested in the program and will follow through. But you are also going to get. . . . You are increasing the probability, as a matter of fact, that you are in fact enrolling a hard to maintain family. With many of them, what you end up doing is spinning your wheels because you set an appointment and . . . you set five appointments and they're not there. . . . But I honestly believe that when you work with—when you work with a group of people that have multiple risk factors operating in their lives on a day-to-day basis that the parent educator also is at risk. Parent educators are at risk because many times they become so caught up in the problems, too. They need a good, stable family that has no major risk factors. You need that to offset it for you. I think that it would be totally debilitating to work with a full case load of high-risk families.*

This is an interesting twist on the universal access argument, the program should be available to any and every family, which is most frequently presented as a political issue or presented on curricular grounds and from the parents' perspective. Parent educators need some "stable" families to leaven their caseloads. It was a sentiment expressed by many parent educators in a variety of ways. The two viewpoints do not conflict, but in fact mesh to form a cohesive rationale that argues powerfully in favor of the universal access model.

After recruiting the "hard to reach," one finds, at the most elementary level, the "hard to maintain" family. The concept can be operationalized in terms of how difficult it is to physically contact a family—that is, to make, keep, and complete an appointment for a private visit or group meeting.

In an age when most of us make use of AT&T and the postal service for scheduling meetings and making appointments, it comes as a surprise to find that other techniques seem prevalent as well as successful.

WW: *Laurie has been cooperative and consistent. She doesn't have a telephone—has not had one for the last 2 years. And so, sometimes scheduling or rescheduling appointments becomes a little bit problematic. If something comes up, it's difficult for her to let me know. And it's equally difficult for me to let her know if*

> *something comes up in my schedule that causes a change. But usually I can stop by the house, knock on the door and just leave a message with her sister or sometimes her brother who's there. If Laurie's not there, I'll just say to them, "Tell her I'd like to come back and see her on Tuesday at 11 o'clock if that's convenient. If it's not, I'll come by and whoever's there can tell me when's a better time." I have found that sending letters does not work.*
>
> LS: *With Laurie or in general?*
>
> WW: *Ah . . . kind of—it's not with everyone. I would say it's about a 40/60 proposition with 40% of it not really working. For example, the last time I scheduled Laurie through a letter, when I got there, she said she had not received the letter. So I don't know. But she was at home so she said, "Oh, sure, come on in."*

Parent educators reported, and we observed, a number of strategies for scheduling families. Almost all parent educators followed the format suggested in the *Program Planning and Implementation Guide* of scheduling the next visit at the end of the current visit. This strategy, although very successful with "easy to reach, maintain and help families," was significantly less successful with our target group. Parent educators used a number of alternate strategies to increase the probability that parents kept scheduled appointments ranging from sending reminder postcards the week before the scheduled visit; calling the day before the visit, dropping by the day before the visit to remind the client of the scheduled visit, to calling just before leaving the center.

The critical element of time (to do all of the extra outreach activities required to work with hard to reach and maintain families) noted with regard to recruitment was a continuing thread that ran though efforts to maintain families in the program. The most potent strategy for maintaining hard to reach and maintain families was simply sticking with a family through all of the early missed and near missed appointments until families had built up a sense of trust in the parent educator and the program. Parent educators reported and a review of records verified that the longer families remained in the program, the easier it was to maintain contact with them. Over and over, we heard comments such as that.

During the first year of implementation of the ECDA in 1985-1986, the St. Louis school district-based parent educators were paid on the number of completed visits. For parent educators serving significant numbers of hard to reach families, this frequently resulted in putting in 5 hours of work but getting paid for only 2 1/2 or 3 hours or, in a worst case scenario, for less than 1 hour.

Predictably, parent educator morale declined and perceptions of job stress increased. The district responded in the 1986–1987 school year by implementing a guaranteed 25-hour work week with a caseload of 55 to 65 families per parent educator. This was a major change from the caseloads suggested in the general program literature that recommends caseloads of 60 families for 20 contact hours per week. With the start of the 1989–1990 school year, the St. Louis district reduced caseloads even further to 50 families for first-year parent educators to a maximum of 60 families for "seasoned" parent educators. Thus, the essential lesson for school districts seeking to implement a PAT Program with "hard to reach" families is to recognize that the time needed to make contact with such families must be built into the official work day. Figure 3.1 summarizes some of these consequences.

CONCLUSIONS

In a word, recruitment policies and practices have prodigious implications for a program such as PAT. The identification of difficult to reach and maintain families poses problems for recruitment strategies. Rather than people reading or hearing of the program through public announcements, coming to a decision that the program is important for themselves and their child, and seeking out the PAT offices and staff, the "hard to reach" have to be sought. We have argued that the St. Louis PAT staff approached the problem with a variety of imaginative and aggressive outreach practices. Recruiting in hospitals, social service centers, and shelters demands an array of special attitudes, knowledge, and skills, as we have indicated in some detail.

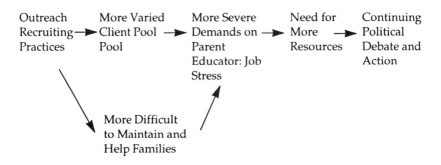

Figure 3.1. The Complexities of recruiting hard to reach families

Such recruiting has important consequences. First, many families enter the program in a way that can be characterized as "others feeling that the program is needed more than the families do." That raises significant motivational issues and increases the phenomenon we have called "difficult to maintain families." Much of the discussion in the next two chapters describes and analyzes the PAT staff attempts to cope with this "new" problem. In addition, such recruiting runs headlong into the issue of the limits of the program, that is, are there some families and children who pose problems too large for PAT as originally constituted and now adapted in the urban community?

Joined with this change in recruiting practice and its outcome is a further significant change in program policy, a change we have only hinted at to this point. The ECDA, established the program statewide and mandated the PAT program for any child younger than 3 years. This meant that many second-and third-time mothers were eligible and "recruited" into the program. White's "teachable moment," the third trimester of the first pregnancy, had disappeared as a given for many families and their parent educators. We argue that this has had a tremendous impact on the curriculum and teaching of the program, in both the personal visits and the group meetings. And more distally, this suggests changes throughout the PAT program. Resources, staff selection, initial training, inservice training, coordination and administration, and so forth are all made problematic to a degree.

chapter
four

The Parent Educator as Teacher

As with most educational programs, the core of the PAT effort lies with the teacher. In this instance, it is the parent educator and the action she takes—what she believes, thinks, and does. Implicitly, we have already begun a discussion of aspects of her background, training, and continuing development in the context of her role in the PAT organization. But now we turn directly to her relationship with the parents and children and her work as a teacher.

Our perspective begins with a brief view from the National Center's *Program Planning and Implementation Guide.* Policy, philosophy, formal doctrine, or, perhaps, ideology are labels for the program's overall notion of how the parent educators should carry out the day-to-day mandate of the program. We believe that these guidelines are an important and continuing practical set of influences on the parent educators' work as teachers.

Next, we raise one of our most important perspectives on the PAT program. We call this perspective "Difficult Family Situations: Reaching, Maintaining, and Helping." What began as our brief on "hard to reach and maintain families" has gradually evolved as we have observed, worked in, and thought about the PAT program. We speak of "difficult family situations" rather than "difficult families," for the former implies more of the possibilities of change and the latter implies something intrinsic to the family. Furthermore, and even more important, we now discriminate three categories of difficult family situations, "reaching, maintaining, and helping." Each category suggests alternative problems and resolutions.

That analysis occasions a line of thought we have called *reconstruing the parent educator role*. More than any other label, *the significant conversation* spells out our conception of the parent educator "teaching." Other aspects follow on this as our emphasis is clarified and extended. Continuing with our intent of having a practical manual, we move next to a discussion of "specific gambits and techniques." We believe we have seen a number of parent educator actions that are worthy of highlighting and worthy of trials in other communities. As always, further layers of context appear around any specific set of recommended practices. Often, these are dilemmas that do not have a simple right or wrong quality, but rather temper or set the occasion for the more specific procedures. We phrase this as "attending to the larger issues." And finally, we try to pull the ideas together into a summary and conclusion.

A VIEW FROM THE PROGRAM GUIDE

We do not intend to reproduce the PAT *Program Planning and Implementation Guide*. However, we believe it is important for the reader to have a brief feel for the standard way of doing the personal visits, for these shape the initial behavior of the parent educators. To facilitate this view we have reproduced as Figures 4.1 and 4.2, the overall guidelines (pp. 31–32) and one illustrative lesson plan on language development (p. 135).

Our reading of the guidelines and these couple of pages, as illustrations, suggests a number of interpretations, both similarities and differences in the program guide/manual and our report/manual. Again we do not argue "good or bad," rather, the array of alternatives possible. To accent what we have done: Our account is full of people, the guidelines are "people free." We deal with what we call "the realities of the program in action," the guidelines tend to be abstracted and idealistic, although specific, useful, and reasonable in our view. We tend to replace what seems like a more businesslike sales and marketing approach and language, in favor of a more educational and organizational social science perspective. Educationally, the guidelines seem to take a more traditional Gagneian or Madeline Hunter lesson planning and lesson type format, whereas we take a more Brunerian and, on occasion, Rogerian flavor. In a word, we feel that considerable controversy exists in the educational psychology of teaching and learning. Robert Gagne, Madeline Hunter, Jerome Bruner, and Carl Rogers are illustrative of that diversity. To us, the domain of teaching and learning is more

Figure 4.1. Guidelines for personal visit lesson plans

The personal visit allows the parent educator to individualize the program for each family and child. It is recommended that visits be held monthly, preferably in the home, and that they last approximately 1 hour. It is important for parent educators to schedule visits to accommodate the needs of families and include both parents to the degree possible.

Beginning with the personal visit lesson plan for a 3- month-old baby, the objectives for each lesson plan are the same. In this and subsequent lesson plans "Standard" follows the word objectives:

OBJECTIVES OF PERSONAL VISITS

A. Maintain rapport with the family.
B. Provide appropriate child development information.
C. Help parents develop observation skills.
D. Support and reinforce the importance of the parents' role as teachers of their child.
E. Solicit and respond to parents' questions and concerns.

The lesson plan procedures outline the five components of the personal visit. The five components are:

A. Establish Rapport
B. Observation
C. Discussion
D. Lesson
E. Summary

Beginning with the personal visit lesson plan for a 3-month-old baby, components A, B, C, and E remain the same. In the lesson plan the word "Standard" follows these components. "Standard" refers to the following:

PROCEDURES

A. Establish Rapport
    1. Greet parents and child.
    2. Reinforce the importance of the parents' role as teachers of their child.
B. Observation
    1. Observe and discuss developmental characteristics and emerging skills.
    2. Observe parent—child interaction, reinforcing parenting skills as they are noted.
    3. Respond to parents' comments and questions.
    4. Continue observation throughout the visit.
C. Discussion
    1. Solicit and respond to parents' questions and concerns.
    2. Discuss what to expect during the coming months.
    3. Identify and reinforce strengths of the family.
    4. Continue discussion throughout the visit.
D. Lesson (see Individual Personal Visit Lesson Plans)
E. Summary

Figure 4.1. Guidelines for personal visit lesson plans (con't)

1. Review and jot down the two or three most important points of the visit.
2. Reinforce parents' feelings of competence in the parenting role and as teachers of their child.
3. Using the handouts for parents, discuss ways for parents to have fun with their child.
4. Discuss topic, time and location of the next personal visit and/or group meeting.

The lesson component of the personal visit is different on each lesson plan and is outlined in detail on each lesson plan.

Throughout the first 3 years of life, the educational curriculum focuses on curiosity, language, intellectual, social and physical development. Handouts for parents and resources for the parent educator to be used during the personal visit, follow each lesson plan. Lesson plans for use by the parent educator are provided for each personal visit, prenatal through 36 months.

ESSENTIAL LESSON PLANS

Twenty-three of the 36 lesson plans are designated "Essential". If a family enrolls when their child is older than 1 month of age and/or if families are not visited monthly, all 36 lesson plans will not be used. In these cases, be sure to use the lesson plans designated essential. It is not always necessary for the lesson plan and the child's age to be exactly the same. Although most children follow the same sequence of development overall, within a given period the rate and sequence of development may vary. Use professional judgment in choosing the lesson plan most appropriate for each child and family.

Age of Child: 1 Month	Developmental Characteristics; Attachment
Age of Child: 4 Months	Intellectual and Motor Development: Hearing
Age of Child: 5 Months	Language Development: Early Use of Books
Age of Child: 6 Months	Social Development; Establishing Healthy Sleep Patterns
Age of Child:7 Months	Motor Development; Safety Proofing the Home
Age of Child: 8 Months	Developmental Characteristics; The Parents' Role
Age of Child: 10 Months	Intellectual Development; Discipline
Age of Child: 11 Months	Language Development; Encouraging Interest in Books
Age of Child: 12 Months	Developmental Characteristics; Developmental Screening
Age of Child: 14-17 Mos	Developmental Characteristics 14-24 Months
Age of Child: 14-17 Mos	Language Development
Age of Child: 14-17 Mos	Negativism
Age of Child: 18 Mos	Language Development; Receptive Language Screening
Age of Child: 19-23 Mos	Language Development; Toilet Learning
Age of Child: 19-23 Mos	Self Esteem; Social Development
Age of Child: 24 Mos	Developmental Characteristics: Developmental Screening
Age of Child: 25-29 Mos	Language Development
Age of Child 25-29 Mos	Social Development

(Revised edition © 1989, Missouri Department of Elementary and Secondary Education).

**Figure 4.2. Essential personal visit lesson plan
Age of child: 11 months**

Emphasis: Language Development; Encouraging Interest in Books

I. OBJECTIVES. Standard (Refer to Guidelines for the Personal Visit Lesson Plans.)

II. HANDOUTS FOR PARENTS AND PARENT EDUCATOR
A. Your Child, 8-14 Months: Language Development. (Refer to Your Child Materials section of this guide.)
B. Techniques To Nurture Interest in Books
C. Language Development, 8 to 14 Months
D. Frequently Understood Words

III. ADDITIONAL RESOURCE FOR PARENT EDUCATOR
A. Book Behaviors of Infants and Toddlers

IV. PROCEDURES
A. Establish Rapport (Standard)
B. Observation (Standard)
C. Discussion (Standard)
D. Lesson
1. Discuss developmental characteristics of a baby 8-14 months with emphasis on language development.
2. Discuss techniques to nurture interest in books and book behaviors of infants and toddlers using the parent handouts and additional resource for parent educator.
3. Model and involve parents in the following activities:
a. Tape record the baby's babbling. Play it back for him. Become excited when you hear his voice. Give parents an opportunity to record the baby's babbling.
b. Point to and name objects in which the baby is interested. When the baby is not involved with an object, name and talk about the objects that are near to him.
c. Make a zip-lock bag book with family photos or magazine pictures. If appropriate, bring a Polaroid camera to use while making the book. Bring three zip-lock bags sewn together at the closed end, and construction paper to fit inside the bag. Using a glue stick, attach the pictures to the construction paper. After demonstrating with one page, give the parents an opportunity to complete the book.
d. Read the baby a simple book. Ask the baby to give the book to one of his parents to read.
E. Summary (Standard)

problematic than the guide implies. As indicated here, this seems especially important as we focus on difficult to reach, maintain, and help families.

More specifically regarding Figure 4.1, we make several comments and interpretations. First, the personal visits are couched in terms of "lesson plans." That seems important in keeping with the idea that the PAT program is an educational program operated through the local school districts. PAT is not a nursing, social work, or counseling program operating out of a hospital or a social agency, although it is being adapted for use in such settings.

The recommended practice of individualized, in the home, for 1 hour, once-a-month personal visits is tempered by our data. And appropriately so, for this is one reason our study was undertaken. As is elaborated here, *individualization* is an educational label covering a multitude of practices, if not sins. Smith has labored that in a number of publications, but especially in the studies of the Kensington Elementary School (Smith & Keith, 1971, Smith, Kleine, Prunty, & Dwyer, 1986; Smith, Prunty, Dwyer, & Kleine, 1987). In our PAT data, we will see this concept stretched to its limits. Almost all of the home visits occurred in the homes, and they usually lasted 1 hour. The once-a-month frequency of personal visits was practically nonexistent in our program. The high geographical mobility of parents in the hard to reach and maintain urban population, in addition to a general underlying lack of stability in the day-to-day structure of their lives, which often made it difficult to consummate scheduled appointments, resulted in an average of five or six out of eight or nine possible private visit contacts for the majority of families that we observed. However, what we did observe were frequent informal contacts, a number over the phone and some in briefly stopping by the homes. These were not recorded as private visits, but they served to keep the parent educator connected with the family and the progress of the child.

The objectives and procedures of establishing and maintaining rapport, providing child development information through conversation and lessons, working on parental observational skills, having discussions with the parents, and summarizing all occurred. However, the variations in each become very significant in our observations and interviews. Additionally, the parent educator as a coach, role model, and agent of change in the mother's development as a person, not just as a parent, was a frequently assumed role, as our observations attested. We believe our accounts provide an important addition to the guidelines.

Language development and discipline were major thrusts within the personal visits we observed. Distinctions of receptive and expressive language, concern with "the little words" (on, under, next to, etc.), reading, and modeling of reading behavior appeared everywhere. Occasional use of audio and videotapes appeared. On occasion, some very creative parent–child language-related construction activities occurred, as indicated later in this book. In regard to discipline, alternatives to the near exclusive use of corporal punishment as a behavior management technique colored discussions of toilet training, temper tantrums, attention span, and responding to parental requests/ demands.

The manual[1] makes only passing reference to what we call "difficult family situations," the topic we move to next.

DIFFICULT FAMILY SITUATIONS: REACHING, MAINTAINING, AND HELPING

Reconstruing the Original Problem

In the initial phrasing of the research problem, "difficult to reach urban families" was the focus. In early discussions during the negotiation of the contract, when Smith first became involved, the conception was altered, mainly by Wells, that some families were easy to get into the program, but hard to keep in, that is, difficult to maintain. The formal proposal contained some of those initial distinctions. In the process of observing families who seemed not hard to reach, in the sense of getting them into the program, and who seemed not hard to maintain, that is keeping them in the program, Smith observed personal visits between parents and parent educators where the problem seemed to be difficulty in helping the parents. A new category, "difficult to help," arose. We see these distinctions among the most important of our results. Such a reconstrual is not atypical of qualitative field research.

More precisely, we use the terms this way. *Difficult to reach* refers to families who do not self-initiate and self-refer themselves into the program in response to the usual announcements in the local media—newspapers, radio, and television. And often, they are families that someone else, usually school or social service people, see as needing the program. The families are perceived to have children at risk of eventually having school problems, what Schorr (1988) called "rotten outcomes." Connotations and stereotypes abound—race, poverty, area of the city, single parent, teenage parents, underclass, and social problems of drugs, crime, and family disorganization. Furthermore, hard to reach

---

[1]The PAT National Center has developed some supplemental materials and training programs in this area.

has metaphorical aspects once a family is in the program: "I call them and no one answers" or "they don't have a phone and I can't contact them." Or "I talk to them and nothing seems to sink in" or "they don't follow through on suggestions." The former we describe as hard to maintain in the program and the latter we describe as hard to help. In our restricted use of *hard to reach*, our accounts of the intensive recruitment efforts indicated how St. Louis is solving that problem.

Difficult to maintain families are those that present large problems in the delivery of PAT services, the home visits and the group meetings. Parents who move about, and mobility is a large problem within the overall urban community, are very difficult to maintain in the program. Much of this occurs in the summertime, the 3-to-5 month period between May and September. We believe that expanding the program to 12 months would help solve this problem. That solution then redefines the "hard to maintain" problem to one of raising resources. And the trade-offs begin to occur—how much increase in resources can one tolerate, or afford, for how much increase in maintaining difficult families in the program? Similarly, one of the most effective ways of maintaining attendance at the group meetings is the provision of vouchers for transportation. How much of a budget for cab fares is the program willing to provide for how much increase in attendance. Such dilemmas abound in our data and analysis. And they are real in our view. They force people at several levels of the PAT program and organization, from state legislators to local coordinators, to make very difficult choices.

"Difficult to help" families are those who make little progress toward PAT goals with "normal" services, those services suggested by the program guide that focus primarily on the parent educator as a teacher of information and developmental expectations. Two large subgroups constitute the general category. Some families seem overwhelmed by outside events—for example, poverty, multiple children appearing too quickly, and single parenthood. A second group seem more psychologically and emotionally impaired. Events from within a person can be catastrophic as well.

Along the way, we raise some of the complications in the dynamics of the program. For instance, if one successfully recruits difficult to reach families, a desirable goal from our point of view, then one is likely to have more families that are difficult to maintain and help. Each of these steps takes more resources. In a sense an anomaly appears: The more successful you are in recruiting, the more problems you create for the parent educator staff. The closer the staff member is to direct service, the more the burden falls. We are reminded of the classic anecdotes of classroom teachers who are successful in working with difficult children often find their classes being loaded with more and more difficult children until their entire teaching program breaks down. We find these issues to be interesting and general practical problems of policy and schooling that have their analogs in the PAT program. As we witnessed the St. Louis program in action, we observed many specific gambits and techniques—some more successful than others—used by parent educators and administrators in working with families living in difficult situations (see Figure 4.3).

Idiosyncratic Aspects of Parents and Families

One of our most important generalizations is "get to know the idiosyncratic aspects of families, accept those, and begin to work toward enhancing the child's development within those parameters." Consider Marjory's case.

LS: *Do you want to tell me about Marjory?*

WW: *Okay. Marjory is . . . let's see, Marjory is right now—Marjory is about 19 years old. She was 16 when I first enrolled her in the program. Um . . . she lived in a household that consisted of her mother, her sister Sue, who had one child, Marjory herself, who had one child, and a brother, Aaron, who was only 2. [laughs] Marjory's mother was still trying to figure out how this happened. She had daughters 18 years old, and 16 years old, and a 2-year-old.*

LS: *And the mother wasn't in the program with her 2-year-old?*

WW: *The mother wasn't in the program although she sat in on every visit. So Aaron was screened. But she felt that she didn't really have enough time for the program, but she was there almost every time I went. She thought it was a good program for her girls to be in, but . . . I don't know if she felt that saying she wanted to be in it was some kind of a comment on her skills because after all she did have three children. But anyway, a very receptive grandmom. Marjory had one child at that time. Now she has two. But at that time she had one, Judy. Marjory did not finish high school. She finished ninth grade. I think she didn't really enjoy school that much, I don't think she was that good at it. I think she could finish but it will take an effort—a real effort on her part. She has a—she has a very . . . calm personality and . . . within her family, she's the one, I think, that her mother and her sister are always saying, "Marjory, you need to do this. Marjory, you need to do that. Marjory! Marjory! Wipe that baby's nose. Marjory!" One of those. But very, very affectionate toward her daughter. And actually very observant of her baby's behavior. She lives off of Aid to Dependent Children. Doesn't have a whole lot of resources. My personal feeling is that she doesn't—she could*

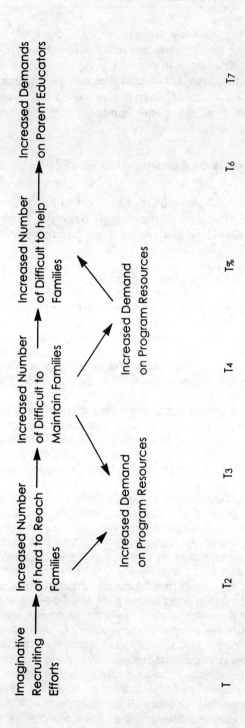

Figure 4.3. A process image of hard to reach, maintain, and help families in difficulty

take care of the physical care a little bit more and by that I mean—and I know kids will be dirty but you wash your kid's face every couple of hours. Didn't monitor Judy's comings and goings quite as much as Cicely monitored Aaron's and Joan monitored Mark's, in that if Judy wanted to crawl out of the chair and crawl up onto the table, well, Marjory would look at her a while, everybody else would cry, "Get back off of that table!" But . . . it's OK. Judy is now 4 years of age. She attends a Headstart Program. And . . . she seems to enjoy it a great deal. Marjory—her children talk very well. They talk very well, because she talks to them.

Becoming a part of that family, talking directly with the daughters who were mothers and indirectly with the grandmother, who also was a mother of a toddler, and working within the parameters of the family constellation requires an artistic interpersonal performance by the parent educator. Knowing that such families occur, accepting their overall lifestyle, and focusing in on the development of the individual child suggest the guidelines for working with such a family. *Idiosyncratic families* is the watchword.

Lessons About Program Success

Images abound of families that are hard to maintain in the program. The reasons vary. These reasons and their consequences in action lead to several lessons about program success. Another of our interviews illuminated the issues. It began this way.

LS: *Before we start on that, Wilma was telling me about the woes of being a parent educator and yesterday's day turned out to be a bust. And you were just going to elaborate. You had three appointments or . . .?*

WW: *Yeah, I had three appointments, none of which—none of which I made. Now, one of them I understand—she's a — she's one of my clients—and . . .*

LS: *Who was this by name?*

WW: *This is Cecilia. You haven't met her before. But she's just begun working and she works a horrible shift, one of those that starts in the middle of the night and goes through to the early morning. You know, one of those kinds of shifts. She takes her kids to the babysitter. And I'm sure she was probably caught up in transit. But the second one was—was a client who is usually very reliable. Josie!*

LS: *Oh.*

WW: *Josie! I called her the night before and she said, yes, she would be there. So I . . . I called her right before I left the office—and the reason I did is because I—when Cecilia wasn't there, I said, "Well, I'll call Josie and see if I can just come a little bit earlier." Well, her boyfriend said she wasn't home. He wasn't sure where she was because he had just awakened. So I said, "Well, you know, we have a 2 o'clock appointment. I'll be there." I arrived at 2 o'clock and Josie's not there. So I said, "Okay . . . tell her I'll call her." I left, went to the elevator—you know, she lives on the eighth floor. Well, the elevator never came. [laughter] So, I went—I walked down the eight flights, which is much better than walking up the eight flights. So I said, "Well, I'll run by her mother's house because I know that she frequently goes to her mom's house."*

LS: *Yeah, that was going to be my next question. She's just around the corner.*

WW: *Yes. So I went to her mother's house. At her mom's house, well, all the snow that's ever fallen in the last week was still on her walk and steps . . . so I—I tentatively made my way up to the door but Josie wasn't there. I had a 3:15 appointment with a new mom.*

LS: *Who's that one by name?*

WW: *Her name is Darla. I called and I said, "I'm on my way. Can you just tell me the cross street so that I don't drive too far because I have not been to this house before?" She said, "Oh, you know, I was just going to call you but I'm just on my way out the door." [laughs] I said, "OK," so—*

LS: *Where she was going?*

WW: *She said she had an emergency with her son. But I asked when's a convenient time to call her back. She told me about 6 o'clock. So I called her back at 6 o'clock, and we've rescheduled for today at 2:15. I'm hoping that we actually make it today. And Josie, I talked with her again. I called her last night and . . . she said she was out looking for—her mother told her about somebody who may do her income taxes for free. So she was trying to find this place. And she said, "I was so sure I'd get back in time." And she said, "I'm just so sorry." So I told her where she could go to get her taxes done because she never did find the place. They do tax preparation at Harris-Stowe State College on Saturdays for free.*

The interview continued:

WW: *So I have her rescheduled for today also.*

LS: *Good luck.*

WW: *Yes, so it'll be a—today will be a better day. And I know that all of this is going to work out because I have a meeting this afternoon and I have everything scheduled so tightly that I know that everything's going to make today because . . . [laughs] . . . because I'm scheduled so tightly.*

LS: *It sounds like one of those "Hope Springs Eternal." [laughter] Actually, one of the other things that your comment reminds me of—and I guess it was something, Josie's looking for the free income tax kind of thing. We'd talked one time, months ago, about the full-time job of being on welfare and the—all of the kind of complications that come in and you've got to somehow make do with less adequate resources and to go find somebody who can do your income tax because you don't have the $ 25 or $ 50 dollars that Block or whoever charges for that kind of thing. And then presumably the emergencies like this of Darla's. Just coping with the problems.*

WW: *Except in Darla's case, she's not on welfare. Darla is a working mom, who again has one of those flexible schedules, where she goes in—her schedule changes up every week and then she's kind of on call, too, so she never really knows when she's going to be at work. It's very difficult.*

One of the more interesting interpretations of this episode from an interview lies in the "lessons about program success," triggered by the reported events. First, one can argue, and we do elsewhere, that the careful preparations and scheduling is an important strategy for making the program work easily and well, yet it does not work all the time. Second, the parent educator keeps working, relentlessly, all the time. The kind of commitment and confidence that this requires goes without saying. As does the supervisory support that is needed also. Third, other important "life events," jobs, taxes, and emergencies always appear in the scenarios. Limited financial resources complicate all of these life events. Sometimes these are overwhelming. Fourth, the parent educator must gear her expectations to incorporate the consequences of these events.

Finally, we would comment on an idea implicit in the interview. One of the latent goals of most of the St. Louis parent educators in situations like this is "increasingly putting the responsibility on the parent." Talking, suggesting, and arranging situations to enhance the possibilities of parents taking responsibility for themselves, their actions, and their children appears in conversation after conversation with parent educators. The general principle borders on the obvious, but implementing it, as in this particular situation, is another story.

A Contrasting Case

Sometimes a contrasting case helps clarify a concept. May's situation has a number of interesting similarities and differences to the hard to reach, maintain, and help families we have been describing. Exploring these variations helps to extend our meaning.

WW: May is not a hard to reach mom. May just absolutely delights in her baby.

LS: Is the father in the home?

WW: No. She's a single mom. And the father's not at home. She said that she doesn't have anything to do with the father. If you ask May what did April do at 9:04 a.m., she could probably tell you. I mean she delights in this baby.

LS: What's the baby's name?

WW: April. The notion that you wouldn't provide—you wouldn't structure the environment, it just never would occur to May that you wouldn't do that. You go into her house, it looks like it's April's house, you know, because she's just very aware of that. Not that she goes overboard, but that she just really delights in this baby. And this baby has been nothing but a source of pleasure. She has an adequate income, she can provide for this baby.

LS: And where's the baby during the day?

WW: During the day, she has a sitter in a private home. She's the kind of mom who—she knew she had to go back to work. One of the first questions she asked me when I called her was "Can you please tell me about . . . some child care arrangements? You know, I'm looking for someone." She had begun to look and to interview people beforehand. She has the financial resources, and this baby is not a drain on her in any financial sense. This baby has fulfilled her is the impression that I get. So her whole approach to mothering and childrearing and interacting with this baby is very different from a mom who feels that the baby was an intrusion. "The baby is a drain, I don't have the time to do what I want. This baby has brought a whole set of problems that I never wanted and I don't know how to deal with right now." This is not May!

LS: The contrast with the Sybils and the Sharons, as it were?

This short excerpt reveals an interrelated set of ideas. Being a single parent without a father present is similar to many of our families. A good job, in the sense of adequate financial resources, differs from many of the mothers. The contrasts appear in "delights" in the child, not an "intrusion," and ability to cope, "problems . . . I never wanted and don't know how to deal with right now." Rounding out the miniature theory of the contrasting case are such ideas as "restructuring the environment" and "not going overboard," and "the baby has fulfilled her." The lesson here becomes: How does one teach other mothers to feel and behave like this? One might argue that this is the endpoint on the "empowering parents" continuum. What kind of "lessons" will do that, accomplish such a goal or set of goals? We note also, that some of the suggestions from the parent educator occurred in a brief telephone call, outside the formal structure of the personal visits and group meetings, but well within the purposes of the overall program. It seems that parent educators are working all the time.

The Turn Around Case

Another of the intriguing and confounding aspects of families living in difficult situations is what we call *turn around cases*. These are the success stories of those who were either difficult to recruit, maintain, or help, but who over time became strong members and supporters of the program. The key phrase is "over time." As we have stressed throughout the report, our perspective is to de-emphasize labeling that suggests permanent characteristics of parents and families. Parents who are initially hard to reach, become less so when the recruiting strategies change. Similarly, families who are hard to maintain in the program become less so when scheduling tactics shift and when cab fares are paid to bring the mothers to group meetings. As the relationship between the parent educator and the parent grows in trust, the hard to help become less difficult.

Comments from our notes suggest some of the parent educator statements on their turn around cases: "Once you catch up with her, the visit is great." "She's just one of those that you have to make up your mind that you have to schedule her three times before you'll see her, but she's okay."

Several categories of strategies and techniques appear in discussions of moving difficult families into strong members and supporters of the program. First, providing frequent and timely reminders of the upcoming visit has been very helpful. More specifically, the techniques include sending reminders on postcards or personal notes, including stamped self-addressed envelopes along with response sheets for rescheduling visits if necessary, and calling a few day's before and immediately before leaving the office for the visit. This last gambit frequently took the form of "Hi, I'm on my way, so look out for me. I'll be there in about 15 minutes." A second broad category we have hinted at before, placing the responsibility on the parent. In our discussions we raised the issue, "if it means more to you than it does to the family, you are in for trouble." Enhancing the significance of the program and its elements (parent visits, group meetings, contact with other parents, drop in activities, etc.) for the parent is a continuing long-term goal. With a few parents this is pushed to the extreme, if you want to remain in the program you will have to do such and such. Significant conversations come in many forms. Frankness highlights the contribution of each party to the continuing relationship.

DIFFICULT TO HELP: THE NEW CATEGORY

As the varied families arose in our observations and interviews, parent educators talked metaphorically of another kind of hard to reach, the families that they had difficulty influencing. These became our "hard to help" category. We collected a number of cases for further discussion. "Not looking forward to the child's development" became the prototypical instance. Others followed. We report them here with some of our initial and lingering questions and with suggestions and recommendations, realizing the tentativeness of the interpretations.

"Not Looking Forward to the Child's Development: Difficult Family Situations and Personal Problems

In memo 33, written after a parent visit with Abbie Thompson the parent educator, the insight that led to the reconceptualizaton and distinction of "difficult to help" appeared in the subtitle, "not looking forward to the child's development." We present the memo, and then we present some additional thoughts about the illustration and the idea. In addition to the substantive points regarding the parent education program, the discussion illustrates well the methodological issues in this kind of research: the flow of empirical data from close observations, to interpretive asides at the time, to later discussion and reflection. Conjecturing and hypothesizing appear at several points. The miniature theories are retested, if not falsified, in later illustrations. The ideas offer problems for later evaluative studies of parts, the tessare, of the mosaic of evaluation.

Several different categories arose as I tried to come to grips with items from several conversations and several home visits. The labels varied from "clients I have not been as successful with as I had hoped" to "parents who don't seem to enjoy their child." The most vivid illustration arose in a home visit with Alice, the mother of 2-year-old Betty. Ultimately, and perhaps most critically for the project on "Difficult to Reach" and "Difficult to Maintain" families, the case seemed to expand the "Difficult" category a giant step to include "Difficult to Help" parents. If the argument is sound it might change the focus of the project and the report to "Difficult Parents: Reaching, Maintaining, and Helping."

But to return to Alice. As I observed Alice and the parent educator in the home visit, I was struck by a kind of affective distance between Alice and her daughter Betty. The mother couldn't seem to quite touch the child with tenderness or warmth. Even when the child snuggled into the big overstuffed rocker where the mother was sitting, a kind of making room for her occurred, but almost simultaneously a kind of emotional ignoring of her also occurred. Verbally, I was struck with her comments that each new developmental event was not seen as a new problem to be solved, but a problem which she didn't seem to have the energy with which to cope. All this, rather than a looking forward to each accomplishment of the child, anticipating the next round of developmental change, and enjoying both the accomplishments and the anticipations. The specific illustrations for much of the discussion concerned naps, potty training in general and "deliberate" accidents in particular, "not looking forward to Betty's move from a crib to a bed" because she would probably wander around or fall out of bed, and Betty's inability to understand and follow directions about toys (which struck me as very well along for a 2-year-old). At the time, one of my interpretive notes was "Everything's a problem, too much on her plate?"

According to the parent educator, the mother has a long history of personal problems, marital difficulties with her husband, and "yelling at, spanking, and beating" the child. How does a parent educator work with such a family? Recently, and partly due to the parent educator's efforts, the mother and father are in a counseling program. Parents Anonymous is another possibility that has been discussed. Friendship networks of young mothers and PAT group meetings were part of the discussion as well. (Memo 33)

We formalized some of our thinking into Figure 4.4, the dynamics of what seemed to be happening in the family and the parent–child relationship. Little of the mother's "early history" is reported here, nor do we accent especially her reports of personal and marital difficulties. The key concepts from the observation that we want to accent are the interrelated items of "not looking forward to the child's development," "affective distance," and "too many problems," that is, too much on her plate for the energy she has. These concepts and propositions are a wor-

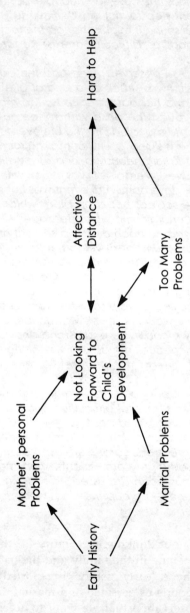

Figure 4.4. Dynamics of not looking forward to child's development

thy intellectual agenda for hours of discussion among parent educators in preservice and inservice educational programs. Paraphrased, Abbie, the parent educator's immediate reaction was severalfold: "Yes, all that is true, I am amazed you saw so much in such a short time," and "Let's talk about it."

As we reflect on the memo, with little fear of contradiction we draw several major hypotheses if not firm conclusions. First, the parent educator had established a bond of trust that went far beyond what is implied in the standard lesson plan item, "establish rapport." Second, the process of trust building did not take place over one or two visits, but slowly formed over repeated interactions within the context of the private visits, group meetings, and innumerable telephone conversations. Some parent educators "live" on the telephone. This parent educator was one of those. Third, up to this point the parent educator's ability to effectively communicate with Alice regarding Betty's development had been less than she had hoped. Fourth, the family's enrollment in a counseling program provided the mechanism to "free Alice up" to focus on her child Betty's development in a positive productive way. Furthermore, the memo shows some of the limits of the educational role of the parent educator and when it is time to refer. Referral is no simple one-time effort. Rather, referral is a skilled process in itself. In this case, Alice's husband was resistant initially. Working through this was its own challenge. Knowledge of local community resources, for example, Parents Anonymous, appears also. Additional examples supporting these more general interpretations appear throughout our data and this report. Figure 4.5 summarizes some of these ideas.

Mothers Who Neither Want Nor Understand Their Babies

As we have suggested, hard to help mothers come in varied forms. Part of being an effective parent educator is perceiving those forms and adjusting one's response to those differences. Among the most difficult to help parents are those who do not want to be parents. In an interview, we talked of two sisters, both mothers in the program. The conversation occurred shortly after the first contact between one of the mothers and the parent educator.

LS: *How old were they?*
WW: *They are 20 and 21.*
LS: *So they're quite young.*
WW: *Yeah. I have some real concerns about the 20-year-old. She has a 6-week-old baby. And she . . . she seems to have no natural instincts for parenting. She—she wakes the baby so*

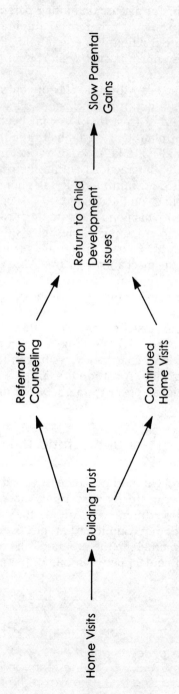

Figure 4.5. Intervention strategies

> *roughly. I asked her if she ever talks to the baby. She said, "That doesn't make any sense to talk to the baby. They don't understand what you're saying anyway." She's going to take a lot of very patient and loving care because I just think that this child has really overwhelmed her. I asked her how she liked being a mother. She's very upset because this baby wakes her up during the night. She wanted a girl because she's convinced that girls don't cry. They wake up during the night, but if you feed them, they go right back to sleep. This baby is an intrusion and a burden to her right from the beginning.*

LS: *The other one is a little different than that?*
WW: *The other one is a little different. She has two kids.*
LS: *And they're sisters?*
WW: *Yes. But the other one has two children. One is just under 2 and the other one is 8 months old. She said she's used to getting up at night because she had to get up with the older one. And really she doesn't get up that much at night. She likes being a mother. Her whole temperament is—you know, you talk about easy babies and difficult to soothe babies, well, with these moms, you can use the same terms, one of them is a real easy one and the other one is much more difficult in terms of her temperament. And both of them, I think are delayed—they're limited to some extent, in terms of their cognitive development. But the older one seems to be much more suited to being a parent than the younger one does.*

It is obvious that this young mother, the younger sister, has not been successful in making the transition to parenthood. She does not have a realistic view of what to expect from the baby. She seems to have limitations in her own general intellectual ability. But she does represent a significant subset of our hard to help group. Parent educators report that one of the first things they try to do with mothers like this is to get them to a group meeting where they can interact with mothers of similarly aged children. Perspective and understanding have a chance to develop and flower.

A poignant example follows in the account of Cassie and her son Russell. In our discussion, a number of key ideas tumbled out and flowed together: not wanting and understanding her child, "turn around case," special potency of group meetings, modeling, and the subtleties of parent educator and parent interaction. Helping the hard to help accents our intent.

WW: *I think she got Cassie from DFS.*
LS: *And they referred her . . . ?*

WW: Hm-hmm. Well, actually they didn't refer her. We go over to the Division of Family Services throughout the month. As people come in to be served, we ask them if they're interested in the program. DFS. has been very cooperative because they send out our flyers in their monthly mailings to their clients. But I believe that Cassie was an on-site registration.

         One of the things that I think was very noticeable was that she hit him a lot. And . . . she—she talked at him a lot. She didn't actually do a great deal until she got up to hit him. So it was—it was a matter of fussing with him and yelling instructions at him. And then when she got so fed up with him saying, "No," and wondering what to do with him, she would grab him and take him out to spank him or something. I discussed—I discussed with the parent educator what I'd observed at the meeting and wanted to know if this was typical of Cassie when they're in the home. How did she deal with it? I talked with Cassie at the meetings. You know, "I bet this must be really frustrating for you." "Oh, yeah, he is so bad." "And what types of things have you tried with him?" And the parent educator was doing that during the home visit. During the group meetings, I would always make a point—I always made a point to talk to Cassie about her son. Whenever he does anything good at the group meeting, I try to make it a point to tell Cassie about it, because I think that what she is doing is focusing in—she was becoming consumed by his bad behaviors. And as a result, that's what she was seeing all the time. She would never see him when he was cooperating.

         And so . . . another thing is that sometimes when he would do something that she didn't like and she would begin to yell at him, I would just kind of walk over and put my arm around her and say, "Why don't you go over to him and show him what to do? Just kind of gently, you know—" And when she did, I'd say, "Oh, you really did very well. Did you notice the difference in his behavior?" Just trying to get her to focus on that. And . . . as I said, we try to suggest alternate strategies to her and then to really call her attention to when things seem to be working, and when Russell was behaving in an appropriate way. When Cassie did something that was really good, you know, you're watching her—she would go over and show him how to do something, then I would make it a point to—to walk up to her at some point and say, "I noticed how you did such and such and such with Russell. You're really getting good at that."

         Russell's behavior at the group meetings is becoming so much more acceptable in terms of how he relates to the other children. For example, his ability to take turns. When *he first came, to talk about taking a turn was totally incomprehensible. [laughs] But he's—and he's still just like any—any 2 1/2-year-old, he still has difficulty playing cooperatively with other children the same age without an adult being there. All of that's there. But his ability to . . . to be compliant when given directions has improved so much that I can't help but think that a great part of that has to do with the program. I can't help but think that, because of the change is so dramatic. It is so dramatic. Cassie seems to be happy whenever she comes to the meetings. Because she's not yelling at him.*

LS: *And . . . here you've got a woman who comes eagerly in one sense to the group meetings who apparently doesn't miss appointments especially, and so . . . and yet is very much in need of the program.*

WW: *And as I say, I'm not sure that without the cab service, I'm not sure that she would not be difficult to maintain. See, what I'm saying is that for this particular mom with her major concern being how to just get along with her child, you know, how do they interact without killing each other, really is what the issue was. Before you can get to anything else, they have to learn how to communicate with each other. And I think that that communication was facilitated—I think was facilitated by her attending the group meetings. And again I'm not sure that we could—that this whole notion about the developmental appropriateness of some of her child's behaviors and the need for her to respond to those behaviors in a variety of ways rather than that one way that she had with him—everything was so—giving demands, yelling, screaming, resulting in a hit.*

    I'm not sure that those points would have been made as clearly or as quickly for her just through the private visit, because she would not have seen him with other children and seeing that, well, he's really not that dramatically different from the other kids. She would have had a parent educator to model some kinds of behaviors for her, but . . . I think that seeing other parents at the group meetings interact with their children, seeing how he could get into a group and with the right— with the right kind of structure get along with that group. I think that all of that has been very helpful in her movement toward a more—a more pleasant relationship with her child. And I think that—now I've just been thinking because you asked me this question— but I think that if we had just been doing private visits with her, that she would have been more difficult to maintain, because I don't think you would seen those changes as quickly in his behavior and in hers. One of the most . . . one of the most compelling rea-

*sons for having group meetings as far as I'm concerned is
that parents get to see their children in different situations.
The other thing is that for those folks who are having a difficult time, they get to see other reactions. They get to see
other ways of handling the problem without anybody ever
having to tell them anything.*

This interview/discussion, as with most of our interchanges, was packed so full of vivid images that the conceptual issues in the larg- er rationale seem more latent than we would like to leave them. Cassie and Russell are almost prototypical in the confrontational and punitive sequence that needed to be interrupted and thought about with many of the families in the program. The group meetings are not just an "add- on" for the home visits. Important in their own right, they provided an opportunity for the supervisor to intervene and help the parent educa- tor. The direct attention by another member of the program staff increased the level of program involvement. The subtleties of parent educator strategies, tactics, and thinking in action are major items. The interaction of the parent, the child, the other children, the other parents, and the parent education staff had different dimensions and qualities not available in the home setting. The social interactionist has another setting for observing, thinking, deciding and acting. What often starts as modeling, as it became more elaborate, became almost a kind of moment to moment coaching of the parent—what to see, alternative possible reactions, brief discussion, and praising of efforts. Other children, other mothers, other situations, other possibilities appear without effort and prescription, and parent education goes on. The importance of the cab transportation solution flows into our discussion as an important con- textual issue for the program.

As our illustrations continue, the analysis picks up on the child's behavior, the mother's immediate response, the array of alternatives, and ways of suggesting and demonstrating some of those.

Looking for a Godmother: A Kind of Neediness

Young, teenage mothers also come cloaked in varied kinds of problems. Sharon is one who, by self-report is "looking for a godmother." One of our interviews raised some of the issues that made her a difficult, but far from impossible, young woman to help.

WW: *Sometimes Sharon acts so belligerent, but then she just wants to hold on so tightly. She told me about her—she gave me some insight into her own life which she said was one in which she had endured a great deal of abuse. And she spent almost her entire life in foster care. Sharon has a lot of—I think that she has a lot of things that she needs to work out. If you listen to her conversation, she says things that are often so contradictory that I don't know which is—which is for real and which is not. I'm not sure that she knows sometimes. But . . . but we're working with her and I'm very encouraged by the fact that she does continue to come to the group meetings. Because she is—she is a very demanding and a very possessive . . . and she does—she does crave—and I'm sure that she needs—a lot of attention. She is one of—she is one of the few clients who requests, "When are you coming? When are you coming?" Asking me, "When are you coming out to my house?" [laughs] And the last thing she said to me when she left the group meeting Wednesday was, "Well, you know, I'm still looking for a godmother." [laughs]*

LS: *Oh, boy!*

WW: *You know, she needs somebody to hug her. And she needs somebody to say to her, "Oh, you say that but deep down in your heart, I think . . ." and to pat her face and to tell her what a great lady she is and to compliment her when she does well. She also needs somebody who will call her when she spins these wild, weird tales. You know, we say, "Now, Sharon." But I think—I'm sure you picked up when she was touching her baby, the kind of roughness that was there. She has not quite learned how to express—I don't think she has learned how to express affection—affectionate feeling. And . . . that's something that we have to work on and perhaps one of the reasons she can't express is because she hasn't been the recipient of a great deal of affection. But . . . but that's one of the things that she needs.*

LS: *Does the program shift from being an educational program to being a social service program in some sense or . . .?*

WW: *Well, I don't think the program shifts from being an educational program but there is—for some people, we do serve a greater social service function than for others. And primarily that's in helping to make contact with the appropriate social service agency. For some families, we—we provide a lot of things, I think, for a lot of families. And what a family gets from us depends a lot on what their particular set of needs are. And so for some people, at some point in the program, we might be doing more of one thing than another at any given visit, but over the course of the program year, our main thrust—the overall picture that you should get from us is that*

*we are an educational program. Although we recognize
that in getting to an educational goal, sometimes you have
to address other issues, just like schools have to go into the
social service business of feeding children sometimes in order
to get to their educational goal. And so we must sometimes
help a family get shoes and get food and that's something
that we have to get to before we can get to discussion of
the educational goals that we've set up. Right now Sharon
has a lot of agencies that are involved in her life. As a matter
of fact, one of the parent educators was attending a staffing
meeting on her with folks from Grace Hill and DFS because
there are so many people that are going in and out of her
life that we need to get some kind of a plan of action that's
coordinated among all of us.*

The adjectives pop out at the reader: *belligerent, demanding* and
possessive, weird tales, *unable* to express affection, and *roughness* in handling her child. The parent educator's response suggests again the kind
of virtuoso performance needed if the relationship is to be established
and maintained and help is to be given. Looking for small indicators of
success, finding occasion to give the woman a hug, telling her with a
"Now, Sharon" that you recognize her tall tales, are the little but highly
significant items in such a relationship. The short account of the multiple
difficulties in referrals, multiple agencies, and having some kind of coordinated plan raises another set of difficulties. The end of education and
the beginning of social service, and vice versa, are vague and changing
boundary lines. At a minimum, we believe Sharon's story would make a
powerful vignette for teaching parent educators—"What do you make
of her? How do you think about such a client? What might you do as
Sharon's parent educator?"

Stable Family but Difficult to Help

Despite our penchant for categorizing and conceptualizing, at times the
characterizing and labeling seems almost ludicrous if not impossible to
do meaningfully. The uniqueness of a number of families facilitated our
move from the conception of difficult to reach families to a view of difficult to maintain families, which gave way to difficult to help families.
Wanda's situation expanded the categories into "stable but difficult to
help." Wanda is a 17-year-old mother of two. She had her first child
when she was 14.

LS: And we've been around on a bit of that. To stay out of the social class issue, you use the word "stable families." Do you want to talk a little bit about what stable family would mean?

WW: A stable family is a family that—to me, is a family that is able to function with whatever resources they have. Somehow they've gotten a handle on it and they're able to go from day to day without being in a crisis situation every day or most of the days. These are families that are able to manage the day-to-day functions so that they have energy left over to really concentrate on their children's development. Who have things well enough organized that they can honor a commitment in terms of when the appointment is made.

LS: Where would this family of Wanda's fall? Are they a coping family or a stable family, to use your word? Or . . . is there some kind of a continuum?

WW: Yeah, there's some kind of continuum. If we're going to go from what I would consider—let me put this way. In terms of my ability to make an appointment with Wanda and to in fact consummate that appointment, to carry that through, she's pretty stable in that regard. In terms of—in terms of coping, I think from Wanda's point of view, she copes very well. But from my point of view, I don't think she copes that well.

LS: Okay, we were talking about Wanda and her view that she copes and your view that she doesn't as well.

WW: When I first met her and her son William, Wanda had just left the elementary school. She was living with her mother. She still lives with her mother. She was planning to go back to her elementary school, to complete school. She just never felt that she fit back into the school, which is understandable. Attempts to get her to complete a GED have not met with a great deal of success. She—a lot of the child care really falls to her mother, the child's grandmother. And . . . well, what I see operating in this family is a whole lot of rationalization. "We could do this but . . ." And the grandmother, Wanda's mother, does it also. Her mother went through a child-care training program and now she babysits with a couple of kids in her home, but it never really did come out the way she wanted it to. At one point the mom was going to school. Wanda was going during the day and the mother was going in the evening. The mother finished her program but she's never been—she's never really done anything with it. Some things, that I would really be concerned about, but it doesn't seem to bother her. She got a job working at a hospital. She couldn't keep it because there was too much—she was on her feet too much. The problem is that she weighs too much.

LS: What do you do in the middle of all of that?

WW:　In the middle of all of that? I try—I encourage her to go back to school. When there is a need to follow through on something, I call her. She will follow through if I follow through with her. For example. William has an apparent language delay. And it took forever for the family to admit that there was some concern for his language, and now, his language is improving but there's still a reason for concern. So I made a referral to an agency for a language assessment. After I made the referral to them, I had to call and say to Wanda, "Have you contacted the agency?" Now I didn't call the agency, I kept calling her. "Did you contact them yet?" So she finally contacted them. When the papers came to her—I had told her what to expect. She's competent to fill out the papers, and her mother is there to help her fill them out. I told the mother, "When the papers come, you must fill them out and send them back in." So when I got there for the next visit, I said, "Did the papers come?" "Yeah." "Did you send them back?" "Well, we were waiting for you to come." [laughs] During the visit we filled out the papers and sent them in." It's a—it's one of those kinds of situations where you have to continually remind, remind.

LS:　As you talk about her, you talk with a more discouraged kind of tone in your voice.

WW:　Um, yeah. You have families where you think you're really, really, really having an impact. This is one if you have to talk about families that you're not having as large an impact as you would like to have, I think that Wanda's is one of those for me.

As we think back through this interview protocol, thoughts and interpretations like "dependency" rise up. Stability is there, but so too is dependency. What to do in such cases? Further thoughts of more comprehensive family-centered programs such as the new "Even Start" idea occur. Would a program that is specifically tailored to both the mother's further educational and career development as well as the child's early development help? Or should there be a rotation of parent educators, where each of us takes one or two of another's "bad pennies" and find that some parents we had difficulty helping, others find easier to relate to and to help? Ideas such as these are part and parcel of the kind of dialogue we see, yet feel needs extending. How "teachable" to parent educators is the vignette?

Concluding Images, Questions, and Speculations

Field research permits the observers to bring the best of their intuitions and responsiveness to minimal cues to bear on the problems under scrutiny. Our practice has been to note these so that they do not flit away, even though one has less confidence in some of these interpretations than in some of the others. But some of the interpretations or second thoughts relate to other interpretations at other times. Such is the case with two speculations caught in earlier memos: "World of TV: "Steel Magnolias' and PAT," and "Self-Oriented Needs." Mostly we ask the reader to think with us about a potentially significant group of parents who look like they are hard to help. Memo 18 is self-introducing.

World of TV: "Steel Magnolias" and PAT

The hit of the season at the Repertory Theater at Webster University, and maybe the best play in the last several years in St. Louis, from my amateur critic's perspective, is Steel Magnolias, *a story of a half dozen women who meet each week at a local beauty shop. The first act is full of dazzling repartee among the owner, a new employee, a mother and grown daughter who both come to the shop, and two other characters, a mannish looking woman and a woman who is the widow of a recent mayor of the community. Gradually, as experiences are told, the character and lives of the women are developed and an image of life in a small southern town appears—all from what might be called a woman's perspective. In the second act, tragedy occurs to one of the members and all are intimately involved. A powerful statement of the meaning of the relationships among the women in the beauty shop occurs. For those of you into some of the recent feminist literature—Gilligan's (1983)* **In a Different Voice**, *Nodding's (1984)* **Caring**, *and Belenky's (1986)* **Women's Ways of Knowing**—*you will find that the play "says it all" in a very effective dramatic production.*

One of the events of PAT that I have encountered over this last year is the prevalence of TV, the soap operas and movies, in the lives of the mothers in the program. The TV is always on when we arrive, and usually goes off at the parent educator's request. Visits are scheduled around particular serials. Some women are up late—two, three, or four in the morning watching the late and the late-late movies. Frequently, so it seems, the young children are part of all this. An occasional comment occurs that the soaps and the movies are more interesting than other things that the mothers are doing. I am not sure I understand the "lived experience," to use a phrase of one of my colleagues, of women in general, much less the women in the PAT program. My impression is that a major set of issues regarding the difficult to reach and maintain families falls into the general domain. What do you think? Any suggestions? (Memo 18)

A woman's perspective, intimate social relationships, and friendships that give meaning to existence seem significant ideas. And these can come from a number of sources. Daily involvement in TV soap operas and late night movies seems the more "real" fare in the lives of many of the woman who are in the difficult to reach, maintain, and help families. If so, that suggests issues far beyond PAT if significant changes are to occur in their lives and the lives of their children.

Memo 13, about "self-oriented needs," links an idea from an early study in social psychology with the current program.

Self Oriented Needs

This memo might be better entitled, "personal hang-ups" of individual parents. However, a number of years ago, I ran into the concept of self-oriented needs in a study of interpersonal behavior in discussion groups (Foureizos et al., 1950). The researchers spoke of needs for domination, status, and expressing emotion or aggression, all beyond what seemed to be demanded by the immediate situation. Some of these are momentary, such as fatigue or aggression that might arise on a particular day from loss of sleep or a quarrel that occurred earlier in the day at work or in the neighborhood. But some are more long lasting dispositions, what Gould (1978) in his Transformations: Growth and Change in Adult Life *has called "childhood demons." These are longstanding conflicts and dispositions, often unconscious or only partially conscious, that each of us brings from our own childhood. I believe they pose some of the most intractable problems in parent education.*

For example, the issue arose in a discussion of a child's temper tantrums and the parent made the comment that she could not stand the child's incessant screaming. The parent was not easily able to perceive, as another parent might, that a calm, but firm not-giving-in, let-the-child-cry-it-out strategy would eventually end the episode. Rather, she would take it for a while but eventually she would blow up at the child. Another parent who is less upset by the crying, finds that she cannot say no, for reasons of her own earlier perceived childhood deprivation to a child's request for something such as a candy sucker or an attractive item on a drug store shelf. Or the parent who has learned a rigid kind of good boy or good girl morality, based in part on spankings or whippings as a child, may have extreme difficulty in foregoing those techniques in her own parenting. Insofar as each of us as parents is "needy," in this sense of self-oriented needs, and some of us more so than others, these needs pose very difficult problems in parent education.

Is the observation and interpretation on target? Do you see things differently? Do hard to reach families have more or different kinds of self-oriented needs? How do you handle such problems in your setting? (Memo 13)

In rereading Wanda's story, and the dependency theme as an interpretation, another illustration of one of Foureizos' self-oriented needs surfaces. Dependency seems both a condition that some parents bring and a consequence of some social service programs. It can be a very difficult issue for the parent educator to handle in any of its multiple forms.

Mostly, we wanted to suggest in these concluding images the open-ended nature of our description and analysis of the PAT program. Eventually, we argue that a continuing research program seems warranted on the intriguing and important issues of the nature of the families in the program and how parent educators might respond to these families toward continued success.

RECONSTRUING THE PARENT EDUCATOR ROLE

Our observations, interviews, discussions, and reflections on the heterogeneity of urban communities and families and our focus on difficult family situations, the reaching, maintaining, and helping groups has pushed us toward what we call "reconstruing the parent educator role." By this we mean that we see differences in emphases, priorities, expectations, actions, and relationships in the parent educator's role from the explicit and implicit positions in the PAT guidelines and initial training. Our interpretation begins with concepts such as *time* and *keeping appointments* and the significance of those ideas for clients and for us as parent educators. Later, *personal relationships*, *significant conversations*, and *informed decisions*, terms not foreign to the overall position of PAT, appear, but with an altered flavor. The discussion continues on through a concern for the penetrating interpretation, supportiveness, affirming basic values, and the long-term relationship. In brief, we are making a case for extending the ideas that originated with Burton White and that evolved in the Missouri version of PAT. As one moves into urban communities and with the subset of families described by our project focus, the program and its underlying conceptions continue to evolve. We believe this is both necessary and desirable.

An Initial View

In an early and long memo, the beginnings of our view extending and reinterpreting the parent educator role appeared. Back-to-back interviews with two sisters, one a long-time participant and the other a new entry into the program, provided the images and the data for the reconstrual. In brief, the linked series of three concepts: *quality of the personal relationship, significant conversation,* and *informed decision* constituted the beginnings of a miniature theory of our view of the parent educator role. A number of other items arose as well. With only minor editing, memo 2 is presented here.

> ### The Relationship Between Parent Educator and Parent:
> ### Origins and Significance
>
> An old and obvious point, but one that is continually troublesome in its day-to-day actualization, is the importance of the relationship between parent educator and parent. One doesn't need to go as far back as the originators of "relationship therapy" (Jessie Taft; 1933, Frederick Allen; 1942, nor Carl Rogers, 1942 and 1951) to justify the importance of the position. Formal organizations such as public schools and mandated programs such as PAT can set the occasion, but it is the parent educator, through her personal effort and skill, who builds the relationship. A parent educator home visit with two sisters, coded as Beatrice and Lillie, the latter new to the program and the former in her third year in the program provide data to reflect on the issue.
>
> Two back-to-back visits were scheduled. When we arrived, Lillie, the first scheduled, was not home, so the intended second interview was begun with Beatrice. The baby present was Lillie's 4-month-old. Beatrice's daughter was taking her morning nap. The parent educator reviewed the status of Beatrice's two children, focusing mostly but not entirely on the 2-year-old. The discussion covered a number of issues. The particulars of the child's self-help skills of dressing, eating, and taking care of herself flowed in and out of the conversation. Health issues, and a concern for dental care provoked a discussion of the dentist's comments regarding sugars and starches. Beatrice didn't understand the latter. The parent educator indicated that the starches break down into sugars and that some rinsing of the mouth and drinking water at the close of the meal might be helpful, as well as the regular brushing of teeth. This made sense to the mother. The water item provoked another large discussion for the mother had been concerned this summer with the child's always being thirsty and constantly need-

ing to "pee pee." As the parent educator raised the possibility of the need for medical attention, the mother indicated that she had already looked into that. The doctor at the clinic, after a series of tests, indicated the child was fine.

About this time the 4-month-old needed to be changed, and Beatrice, the aunt, changed the infant's disposable diaper. This led to a brief discussion of pampers, handiwipes, and talcum powder and the earlier regimens of cloth diapers, sponges, and the more difficult battles with cleanliness.

Shortly thereafter the 2-year-old awoke and joined the group. Beatrice has been in the process of toilet training her for the last 6 months, and this provoked a long discussion. She tends to both praise, a soft handclapping at success, and punish, a swat or two, for wet or dirty training pants. Beatrice indicated that she did no punishing this last summer when the child had been eating too much fresh fruit and had had diarrhea. The parent educator joined in the discussion with the pros and cons and some concern over the need for punishment in these instances. The observer's inference of the parent educator's perspective was that the ultimate choice was the mother's, but it was the parent educator's responsibility to help make it an informed choice. That seemed significant. Meanwhile, almost as if it had been scripted, the child indicated to her mother that she needed to go to the bathroom. The potty chair was set up in the next room, out of sight for privacy, and the child successfully accomplished the task amidst praise, the mother's cleaning out the chair, and the using of a spray deodorant in the room. Meanwhile, discussion of motor skills, games and action songs (e.g., "eency weency spider"), books, and language skills and development occurred.

Shortly, the scene changed and Lillie arrived with her nephew, Beatrice's 3-year-old son from nursery school. The second visit began amidst Beatrice's leaving to help another of the relatives, in a nearby apartment. Lillie was left with her 4-month-old son and her niece and nephew, Beatrice's two children. The parent educator developed an hour's discussion regarding the program, the 4-month-old infant, and her long- and short-term hopes and intentions. Part of this involved the parent's signing the appropriate forms and releases. Concurrently, the 2-and 3-year-olds played with several toys—blocks, telephones, and a manipulative button, pushing toy which the parent educator had brought along as part of her "professional equipment." The observer joined the children on the floor during these activities. Most significantly, within this time the parent, Lillie, talked briefly but poignantly about an earlier child of hers who was being raised by a relative. The circumstances were only partially related, but one of the observ-

er's inferences concerned the considerable guilt that seemed to remain and the beginnings of trust shown to the parent educator. The parent educator had known about the other child and some of the particulars from earlier visits with the family.

Theoretically, the visit provoked Figure 4.6. The central concepts are personal relationship, significant conversation, and informed decision. They are related in the form of hypotheses: When a strong personal relationship exists, as with Beatrice, the probabilities increase for a significant conversation about child development, and this leads to a higher probability of informed decisions. Further conjectures include the consequences of altered parent–child interaction and increased use of health services and educational services. The final hypotheses are that these result in increased probability of improved child development outcomes.

On the antecedent side of the personal relationship conception, represented in Figure 4.7, is a tentative set of hypotheses from the observation of the interaction with Lillie, in the second interview. A series of conjectures arose on the "beginnings of the establishment of a personal relationship." The elements include "background or contextual factors": prior involvement with the extended family, support for the parent educator from the sister (Beatrice), and the parent educator's prior knowledge of Lillie and her circumstances. Several elements lay in the mother: the recent birth of her child, the array of emotions related to an earlier child, and her current experience of "now" being a mother. Finally, lying within the parent educator were elements of clear presentation of the PAT program and its possibilities, the necessary permissions, and a clearly visible demonstrated interest in, concern about, and involvement with Lillie's child.

The two figures can be linked together into a more complex miniature theory of the origins of personal relationships and the consequences of significant conversations.

In the current program and in future implementation of the program in other urban communities, I would argue that the ideas in both their concrete and abstract form are important. The ideas provide me, a relative newcomer and outsider, with a way of talking about the PAT program that I had not had before. The ideas provide a kind of model to guide what I would be trying to do if I were a beginning parent educator. Or they suggest what I as a trainer or supervisor might be working toward with new parent educators. (Memo 2)

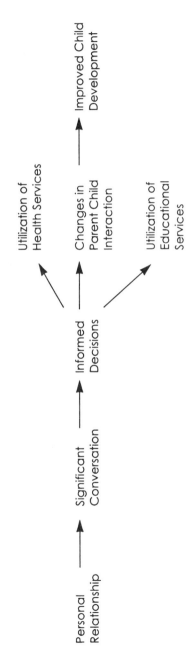

Figure 4.6. Consequences of personal relationships between parent educator and parent

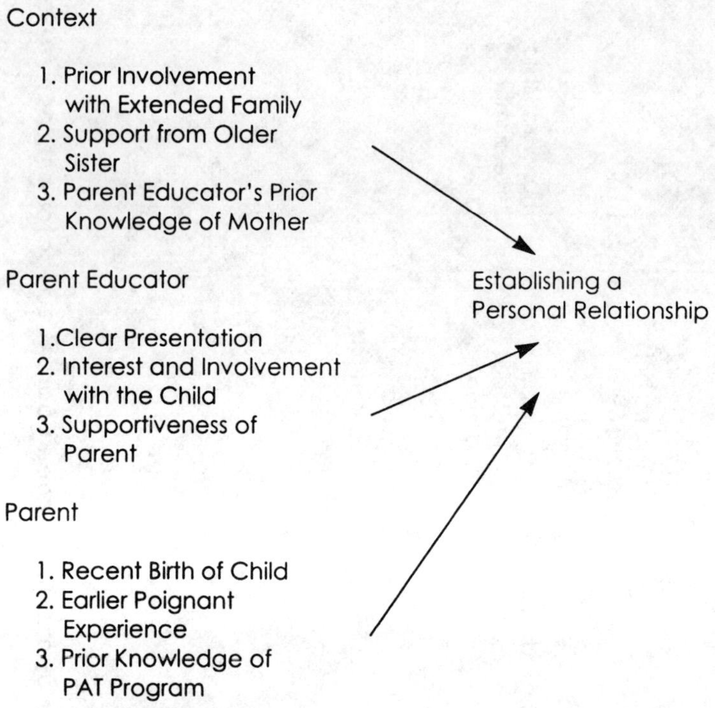

Context

    1. Prior Involvement
       with Extended Family
    2. Support from Older
       Sister
    3. Parent Educator's Prior
       Knowledge of Mother

Parent Educator   Establishing a
                                         Personal Relationship

    1.Clear Presentation
    2. Interest and Involvement
       with the Child
    3. Supportiveness of
       Parent

Parent

    1. Recent Birth of Child
    2. Earlier Poignant
       Experience
    3. Prior Knowledge of
       PAT Program

Figure 4.7. Antecedents of a personal relationship

The contrast between the two mothers provided the images for the thinking. In the first instance, the well-established relationship highlighted the specific tactics used by the parent educator as she worked toward establishing the acquaintance and the trust necessary for reaching the long-term objectives of the program. Each hour, in different ways, had a quality that seemed different than what is usually called a "lesson" in a schooling or educational framework. "Significant conversation" seemed to fit what was going on.

The unstated implications seemed those of more of a meeting of equals, talking almost informally about important aspects of a child's development, but with clear-long and short-term purposes. The parent educator was not "telling" or "instructing" the mother as a teacher with a class of pupils might, yet she surely was "teaching" or "educating" the parent. The style implied the kind of parent empowerment that is one of the long-term goals toward the even longer term goal of the child's fuller development. Clearly too, the parent had her own ideas about a number of aspects of the child's development (e.g., health, physicians, clinics, toilet training and the rewards and punishments she used). The parent educator's ideas became a part of the total situation, but neither the dominating one nor the one right way of doing things. She clearly was helping the parent make a more informed decision.

The second personal visit highlighted one instance of a parent educator setting the conditions for the kind of long-term relationship that would occasion the type of learning she hoped could be accomplished with the parent. One of the significant items, the mother's first child who is being raised by a relative, happened to be known to the parent educator from her earlier contacts with the large extended family. With other clients this is the kind of information that is slowly acquired. Yet, it is the kind of information that is very crucial for understanding the views and the motivation of the mother with regard to the child who is in the program. Without such knowledge, the mother's behavior and interaction with the child does not make sense.

Although this theorizing grew immediately out of the particular sequence of two provocative parent educator home visits, the seeds were sown in the observer's long-term background in psychology and clinical educational work with children, and the prior individual and group meetings he had within the research in the parent as teachers program. Furthermore we have not sketched here other home visits and group meetings that extend the ideas, both in their current form and in modifications for special circumstances. At a minimum, special discussion might follow concerning family situations that involve easy and hard to reach families, easy and difficult to maintain families, and easy and difficult to help families. As we have developed these conceptual categories we have made further distinctions within them. Each of our extended illustrations in prior and subsequent pages can be played off of the overall conceptions presented here. A return to the PAT guide would give additional items for reinterpretation and discussion. The mix of this kind of inquiry with its "generation of grounded theory" that we are practicing and the concept of *the reflective practitioner* that we are also advocating flows into our reconstrual. The instructional possibilities within beginning and advanced education of parent educators seem extended mightily and suggest reconstruals at this level also.

In short, we believe the implications of such ideas as these are highly significant for parent educators working with parents who are hard to reach, maintain, and help. The implications ripple through issues in "training" parent educators, developing "curriculum," and carrying out "evaluations" of the program.

Elements of a Theory of the Parent Educator Role: A Potpourri of Observations and Conjectures

A *potpourri*, to quote Webster, is "a mixture, as of spiced flower petals in a jar." We have a number of "spiced petals" regarding the role of parent educator. Once again, they blend observations, reflections, and conjectures. We hope they stimulate parent educators to think about their role and we hope that innovators in other communities see some of the intriguing possibilities in their adoption and adaptation of the PAT program for their own schools and communities.

Emotional Components of Being a Parent Educator

One does not have to be around parent educators and families who are hard to reach, maintain, and help for very long before seeing the array of emotions that cut through home visits, group meetings, and play groups in the PAT program. We find these very difficult to describe and discuss but very important. Our potpourri opens with a mix of memos and interview comments. The key comments focus on "enjoying the children," "supportiveness" as one parent labeled it, and "compassion," as phrased in a research report being read during the time of the visits.

Enjoying the Children

In a sense, it should be obvious, but it is also not evident in every personal visit that parent educators make. In the field notes of one occasion the "it" was recorded as, "The PE has a playful enthused way about her. She really enjoys the kids and their interests and activities."

The observer and the parent educator had climbed the stairs to a second-floor flat in a free-standing building which was only one of two that had survived the razing and the boarding up of buildings on the block. The stairs were worn, wooden, and encased in walls of broken plaster. I wondered about the children going up and down with no handrails on the steep steps. Upstairs, a front bedroom was screened off with a sheet, and we worked in a second room that was combination bedroom and parlor. A dining room and kitchen disappeared in the back, darkened with pulled shades and no lights on. We sat on the floor, which was superficially clean in the sense that it had been swept, but on a rug that had years and years of grime woven into the fabric, with the three children, aged 3, 2 and 10 months. The lesson was geared to the general development of the 2-year-old. The kids were immediately into the box of toys and materials the PE had brought along. They knew her and her "toys" from prior visits. She cautioned them with a "One thing at a time." She had the 2-year-old "reading" the book Babies with responses to "Show me . . . the baby who is sleeping" and so on. With the right hand and voice she urged the oldest to wait and let his brother answer and to help only when he needed the help. Later, two buckets of blocks were dumped over and the mother joined in the hand and eye coordination exercise of stacking the multiple kinds of blocks. And still later, the lesson shifted to language activities of "put the block under mama's chair, on top of the dresser, by the door, next to the fan on the floor, etc." Finally, the PE did a simple activity, but one with multiple child development goals, a kind of precursor to "Simon Says." She asked the two older children to "stand up, wiggle your fingers, wave your arms like an airplane, one foot up, now the other foot, touch your toes, jump, etc."

But through it all, the central image to the observer was the simple pleasure in the children exhibited by the parent educator. The hypothesis is that that kind of attitude and behavior is significantly related to both immediate rapport and to long-term involvement by the parent. We would also hypothesize that that kind of attitude is probably more a part of the selection process of parent educators than of the preservice or inservice training program. (Memo 61)

Poverty is a part of the urban scene. In a fundamental sense, it recedes into the background with a parent educator who enjoys the children, who has materials interesting to the children, and who progressively involves the parent in the activity. Multiple kinds of learning occur.

Another parent presented a different aspect of the emotional quality in her relationship with the parent educator. *Supportiveness* was the label we attached to the experience. A memo developed the idea.

One Parent's View of the Value Position of PAT

Recently I had a chance to talk with a parent in the program. She raised an issue that I had not heard before. It seems important enough for further discussion. As Susan expressed herself, one of the most important aspects of the program was not the information which she received (and which she was not discounting), but only raising to emphasize the supportiveness of the parent educator. And this was not just a supportiveness to her personally as she had all the problems one has with three young children. Rather, the supportiveness was for the value position and lifestyle she had chosen. Among some of her friends, marriage and children, and particularly more than one

or two children, was a way of life not as good as careers, larg-
er houses, material things, and personal freedom. Implicitly she
perceived herself as under criticism if not attack from large
segments of late 20th-century American culture and society. In
her view, the parent educator and the PAT program were
affirming and supporting her choices and lifestyle.

Around the university, I tend to meet young women who
are electing some other alternatives, at least for the moment,
and some are quite strident about it. I can remember class dis-
cussions of "education, careers, and families" and the great
resistance among many of the most articulate students that
"family" was a mix of quaintness and negativism, something to
be shunned. And now I was hearing a very articulate young
mother of three seeing the PAT program affirming her choices
and lifestyle. (Memo 23)

If these comments are generalizable, and we believe they are, PAT offers
another dimension of an emotional relationship toward empowerment
to some individual mothers well beyond the basic concerns for providing mothers with information.

Further thoughts on emotional relationships within PAT
appeared in related reading as well as observations of mothers and children in the program per se.

Compassion

Recently, and for other purposes, an essay on "ethics, field
research, and alternative paradigms," I was reading the soci-
ologist Laud Humphreys' monograph The Tearoom Trade
(1975), a participant observer study of homosexual behavior in
a restroom in a public park. It is a fascinating book on a num-
ber of grounds. But the point I want to make here arose in a
comment by one of his critics, Barry Krisberg. "One feels a
tremendous sense of uneasiness while reading Humphreys'
ethnography . . . Perhaps the root of the dis-ease is that one
senses that the sociologist appreciates his deviant subjects but
is not compassionate with them. To be compassionate, is
seems to me, requires that the researcher understands the fun-
damental passion or suffering of his subjects. This lack of sensi-
tivity to human suffering leads the 'hip sociologist' to ignore
important dimensions of the social problem which he is
describing" (p. 225).

In trying to fathom the issues of "hard to reach and difficult
to maintain urban families," some of the parents of the parent
education program and the central subjects of the research
project, I am curious as to your reactions to the issue of com-

passion. What are the consequences of being or not being compassionate? Do we miss something significant in our analyses and discussions? Is compassion really sensitivity to "the fundamental passion or suffering" of one's clients? Webster's dictionary speaks of "sorrow or pity excited by the distress or misfortunes of another." Is empathy a better word? Is there a conflict with being a "professional?" What difference does it make in what we do as parent educators or researchers? (Memo 10)

Compassion then becomes another possible way to think about the complex relationship between parent educators and their difficult to reach, maintain, and help parents.

Finally, one of our long interviews raised further observations and reflections on emotional aspects of the parent educator and parent relationship. *Rapport* was the idea that triggered the discussion into antecedents of the relationship. When parental actions, beliefs, and values match program values, supportiveness and compassion are easy. When the match does not occur, dilemmas arise regarding perceptions of "being critical."

WW: *But in the very beginning, just getting that rapport going can be . . . is affected by how parents perceive that the parent educator perceives them. "Do they think that I'm not doing it right?" This program—just if you look at it in terms of common sense—it makes sense if this program works, life is easier for a parent educator when you're working with a family that has a very close match between the experiences of that family and the kinds of experiences that the parent educator has had. When the general goals of the family are consistent with the goals of the program, when the childrearing strategies that the family has been exposed to, and that they were probably raised under, they have notions about how they're going to raise their children that are consistent with the kinds of things that we suggest, then those visits go—easily with minimum disruption, minimum problems, etc. I think that as those matches become further and further apart, the probability of . . . the probabilities that you're going to have, certain other problems cropping up becomes greater. And for example—and I might be all off on this—but, well, for example, I think that if you go into a home where families—the mom really doesn't believe in spanking, she doesn't believe in corporal punishment so much, and you go in and you talk about all the different other ways to help children control their behavior, and you say corporal punishment—you don't even bring it up really, but if it comes up, you say, "Well, we don't recommend it," that's not so difficult for that family. As a matter of fact, what you've done is validate that mother. I think that it's significantly more difficult to go into a family where corporal punishment is a part of the history of that family. And most folks in that family have turned out reasonably well. Nobody's a mass murderer or anything because they received corporal punishment. And so it's really been a pretty viable option for them, they've done pretty well with it. When the subject of corporal punishment comes up, you say to her—even though you never say, "That's wrong," you begin to present all these other options and you should use corporal punishment as a last resort—even though you have not said it, I believe at some level you are sending the message to that mother that what she's doing is not right.*

LS: *Yeah, it's just like if you advertise the magnet schools enough, you're going to have a similar implication.*

WW: *So you're saying that what you're doing is not right. And so while we say, and while in our hearts we believe, and we try very hard not to be judgmental, and not to—not to say that one set of values is better than another, the very fact that with the one family what we do is validate what they previously believed and with another, we begin offering a whole set of other options, puts a wedge in with the one where there is none with the other. What you have to do with that second family takes a lot more effort. It takes a lot more ability to finesse and negotiate, to keep things on an even keel with the second family than with that first family where everything kind of meshes together. So the way you present information really becomes critical with families where you're suggesting some new things, some brand new kinds of notions to them. That's one of the things that contributes to making a family harder to serve than another family. And then the real problem comes up when there's a family that's got a whole bunch of those things. [laughter] That you're having to somehow try to introduce new patterns and new notions into that family without implying to them that what they've been doing is so wrong that you're being judgmental about it and getting the family on the defensive.*

LS: *In a sense we are back to trust, the mutual trust of parent educator and parent.*

Once again, we believe our interview/discussion has tapped into one of the most difficult and little discussed aspects of the PAT program, the dilemma of conflicting values and beliefs and the intellectual and emotional problems created for the parent educator. Personal relationships, significant conversations, and informed decisions are put to the test. If the parent and the parent educator have built a strong personal relationship then, as equals in one sense, they can enter into conversations about some of the most significant and important beliefs each holds. The exploration of differences, conflicts with other personal beliefs, and conflicts with other members of the client's family, for instance the child's grandmother with whom they may be living, or even more critically whose house they may be living in suggest the array of items in a "significant conversation." Out of this comes an "informed decision" and actions with, toward, for, and sometimes against the child and his or her development. Education, as we conceive it, is not an easy conception or practice.

Penetrating Observations and Comments

The repertory of skills within a parent educator's overall framework is large. Interpretations have a long history in the counseling literature. We note one such episode from our records that got recorded in a memo along the way. We tried to formulate a more general model (Figure 4.8) for further discussion.

Making the Penetrating Interpretation

This memo arises out of a visit and discussion with a parent educator from a community outside the urban centers at the focus of the study. It is part of the strategy and tactic of taking good ideas from wherever one finds them and integrating them into the narrative and theory of the study itself.

The parent educator made the comment, "You don't seem to be enjoying your first child (now 30 months) as much as you did a year and a half ago," that is, before the birth of the second child. The observation arose in the midst of a "significant conversation" (Memo 2a). It followed on some comments by one parent that recent months had been a "nightmare," regarding sleeping problems and temper tantrums, and the parent educator's observations that both parents had much less tolerance now for the older child, who they had earlier idealized and had made the center of their existence. Their verbal behavior toward her now tended, on a number of occasions, to be highly directive, critical, and defensive. "Do this, don't do that, do it now, I'm tired of this and that." For those of you familiar with classroom interaction schedules, the comments would be 5s, 6s, and 7s on the Flanders Interaction Analysis Schedule (Flanders, 1964). This is not to argue that most if not all parents engage in such behavior on occasions. The penetrating part was the noting of a difference in the behavior over time and the decision to make it a part of the conversation.

The second parent denied the validity of the generalization, presented counterevidence, and became angry in a controlled way with the parent educator. Discussion continued regarding items such as the center of attention idea, the possibility of sibling rivalry, the role of parent fatigue and busy work schedules, the time spent with the child, etc. No formal resolution was called for or occurred in the visit. Group meetings and play group meetings in the next few days indicated a marked change in the behavior of both parents toward the child. A later comment from the denying parent appeared in the form of "You were right."

The general argument being made here is that from time, to time parent educators not only do, but should make "penetrating observations" as part of their home visits and that they should realize that denial, hostility, and a change in behavior toward the child can occur. I have barely explored the circumstances under which such interpretations might occur, how one might handle the negative reactions of the moment, nor have I raised the special problems in the applicability of the idea to urban underclass participants in PAT. What do you think? (Memo 9)

The memo provoked several reactions that seem both relevant and important. First, a concern was raised for the competing demands and pressures upon many of our families with difficulties. This context of frustration can increase the likelihood of the more directive, critical, and defensive behaviors on the part of the parents. Second, in the illustrations raised in the memo, the changing behavior of the parent, and the perceived changes in the first child after the arrival of the second aroused further emotion. In many of the hard to reach families, the discrepancy is between the parents and some external standard of "good parenting behavior." Finally, as the situations differ, the outcomes may also be different, and different models need to be drawn.

Counseling and Parent Educator Relations Over the Long Haul

A very interesting dynamic occurs within the hard to reach, maintain, and help families as the parent educator remains with the program for a number of years. A complex and subtle shift occurs in the nature of client's learning, in the shifts in load due to the selective retention of families, and in the change in recruiting through parental recommendations, requests, and selection. Our interviews elaborated on the issues.

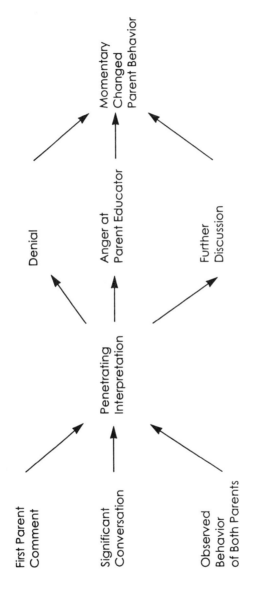

Figure 4.8. A miniature theory of the penetrating interpretation

WW: *On the current list, I don't have any hard to reach families because all of my families have been with me for years. There are some who are harder to reach than others, but one of the things about my current caseload is that most are people I have been with for 2 or 3 years or who were referred to me by someone who has been with me for 2 or 3 years. They insisted that I be their parent educator because of the way they found out about the program. I always had more families than required. This occurred in part because new parents who had been referred by someone in the program would specifically request that I be their parent educator. A second factor was that I continued to work with families for whom I knew I might get little or no reimbursement. For an individual such as Karen, whose life was so hectic, being on a nurse's schedule, she was really head of the household. She lived with her mother and father. And it was just hard to catch up with her. If I caught her at home on the phone, she would talk for a half an hour. And when we met we always had—you know, we had great visits in terms of her child, always had a wonderful visit. She was always full of questions, always very responsible, but hard to catch up with. You know, just hard to catch up with. That's—that's a hard to maintain family in that her life was just so full of so many things that what she really needed was a monthly newsletter and a drop-in program that she could use when she had time.*

Now, in retrospect, the ever busy Karen is an interesting, but positive, subcase of a "hard to maintain" family.

The parent educator who works with difficult families must assume many roles other than educational consultant to the child's development. The following interview illustrates the parent educator role as counselor over the long haul.

WW: *The household consists of Jennie, Art—he's Sandy's father—Marion and Sandy. Art does seasonal work. Art and Jennie have different ideas about how to rear children. Art will tell you, without very much prompting, that he comes from what he considers and probably was an abusive background—received a lot of corporal punishment. But he says he wants more structure. If he tells his 2-year-old to do something, he wants her to do it right now. He thinks that Jennie is much too lax, that she talks too much, which from my perspective Jennie's doing just great. She uses reasoning with her children. She applies sanctions rather than punishments as a rule. So there's this tension between them. And when I go on a visit, invariably Art is there, and we get into a "Now, Wilma, tell me. See, what happened was Sandy did this." And then he wants me to tell him who's right, or what he should have done.*

LS: *He wants to drag you into the confrontation.*

WW: *He wants to get me into the middle of the dispute. And so what I have tried to do is—first of all, I tell him that I'm not going to get into the middle. "But what we can do is we can try and pull back from the situation and see what's going on—and talk about what all three of us know about how your child is developing, what she's capable of and not capable of, and see what kind of compromise we can make here." And he is—he is amenable to that.*

LS: *What does he make of the inconsistency in terms of his—you didn't use the word anger but just his concern about the way that he was raised, and yet the fact that he does the same thing with the kids?*

WW: *He says, "Yeah, I know but . . . but they've got to learn some discipline." He's just not able to pull it apart really yet. But as I have told him the first step is recognizing the problem and he's doing that. Then the next step is to try to act on it. Behavior patterns are difficult to undo. So therefore you have to make a conscious effort to do it. He's making a conscious effort now. One of the things that I've suggested to him is that, "Let's identify four or five different things you could do in response to a child's behavior. And before you jump to the one that you would use automatically, try the other ones. Give yourself a chance to get them into your behavioral repertoire so you can begin to feel comfortable using them. But make a conscious effort to give all of those a try before you revert to what would come naturally to you as a response." And he's been trying to do that. Although he still has a problem. He now says, "Well, what I've learned how to do is I walk away." Which is a big step. He says, "I walk away from it. And I don't come back until I feel calmer. And then I can talk."*

In summary, several elements stand out. First, the parent educator defines her position in clear unequivocal terms—refuses to be drawn into argument on either side, again providing information so parents can make informed decision. Second, she maintains the program focus by basing observations and suggestions on what parents know about the child's developmental status. Third, she gives specific feedback—specific things to do so the parent can get specific feedback from actions. Finally, she begins where the parent is but has high expectations for continued change. A quality of concerned interaction among peers seems to be a key latent subtext in this account.

A major consequence of a long term parent educator–parent relationship is the susceptibility of the client to direct influence attempts. In one interview we returned to a parent who had missed an appointment.

WW: Yes, I'm out of time. I've got to get to Josie again.

LS: Okay. Good luck with that.

WW: Oh, she's going to be there today.

LS: All right, I'll check with you on that on a later time.

WW: I was going to say they might disappoint me the first time around but when I call them back and say, "Now we really have to get this appointment in, they're usually there." [laughs]

LS: Okay. You just dissolved the whole difficult to reach and hard to maintain concept. I think I'm out of business.

WW: No. No. But see, that's only because Josie has no business being difficult to reach and hard to maintain since I've known her for 4 years. This goes to show that the whole problem really may be one of persistence. But there are some families that you just have to make up in your mind that you're going to schedule three appointments to get one in. If you can get that in your head, it saves a lot of your own personal turmoil. . .

LS: Oh, yeah, they're caught up—

WW: Going to get caught up that way. And when you have a whole set of problems besetting you, the probability that things are going to come up unexpectedly increases. I often feel that it's not an intentional response on the part of the parents. It's their reaction to the situation. And it has no personal reflection upon the esteem in which they hold me or this program. It's their priorities in life, and I have to accept my place in the list and learn how to deal with it.

LS: But that's a good point, it's the sort of thing that every teacher's got to learn that when the kid gets mad at you, you can't take that personally. In many instances, there's something else going on and you happened to be at a convenient point.

In this potpourri we have stressed several elements needing additional thought and reflection, if not research, as program personnel continue to construe and reconstrue the role of the parent educator. Varied emotional qualities loom large—joy and pleasure with children and mothers, supportiveness, empathy, and perhaps compassion. The making of penetrating observations has potential benefits and hazards. Over the long haul, images of the complex interrelations of teaching and counseling appeared in our observations and discussions. All these ideas seem important as the program evolves and develops.

Specific Gambits and Techniques: Another Level of Theory

Our data contain a number of quite specific "gambits and techniques" relevant to the broader ideas we have developed in the rethinking of the parent educator roles. Most of the ideas developed within the context of a specific home visit or conversation with a specific parent or parent educator, and we present them this way, but we believe they are worthy of more general consideration and application. They run the gamut from variations in scheduling home visits to ways of opening a discussion in a home visits to role modeling.

Scheduling Home Visits: Stopping By

As we communicated earlier, in an age when most of us make use of AT&T and U.S. Postal Service for scheduling meetings and making appointments, it comes as a surprise to find that other techniques seem prevalent as well as successful. Some families don't have telephones. Others have intermittent service. Some parents seem to pay little attention to their mail, including PAT announcements. Often the most expeditious technique is "stopping by" when one is in the neighborhood. Almost needless to say, the additional time taken means that program resources are strained. The patience and flexibility also might be conceived as demands on personal energy and resources.

"How's She Doing?"

One of the pervasive, and seemingly very successful, gambits in the personal visit is a very simple but seriously stated, "how's she or he doing?" Invariably it provoked the beginning of a meaningful discussion. Memo 29 detailed the observation and preliminary analysis.

> Beginning a parent–child home visit is no problem to the experienced parent educator. Most of the sessions, after a brief getting settled, seem to open with a variant of "How's he doing?" This usually brings forth an "all right" or a "pretty good" or some particular account of an event or an accomplishment. The gambit does several things: It focuses, at least initially, on the child and his or her development. But it can alter the parent educator's intent for the meeting for the discussion sometimes takes on an important life of its own.
>
> On occasion, this diversion may happen in part because of my presence. During a recent visit, the parent showed the parent educator a birthday dress she had designed and sewed for her daughter, Mary. Shortly, other creations of the mother were brought forth, some new to the parent educator and

some for my view. Felt boards and cut-out figures, homemade costumes, and the possibilities of pretend dramatic play with a highly verbal little girl moved in and out of the conversation and the Denver screening which was the "topic" of the morning. The mother's creative craft talents have been worked into an array of activities in PAT and in other groups and center activities.

But the "real problem" involved the parents, and especially the mother, wanting to raise their child differently from the way she and her husband had been raised and the conflict that that precipitated with both sets of grandparents. The mother's noncorporal punishment policy, among a larger repertory of "indulgent" parent practices, contrasted sharply with her own upbringing and was spoiling the child in the grandparents' view. The mother detailed a number of items which she perceived to be at the heart of some of her own self-esteem problems, in spite of her very obvious intellectual and creative abilities.

Or is the "real problem" the parent's need to work through the dynamics of one's own troubled parent–child relationship from years ago? The psychiatrist R. Gould in his book Transformations: Growth and Change in Adult Life *(1978) talks about the "childhood demons" that each of us carries around and into our current activities. Parenting seems an obvious place for importing such "demons." Is this what is going on here?*

Needless to say the Denver didn't get finished. What is one to do? At the moment? And over the long run? Thoughts and suggestions? (Memo 29)

The memo started out as a commentary on a very successful practice, beginning the home visit with the simple question, "How's he or she doing?" The parent was able to present a number of sewing and craft projects related to the child's activities and some projects involving the PAT center in which she was strongly involved. But, and this seems an important "but," it also opened the discussion to a comment about the mother's relationship to her own parents and to practices with which she did not agree and did not want as part of her relationship with her own children. The parent educator decided to "run" with the issue at hand and hold the Denver Screening, the planned activity, until later. Images of what educators call "the teachable moment" also went through our heads and later reflections. We find ourselves very supportive of this kind of parent education—flexibly changing plans, building on a significant issue and moment, and helping the mother sort out the immediate problem(s) with the child and the grandparents, and perhaps most significantly, the mother's long-term perceived self-esteem problems.

Any immediate gambit has the potentiality of skipping very quickly, like the flat rock tossed on the surface of the pond, in unusual directions and creating multiple ripples as it touches down each time. In our view each of those ripples is probably a very important part of the parent educator's task. The demands on the teacher then increase, and here the parent educator is really a "teacher" in the best and deepest sense of that label. She must hold this "lesson" in her head and notes, be prepared to return to parts of it in later meetings, and eventually weave it into the long-term grand design of her curriculum and teaching. As everyone who has ever taught knows, this is one of the times that teaching becomes a creative peak experience. Increasing the frequency and the quality of these parent educator and parent times and occasions becomes an issue for supervisors and administrators as well. We are suggesting items toward a continuing educational program for parent educators. And we are implicitly asking when, where, and with what resources will this continuing education be carried out. There is more in the simple question "How's he or she doing?" than first met our eye.

Straightforward Style

Our discussion of the cultural implications of standard English led us into a discussion of how a parent educator mediates among the multiple worlds of race, class, and personal options. *Straightforward style* became the label encompassing the concrete actions in such complex situations.

LS: *Do you see any resistance among the parents to that at all? Or how do you handle that big issue when you're dealing with a parent who talks to you in a more colloquial dialect, at that point?*

WW: *The way I approach it is I tend to be a very straightforward with . . .*

LS: *I haven't noticed that. [laughter]*

WW. *: . . . with the people that I work with. Otherwise, it's less productive, and also it tells—I think it tells people something about your assessment of them, that deep down you think maybe they can't handle it. For example, on the visit that I was just on this morning, we got into a discussion of the importance of reading to your children, the importance of encouraging the use of elaborate language from your children and in parents' use with their children, and using standard English. I just told the parents that in order to compete —in order to do well—if one of our goals is to try to make sure that when our children do get into school situations that it is fun time or comfortable time, as free of stress as possible, that one of the* *things we have to do is give them the tools, to bring that about. I just say to parents quite frankly that one of the things we have to stress is the use of standard language. This all came up because Mom is taking—she was scheduled to take the GED test this summer. She didn't take it. I was encouraging her to go back and take it and she was saying she thought she was not going to do well with the vocabulary section. But during the course of our conversation she said something like "Well, I ain't going to do that—oh, I mean I'm not going to do that." I said, "Oh, see, you'll do well. You see how you just self-corrected yourself." And that's how we got into the conversation about the value of standard English. One of the things that we as Black people, as poor Black people, often don't do is teach our children the second language. We talked about reading books and the need to read more books to our children. These are things that we need to do if they're going to function or have a less stressful time when they go to school. They were in total agreement on that.*

The issue of standard English is discussed in more depth later, but here we elaborate further on the parent educator's straightforward style. As difficult and sometimes contentious issues come up, being able to express a point of view "quite frankly" seems a major tactic worth reflecting on if one is a parent educator. In this instance, Wilma surrounds her belief with other concepts, beliefs, and hopes: "elaborate language," "compete," "to do well," "fun time at school," "give them the tools," and have "a less stressful time when they go to school." In her view, the parents "were in total agreement on that."

We find ourselves moving toward both a broader perspective on parent education and also a much more concrete and specified array of quite particular actions. Readers should have the grist for further discussion and debate as they articulate their own positions.

"Meeting and Greeting": Unflappable Flexibility

In thinking about the recasting of the parent educator role, it is helpful to use a set of "usual procedures" and then to contrast those with a particular case.

WW: *Generally when I go in, I first—it depends on the age of the child. One of the things—with the older kids, when I come in, usually they meet me somewhere between the door and wherever we're going to sit and want to know where's my bag? Where's my stuff? Where are my toys? What did I bring them? And so . . . so we attend to that first off.*

LS: *You're really a bag lady?*

WW: *Yeah. [laughs] Meeting and greeting. And then I think it's really important that I talk—I ask the mother how she's doing. How are you as a person doing?*

LS: *To the mother?*

WW: *To the mother. I ask the mother, "How are you doing? How are things going for you?" If they're in school, I'll ask, "How's school?" If they're—if I remember something from last month that they told me, I ask, "Did you get that new dress you were talking about?" Or "How did that cake come out?" But something that's very personal for them. I often—one of the things I always ask is "Have you been out to a movie or somewhere lately?" Or "Have you had some time to just be yourself and not be a mother for an hour?"*

    And then we talk about how the kids—"Tell me what's going on with the kids. Bring me up to date." And I try to tell them some things that I've noticed. Something like "He's really doing a lot more talking" or "Boy, he seems to have grown a whole lot," and "He just seems to be so much more active."

    And then I do try to lay out my agenda—what we really want to talk about today is such and such and such a thing. Then we want to do an activity. I'll want you to do it with him for a while. And then, "If you have any questions or something comes out, naturally we'll talk about that. But those are the two main things I want to get—we want to get through today. Was there something that was a concern to you before we start?" And then we can get the agenda laid out, so we don't stray too far from it. Sometimes there's a concern that comes up. One of the last things I try to ask is "Did you have any questions before I leave?" And if they don't, schedule the next appointment and . . . invite them to a group meeting. I always—on my calendar, even those that I've been seeing for three years, I always write my name on it. So that they can see me writing it because I think it stands out a little bit more. And . . . a lot of the times I circle the phone number and tell them if they need anything, to please give me a call.

Our analytical world gets more and more intertwined and complicated. This time we put the label "Meeting and Greeting: Unflappable Flexibility" on a small part of one of our discussions and trace out how a parent educator home visit might move. Earlier we were urging a "How is he or she doing?" gambit regarding the child. We thought that was powerful. Now we are extending that gambit to the parent herself with a "How are *you* doing?" This question gets coupled with all kinds of parent educator recollections—some personal and some educational and professional about the parent. Then back to the child and then to a possible agenda—a kind of lesson plan for the hour. But interwoven are requests for immediate "concerns" that the parent might have and "questions" that they have but haven't been able to ask. Finally, the all important scheduling of the next meeting occurs. In a sense we are talking about parent educator flexibility, but also, as the almost breathless quality of the long interview comment implies, a kind of "unflappableness" also seems ever present. Individual styles come to have important and provocative patterns—ones that we would recommend to others for careful consideration.

A Return to Broader Images of the Parent Educator Role

In the process of any reconstrual boundaries of conceptions and outlines as ways of communicating continue to collapse and be reformed. Such intellectual events happened continuously in our dialogue and thinking. At this point we return to two very wide-ranging conclusions and suggestions about the parent educator role. In the next section, we build on a continuing practical activity in the day to day work of the parent educator. In the section on role modeling: a larger instance, we raise a surprising view that some parents, in that category of difficult to reach, maintain, and help urban parents, held of the parent educator. We extend the usual educational use of the conception of role model.

On Participant Observational Inquiry

One of our memos addressed another aspect of the parent educator in action. In it we attempt to generalize the specific acts of parent educator observation to a much broader inquiry stance and thereby extend the power of the approach.

This is one of those memos that might be redundant for most of you, but for a "once-upon-a-time educational psychologist" I find myself being continually surprised by the potency of participant observation in the day-to-day work of the parent educator. By participant observation in this context, I mean essentially that a practicing parent educator works in a natural setting, observes the parents and children in their homes, talks with them about important events in their lives and the life of their child, and writes up a short account of each visit in the form of a few sentences and paragraphs. In general, it is a qualitative inquiry approach to children and parents.

Part of the clarity and the power of this approach can be seen in contrasting it with other approaches to child study and child development. Teachers rarely see the child in the home setting, or talk at length with parents. In part, this memo was occasioned by the comment of a kindergarten teacher who talked of the PAT program and of her own discomfort with the thought of doing home visits. (Obviously the school setting has its own importance as does classroom teaching. I am not disparaging either. Just making the point that there is a difference.) Many counselors working with parents seldom or rarely see the children of clients, and even more rarely observe in the context of the home setting. They are forced to rely on parent reports of what goes on, rather than having the chance, as do parent educators, of observing for themselves. In part, this memo grew out of noting the differences in the verbal behavior of a parent and noting what the parent actually did with the child. At times, all of us paint verbal pictures different from the reality of overt activity and interaction with our children. Finally, I would contrast participant observation with the kind of "observations" made by test and measurement psychologists. As one who has given his share of Binets, Wechslers, Rorschachs, TATs, and Bender Gestalts, I find these attempts to get at "dispositions" of children important for all kinds of purposes, but they are different from observing particular and specific instances of the child's interpersonal actions and interactions with parents and siblings. And sometimes they are less help than direct observations of behavior and action when one tries to work out plans for parents helping their children.

The educational world of parents, children, and teaching is full of different and partial pictures created by different theories and approaches to children and their development. I am making here the simple point of not disparaging our parent educator view of reality created by careful qualitative participant observation. (Memo 11)

Participant observation, a kind of qualitative inquiry, has gone from the negativism of "anecdotal records" to the loftier realms of ethnography and action research as practiced by anthropologists and educators. We believe that parent educators have a major opportunity of coming to know children and parents through the simple but careful observation of the activities of child and parent and the opportunity to talk with parents about their personal views, ideas, and emotions that make up the task of parenting. Learning to move these observations and ideas into action programs for improving parent-child relations and the child's development is the necessary next step, one that is underway daily in the talk among parent educators and in the formal instructional programs run in each of the local centers. If we needed an illustration, the multiple interview/conversations between the two of us, relying heavily on Wells' extended observations and thoughtful reflections toward action, and the multiple memos written by Smith as he observed and talked with participants in the program, and the elaboration of these as we have developed our initial report and now book should indicate one direction these efforts might take. Throughout, we have accented detailed concrete particulars of the activities and interactions of participants and our attempt to make more general—conceptual and theoretical—sense of those particulars. At its farthest reach we are arguing that educational programs should be inquiry-oriented at every level, reflecting a general stance and rationale argued some years ago by Schaefer (1967) in his *The School as a Center of Inquiry* and more recently by Elliott (1991) in his *Action Research for Educational Change* and Cohn, Kottkamp, and Provenzo, (1987) in their *To Be a Teacher*. Parent educators are ideally situated to move in such directions for the enhancement of their work with parents and children. Participation in the excitement and ferment in this aspect of professional education has long term implications for parent educator motivation, understanding, and improved practice, goals at the heart of practical efforts to influence child development with parents of families difficult to reach, maintain, and help.

Role Modeling: A Larger Instance

Parent educators at their best are special people in the lives of their families. Memo 21 caught a dimension of that special aspect of being a parent educator.

> Much of what one hears about "modeling" in the PAT program concerns the parent educator modeling for the parent the specifics of techniques of working with the children. For instance, this is how one might read and talk with a child about a book, here is a homemade game of matching objects for color or texture or shape, and here is a way of working on puzzles. But that is not the kind of modeling I want to raise here.
>
> Many of the mothers in the urban population have an array of problems that border on the limits of "impossible to cope." Kids, finances, housing, living arrangements, boyfriends or husbands who are either not around or who are difficult in a multitude of ways suggest some of the aspects of single parenting. Another way of phrasing the dilemmas, in colloquial terms, is that many of the women "need to get their act together." And that is a difficult task.

I have observed a number of the mothers interacting with the parent educators. The quality of relationship I have commented on before. Sometimes cloaked in humor, sometimes in seriousness, but always with an expression of depth. I have been privy to small comments either made by the mothers or the parent educators. Some of the latter have been informal comments "along the way" to me directly or to other parent educators in a variety of contexts. They refer to telephone calls made by the parent to check out an event or an idea, calls concerning family relationships or boyfriend relationships, or those about the pros and cons of moving from one location or another. The image that arises is that some of the parents see the parent educators as having their act together—their appearance is well kept, their dress has a professional look about it, they have a job and are enjoying doing it, a competence appears in what they are about, there is a purpose and a meaning in their lives.

While parent educators have their own problems as everyone does, most of them are conveying significant images to parents most of the time. I am not sure how one measures such relationships. I am even less sure how long it takes for such influence to appear nor how to measure the impact on the mothers, but I believe the events are occurring. The parent educators are in part role models for the parents. I believe that this kind of modeling is very significant for the program.

As I look back on earlier memos I think that this might be seen as an elaboration and revision of Memo 2a and Figure 2.1. Pieces of the puzzle that is PAT continue to come together. (Memo 21)

"Getting one's act together" and "having one's act together" are two colloquial ways of describing points on what we perceive to be an important continuum. Often without intensive thought or reflection parent educators are models, in this larger sense, for many parents, parents in difficult straits of multiple sorts. In the more successful instances of parent educators becoming models of a desirable and perhaps enviable "lifestyle" all this seems to happen "naturally" as the parent educator goes about her work in an organized, task-oriented, yet sympathetic way. The implications reach out in multiple directions. Insofar as the parent educators come from the local community, and many do, the possible closeness of identification increases. The community ramifications are well beyond parent educator roles. Questions arise as to whether "having one's act together" is a selection or an educational issue for a program such as PAT. Probably both would be our middle of the road interpretation. How should PAT training activities and programs try to teach toward such an objective? Attempts to "deliberately" try to implement this dimension of the parent educator's role suggest important continuing inquiry problems. Our conjectures run on and on.

As we have moved toward a general perspective on the role of the parent educator we have found ourselves commenting on several levels of generality. Many of the items are not new to particular parent educators, although we would argue, insofar as the items arose in quite specific situations with individuals, the entire repertory is probably not in the heads and skills of any one parent educator. Adopters of the program should find the particulars helpful in thinking about their own situations, as should those educating preservice and inservice parent educators.

SUMMARY AND CONCLUSION

In this chapter we continued to present in considerable detail our observations and reflections on the PAT program as we have encountered it in St. Louis. Our central theme has been the parent educator as teacher of families with difficulties. We looked initially at a few examples from the formal program guides, then we launched into a reconstruction of our original research brief by enlarging the "difficult to reach and maintain" categories of families to include the "difficult to help" group. This enlargement then demanded a reconstrual of the role of the parent educator. This is the kind of "grounded theorizing" we see as being one of the most important in our findings. We tried to present illustrations and ideas that varied in generality and specificity. Throughout the ideas were tied quite closely to our observations presented in the form of memos written during the 18 months of the project and to our views as they appeared in our year-long series of "interview/discussions." In a sense, the memos tended to give a bit more of Smith's growing views and the interview/discussions tended to give more of Wells' well established views of 5 year's experience as a parent educator and coordinator in the program. Our inside/outside perspectives on the parent educator as teacher were increasingly brought to the fore. We believe that that not only has served us well but that it will serve well those who hope to adopt or adapt the program in their own urban areas.

chapter
five

The PAT Program as Curriculum

The subtitle of this chapter might be "format, substance, and reactions" for we want to present several kinds of discussion regarding the PAT program as curriculum. The two major formats or means of presenting the program are personal visits and group meetings. We make some comments about the differences between these two settings, but mostly we want to focus on their similarities. In a sense, we have had much of our say about the personal home visits in the last chapter. We raise now some issues, problems, and resolutions in teaching groups of parents. But the main point we want to make concerns the substance of the meeting whether in a personal visit to the home or in the context of a group meeting in the center at one or another of the schools. In no way do we try to replicate the content of the 36 lessons from the revised program guide. To enter the discussion, we raise an interpretation of some issues in the nature of goals and objectives when one studies an urban setting with the particular focus of difficult family situations. In a sense, things are not "really" different, yet they are. An ephemeral tone or emphasis occurs and all of a sudden one gets the feeling that something significant is happening that is different from what one has expected.

During an early group meeting on the topic of language development, a number of these ideas surfaced, in the observer's mind, as a set of dilemmas regarding objectives and priorities among objectives within the parents as teachers program.

It seems to me there's a reasonable debate as to how much these sessions ought to be conveying information, how much they ought to be doing some kind of intellectual development, how much they should be doing some kind of personal not quite therapeutic integration of feeling and ideas about things, and then how much a kind of direct skill development, as in the construction of flannel boards or puppets, should be going on. Apparently different sessions deal with different aspects of all of this. But things seem loaded on the informational part.

Further, then there's a whole pedagogical strategy in terms of how one teaches whatever it is that one wants to teach. So far almost all of the sessions have been very heavily involved in telling and occasionally showing and telling, but not a lot of discussion and batting back and forth of ideas and personal views. On occasion at other meetings some of the women have done some of that. We're sort of back to objectives, curriculum, and pedagogy. And there you are. (4/21/88)

Without realizing it at the time, ideas such as these set the context for much of the discussion that is to follow in this interpretation of the PAT program as curriculum. In our view, there are major value issues at stake in how the goals and objectives are phrased. With our population of parents and children, the move from more informational aspects of curriculum to intellectual and social skills of both parents and children seems very important and in need of discussion among parent educators, their supervisors, and those doing preservice and inservice educating.

CURRICULAR GOALS AND OBJECTIVES: A NESTED VIEW

Even when goals and objectives are stated at different levels of generality, it does not follow necessarily that they are in conflict. In our view, they may be "nested," that is, the relationship may be that of small parts to larger wholes. Practically, a clarity and logic exists in seeing school success as the overriding goal of the PAT program. Parents, parent educators, and even state legislators who write the legislation and provide the funding anticipate that the probabilities of school success will be increased by participation in the program. However, a total focus here can be a short step to a kind of assemblyline image—the child in PAT from birth to 3 years, preschool, Headstart, or day care for the next couple of years, kindergarten success at 5 and on into successful reading, writing, and arithmetic in the primary grades—and on and on and on.

Quality of life in the present moment of time is a not completely mutually exclusive alternative to the future time orientation implicit in school success, but it is a change of emphasis. The dilemma seems real and important (Berlak & Berlak, 1981). Additional complexities appear when one begins to speak of race, class, and gender constraints and opportunities. When "middle class in an integrated society" is seen as a long-term goal, a view implicit in some of our observations and explicit in some parental interviews, then the PAT program takes on a different complexion. One's location in our society gives nuances and emphases in priorities of goals and objectives even in a program such as PAT. Several of our memos and conversations captured the concrete images that led to the overall view. The first of these we labeled "The Bottom Line: Preparation for School Success."

> Perhaps because of the dominance of the economy and the corporation in the lives of all of us, their labels have become the metaphors for those of us in education. I resisted the temptation to say "for those of us in the education business." As I understand the "bottom line" label it refers to the fact that most corporation reports, after all the glowing verbiage of company intentions and activities, put the profit and loss statement on "the bottom line." The power of the image is that that is where unadorned "truth" shows.
>
> The metaphor can be used with the PAT program. In all discussions of "taxes and tax-supported programs," "the welfare family," or "the welfare mess" as it is sometimes called, "crime and drugs in the urban community," and "laziness, idleness, and uncaring parents," the bottom line, so it seems to me, the part that cuts through all the negative verbiage, is that the youngsters will all end up in the public schools at 5 and 6 years of age. For 6 hours a day, 5 days a week, and 40 weeks a year the child will be the school's responsibility. What can be done to minimize the potential for school problems? That point must always be kept in focus as the core of problem-solving efforts.
>
> Is that what the metaphor "bottom line" means for PAT, the issue that won't go away? And is that then the major justification for PAT efforts? (Memo 8)

Our interview/discussions followed up on the memo, in the form of a set of comments that we labeled, "purposes: present time versus future time orientations."

In our view, purposes of programs such as PAT often get phrased in very general and oversimplified ways. "PAT as school readiness" provoked a discussion of the complexities in goals and purposes.

LS: *Let me turn it around another way. Do you have any prob-
       lems of phrasing the program in a sense as—or construing it
       in its most narrow sense as kind of a school readiness pro-
       gram? As you play it through your own head and think about
       the purposes of PAT, it seems to me that one argument
       would be that it's to improve school readiness. And you're
       shaking sort of "yes" to that. Is that too narrow? Is that too . . .
       school-related or . . . ?*

WW: *I think that there are several purposes of the program. One is
       that sometime—well, let me step back. Sometimes as we talk
       about school and just life in general, I think we spend far too
       much time focusing on future benefits and not enough on
       present benefits. One of the major results of the program I
       think is just to make this whole business of being a parent
       more enjoyable right now. There's a great value to having
       happy, healthy children right this minute. There's a great
       value in supporting parents as they try to do what's best for
       their children today.*

       *I don't have a real problem with saying that it's a
       program . . . whose goal is to help children be more ready
       for school. Where my problem comes in is with how some
       people might interpret that readiness. Some people are
       going to interpret that readiness as being directly related to
       paper, pencil, control techniques, sitting down in chairs, you
       know, very, very structured. And I think that helping children
       get ready for school is helping them to develop a sense of
       curiosity, helping them to be able to see relationships, help-
       ing them to . . . to be willing to take a risk or have a good
       sense of themselves and so be willing to go out and explore,
       all of that is a legitimate goal with this program. And to help
       parents understand how they can facilitate that.*

Now, as we reflect on these comments, we find that the more
obvious goals parents have for the program closely parallel those
expressed in the interview; that is, to support parents in their childrearing roles and to help parents support their children's maximum development so that they are well prepared for the school experience.

We would reemphasize the briefly stated broader set of issues
raised in that discussion—curiosity, risk taking, sense of self, and willingness to explore. In our special sample of families, those parents who
are having problems of coping because of personal reasons and reasons
of difficult family and home situations, these goals become more problematic and more difficult to attain. Dilemmas for the parent educator
continue.

In addition, some parents have more far-reaching goals in mind
when they participate in the program. Many speak of wanting their chil-

dren "to do better than me," "to get away from this neighborhood," and "to be able to get a good job." These long-term aspirations help organize the day-to-day goals and activities and provide the parent educator a way of talking and working with parents, even when their children are in their first 3 years. Success in school is pivotal for these aspirations.

Other parents are less explicit verbally, but the observer saw nuances in one mother's comments and behavior. Postmeeting notes caught some of this.

> In the hour visit, the mother was very articulate in her discussion with the parent educator over a number of issues—language development of the children, her strategy for toilet training, and her disciplinary approach. She read Bible stories to the children, and her sister had a Bible lesson each day with the children for whom she baby sat. She and her husband worked steadily at the toilet training and one of the older children had been very clear when he had to go to the bathroom and trained easily at 18 months. As she told her 3-year-old son James not to jump off the chair or up and down on the carpet she included reasons—the lady in the apartment downstairs is sick. She asked the child to apologize when he had crumpled one of the parent educator's worksheets. James said, "I am sorry." He had been swatted twice, told in no uncertain terms that he was not supposed to do that, and he was required to sit by the chair on the floor. All this reflected an elaborated language code.
>
> The mother talked about the records needed by the oldest child before he could enter school this fall. She felt that things were more complicated now than they had been when she entered school, although that was in a small rural town outside the city. She inquired into the PAT group meetings and indicated that she might be able to alter her work schedule in order to attend.
>
> The intuitive image I had was that the big agenda was the long-term perhaps generational, goal of being a middle-class family in an integrated society. And PAT was part of that. If all that is true, in this instance, and if there are other similar instances, then the program has another level of depth and importance. (LMS: Summary Observations)

Finally, after a long hard day, when end-of-the-year fatigue had mounted as well, one parent educator made a number of comments relevant to this discussion. More generally, parent educators also bring, in addition, their own personal goals to the program. The following expression of doubt regarding the success of the program suggests that

this parent educator's goals for the program extend beyond simply helping parents to enjoy their children more and helping to prepare them for
future school success.

> LS: Do you think that the PAT is making a difference?
> PE: Well, I would hope it would be.

She went on to explain what she felt she was accomplishing.

> PE: . . . we're at least telling parents what to look for . . . and
>   they can really honestly assess the situation themselves and
>   say, "Yeah, she's doing this" or "She's not doing that" and
>   "What can I do to encourage it?" I see that. But . . .
> LS: In the success stories that you've had, what seems to be the
>   element?
> PE: Well, what I consider to be successful . . . is getting back in
>   school after dropping out.
> LS: So part of your focus, even though you may be doing lan-
>   guage lessons or motor lessons about the child, is trying to
>   get the mothers to think about themselves and where they
>   are and what they're doing? Is that a fair statement?
> PE: Definitely.

We have barely begun the discussion of the complexities of
issues surrounding goals in a program as broad and challenging as PAT.
We find ample room for each parent educator to construct creative and
worthwhile "lessons"—activities, demonstrations, and conversations—
and to exercise professional judgment in so doing. Our "manual" should
help other educators in other communities begin to think through their
own situations in similar fashion. We believe this to be an important
"adaptation" of the PAT program.

In the memo and the conversations with parent educators, the
complexities of goals and objectives of parent education are highly visible. We phrased that tentatively as "a nested view," that is, objectives
are interrelated with each other in ways not necessarily linear nor necessarily in conflict. No one quarreled with the idea that the program
should help children when they enter school. A "but . . ." often seemed
attached to the simple agreement. When pressed, many parent educators expressed, as Wells did here, a strong concern for "present benefits," an improvement of the life of parent and children at the moment.

Wells also stressed that preparation for school needed a broader
definition than the sort of paper-and-pencil readiness. For her children's
readiness included a sense of curiosity, willingness to take risks, going
out and exploring, and a good sense of themselves. Nested in "school
success" are a series of difficult to define and measure, but exceedingly

important outcomes of the preschool years. And these have floated through professional education for many years in the form of *Emotion and the Educative Process* (Prescott 1938, 1957) and *A Teaching Program in Human Behavior and Mental Health* (Ojemann, 1955, 1958, 1967). Often more implicit than explicit, we find these objectives very present in the thinking of urban parent educators.

Other parent educators were quite explicit that parental help often was focused on the parent per se, for example, getting back to complete their own schooling from their early dropping out. The implication is that doing that would result in more self-esteem and economic stability and would eventually rebound on the child's development.

Other parents saw urban society as more complex than the rural communities in which they were raised and they carried out an agenda of Bible stories, simple concern for neighbors and politeness to them, and elaborated language explanations for helping the child move into a more economically secure integrated society. Multiple aspects of the parent education program seemed to facilitate that.

Our hope here, in this kind of reporting and interpreting, is to open discussion among parent educators to the subtleties and the importance of reflecting on and possibly reconstruing their views on the complexities of nested objectives of parent education programs.

CURRICULAR FORMAT: GROUP MEETINGS WITH URBAN FAMILIES

First Views

Unpacking the latent dimensions and dynamics of group meetings has much in common with the reconstrual of the personal visits to the homes of the families. Our observations and interviews produced a number of significant ideas regarding attendance, topics, teaching tactics and strategies, and parent and parent educator relationships. We begin the discussion with a view of an early meeting and then a long excerpt from an interim report written by Smith after the first semester in the project.

An Initial Group Meeting

We seem to be aligned, consciously or unconsciously, with those who argue that no episode, meeting, or set of events is meaningful without a context. Our notes always seem to capture contextual flavors. Even with that stance, the issue of "minimal resources, poverty, and innova-tive programs" was not especially salient when the initial parent group meeting was the agenda item for the day. But again, it would not go away.

> I'm on my way down to the Branch School for the first of the parent meetings that I will attend. It's a wet, rainy, snowy, cold, blustery day, temperature in the 30s. It's about as uninviting as one can imagine. I would guess that there's going to be mini-mal attendance at the meeting. I'm not sure whether immu-nization and that kind of health program will draw parents in general. I'm not sure whether this weather will keep off anoth-er bunch. It'll be interesting to see who gets there both by way of parent educators and by way of parents.

As Smith drove, reflected, and recorded, images floated by.

> In the middle of all this I still have an image of the tall, thin assis-tant principal of the Branch School, looking at me with a smile, about the parents who are difficult to reach and maintain, as though I was on a fool's errand. She didn't say much at all, she just looked and smiled. But I was really left with a remarkable image.

Other thoughts from a prior day intruded as well.

> Partly as a result of my visits and partly as a result of talking with the evaluators I'm struck with the general poverty of the pro-gram. There just aren't resources to do all kinds of things. That working on a shoestring is something we've done over the years, yet there's the feeling I have that I'm too old for it at this point.

Implications appeared.

> I don't know quite what to make of that personal feeling on the one hand and the nature of the reality of many people's lives on the other hand.

That larger issue was not followed up then. Rather the notes skidded back into the project per se.

Mixed with it and contributing to it is the kind of initial program enthusiasm that the director has where all things are possible and obtainable and one's expectations and hopes and agendas all seem to grow faster than the resources to implement all of that. Somewhere along the line the quality of the work suffers in multiple places and multiple ways whether it's the actual implementing of the program or whether it's the evaluation of it in some form that makes long-term sense. (2/19/88)

These thoughts were not dispelled by the group meeting of the morning. It was as though the events of the group meeting moved like a bulldozer through the woods of the scattered thoughts. The notes pick up on the observer's drive back to the university.

The meeting was a real interesting one, on multiple grounds. First it was very difficult to get parents there. Four finally showed up, all part of some interrelated extended family. A man and three young women. They brought three children with them. All seemed to be preschool age. They came late and left early. Mixed in with this was a film and projector which didn't really work very well and which wasn't shown until after the parents and the kids had left. It was an old film, an old projector, and allegedly it's the film that was giving the trouble but I'm not totally sure of that. The coordinator was a bit embarrassed at how all of her best laid plans didn't work out.

The woman who was the presenter tried to run an abortive discussion, but from my point of view talked way over the heads of the people and they didn't either understand much of what she was saying or seemed also not to like her very much. There was a general uncomfortableness in that pre-period as everybody was waiting around.

The film itself she described as perhaps the best public health film ever made. My feeling was that it was quite interesting with Cliff Robertson playing the role of narrator, kind of like the hitchhiker in the HBO films. There were little vignettes of kids growing up from birth to 6 or 10 or 12 when they caught one or another of the diseases—whooping cough, polio, etc. Then the consequences would be spelled out and would be developed. All of that seemed to me went along very nicely.

The flow of the notes caught the improvisation within the meeting and the building toward an alternative set of positive consequences.

Afterwards we had a discussion with the two or three parent educators, the coordinator, me, and the presenter. That, too, seemed to go along very nicely and was perhaps the real strong point of the whole morning's effort. That is, the parent educators, the several who stayed, got a chance to ask whatever questions they wanted and those varied all the way from when shots are given to other diseases such as a fungus that one of them had run into in one family. That seemed again to be important as the parent educators get increasingly aware of the general area of child development, in this instance, health problems particularly. Olive, the presenter is a very literate and knowledgeable woman who was trained as a nurse and is now doing mostly educational promotional activities.

The mixture of continuing education for parent educators as well as the education of parents seems a little talked about issue. As beginning parent educators stay with the program over a period of time, their own knowledge and skills are built upon continuously in quite relevant ways.

In quite concrete and specific form, data continued to emerge on the central issue of our inquiry, the difficult to reach, maintain, and help urban families and ways to improve the program for them.

The coordinator referred again to the transportation problems which seemed to be acute. In addition, she referred to the fact that one other family or cluster of mothers and children who were supposed to come were waiting for the delivery of diapers or related things that didn't arrive—weren't to come until about 11:00. The group that did come was caught in the fact that some emergency, that wasn't defined or related to me, came up. Since one person was driving, everybody had to leave. (2/19/88)

Images of earlier innovative projects arose and floated troublingly through the observer's head and ended up in the recorded summary observations and interpretations.

I'm left with this ungodly feeling of being back in the Rural Highlands [Smith & Pohland, 1974] when we were doing the computer-assisted instruction program and "nothing" seemed to work right. And "nothing" related to practically every item in the total system. Coming to grips with that I would guess is going to be one of the most difficult problems in the whole affair.

Other more successful lessons tempered these early interpretations. But, at the moment, other conjectures arose and became a part of the evolving problem and interpretation, as did the observer's general orientation—personal and professional.

It also seems to lead to an attitude and a point of view of "That's the way it is" or "There's nothing you can do about it" or "You live with it." That is so alien to the way I personally want to live and the way I personally want to organize whatever activities and projects I'm involved in.

The notes continued, with thoughts that broadened the array of ideas and possibilities.

In a similar vein, before the meeting we were talking and Olive was raising issues about a teenage program that they have in the high school that involves at least four high schools and maybe 40 or 50 kids who are being trained by the public health department to act as peer leaders and peer counselors in programs regarding all kinds of health problems and issues that run the gamut from nutrition on the one hand I suppose, to teen pregnancy, to date rape, etc. Part of the issue is that they pay the kids to run groups and they figure that other kids will listen to other kids, and the consequences tend to be better, although relatively undocumented in her program, so she said, than if the people themselves were trying to do it directly. She cited the case of one outstanding success in the program, a young fellow who's now in college who had been booted out of almost every high school in town who finally got caught up in the program. His grades went up, his activities went up, and so on. This case was countered with another case by the coordinator in another part of the program where there seemed to be a mix of ambition on the part of the child, or the young person, a quick intelligence, support from family and/or teachers, and an ability to see and use opportunities like these programs. (2/19/88)

The "group lesson" raised other ideas.

Mixed into all of this is the array of social agencies and services that run out of the schools, the health department, the social services, the government offices, and so on. These are so multiple and targeted and overlapping and partially utilized that I can't even begin to understand at this point. There is a fascinating mix of individuals and personality characteristics who are able to provoke the use of the word ambition on the part of both of the women, which mixes with opportunity and support and availability and things of that kind. (2/19/88)

In summary, a group lesson that seemed not to reach its manifest purpose was improvised into a training opportunity for several parent educators. As we explored the "problems" of the lesson we found ourselves in the middle of the issues that brought us to the inquiry—clarification in the developing and carrying out a program for difficult to reach, maintain, and help urban families. On a cold and bleak day, getting families to the center mixed with equipment that didn't work well, and teaching that seemed to pass the clients by. Most of these problems and dilemmas return and possible resolutions are presented. For the moment, a series of simple ideas follow easily: better trained outside presenters for this kind of population, equipment that works, transportation that is functional and stable. These suggestions become "new problems" and spawn further conjectures—community concerns, increased funding, adult and professional education and training, and so on!

Further Complexities in Urban Parent Education Meetings

To speak of urban parent education meetings in general terms tends to lose the flavor of the events. As this quality of particularity declines, it is also difficult to think about recommendations for improvement of a program. The summary observation and interpretation notes of a meeting in early March, as the inquiry was just underway, give considerable detail and some interpretations toward recommendations as seen by the outside observer. The notes almost approach the form of a "memo." It's 6:37 on a Thursday evening, and the context was this.

I've just left the university, and I'm on my way to the Hawthorne Center. The weather is atrocious. We've had rain all day today and it's gradually turned into a sleet and ice storm. The parking lot was very slippery underfoot and all the cars were totally covered with ice. It took me a while to get all that cleaned up and organized. Now that I'm out on the road there's nothing much happening but a little drizzle, and the roads themselves are wet but not frozen. It's an incredibly miserable night. I checked my mailbox to make sure there hadn't been a call from Helene, the coordinator of the Hawthorne Center. I'd talked with her earlier today and she said the meeting was on because they have some invited people for the topic of nutrition. She'd already had some calls from people who are not going to make it so there is a real issue as to who will be there and what kinds of things will happen at the meeting. My guess is it's going to be another one of those minimally attended meetings. It took all my strength to get up and go. I'm not sure that if I were a parent I would have been up to it. I'm down to the main north–south road and the traffic seems to be moving relatively simply, easily, and sparsely. It's really not all jammed up. The worst problem is seeing where the lanes in the highway are, as different streets like the Interstate Highway branch off, and you end up going from the middle lanes into the side lanes without realizing it. (3/3/88)

The sun, or moon, doesn't always shine on educational programs. Complications come in many forms, and even affect program observers and researchers. Having outside presenters makes one hesitant about canceling an evening's program. Multiple forms of the "damned if you do and damned if you don't" dilemmas are part of the reality of an educational program. Helene decided to go ahead.

The notes picked up 2 hours later.

It's now 8:37 and I've just left the Hawthorne Center.

It turned out to be a very pleasant and informative evening. Only three young mothers with their children showed up. There was one parent educator with her girl of about 12 and Helene with her two children, a boy of 9 and a girl of 8. The nutrition program was very cleverly done with people in costumes acting out the parts of the four basic food groups and a talk and discussion with very lively young women. The presenters are all students—dietitian students at a local university, working out of a local hospital.

The key item, though, relates to how to get parents there. And the big truth of the evening, I suppose, is that all three of the mothers were clients of Abbie Thomas, who was the only parent educator who was there tonight. She's a large, hefty, considerably overweight woman who is also very bright and very creative and full of fun and vitality. She relates easily and well to the mothers and they seem to relate easily and well to her also. None of the other parent educators showed and none of their clients showed. Most of the parent educators don't like night meetings, and most of them want to be paid extra for putting in those hours. Abigail apparently enjoys the job very much, apparently gets lots of her own needs satisfied in the program, and goes along an extra mile in terms of being active and participatory and helpful. It's almost as though she were an assistant coordinator. Whether she has those kinds of ambitions I don't have any idea. It was evident to me that she works very hard at making the whole program enjoyable. (3/3/88)

The notes continued and shaded into a series of interpretations as the observer reached for some preliminary understandings of what seemed to be happening.

*There's another dimension also in that the parent educator is a
very highly trained woman for that level of job. She has a
teaching degree from City University with some prior work at
another local university. She was in and out of school back in
the late 1960s and early 1970s and alternated working as well
as going to school. She grew up in this part of St. Louis and
mostly recruits and works with families in that area. She indicated that she does recruit as far north and downtown as the
public housing apartments because she ran into some high
school kids from Tech High who were there when she was
recruiting there. She commented also that she is a good
recruiter as well. She also indicated that she's selective about
her cases and clients. She didn't spell that out.*

Growing up in the area, a mixed educational and work career, recruiting
in the high schools, feeling good about her abilities to recruit, and having the autonomy to be selective regarding taking clients are all interesting leads for understanding the nature and role of the urban parent educators who work at the cutting edge of the program.

The next paragraph of notes took up a particular line of thought
among the several possibilities regarding the evening's experience.

*There needs to be some kind of long biographical look at the
women who are able to bring their people out and the ones
who are not. It interplays with their whole attitude toward the
project and the amount of energy they're willing to expend on
project activities. That's got to integrate in some way with
where they're going professionally and what they want to do
more generally. (3/3/88)*

In the beginning, we did not play out the possible relationships between
the recruiting, maintaining, and helping of the parent educators and the
focal issue of the recruiting, maintaining, and helping of parents with
their young children. Abigail Thompson seems a clear example of some
of those relationships and complexities of personality. She returns from
time to time in our story and analysis.

The notes shifted to a focus on the several parents and what
they seemed to enjoy and get out of the program and the much broader
reaches of the underlying public policies related to the PAT program.

*That personal touch and the interest of the young women in
each other seems to be part of it. I was told by Jean, one of
the young women, and by Abigail that they've also set up a
play group on Tuesday morning and Friday afternoon, or vice
versa. Essentially the women have quite small homes and also*

have only a few toys for a large number of children so they made arrangements to meet at the play center at Hawthorne and, in effect, have what amounts to a co-op nursery school there. This enables the facilities to be used a little bit more and it also builds in other aspects both socially in the program and also in terms of the kind of development and knowledge that are occurring with the kids. It's some kind of warm, caring, human element that has got to run through all of that.

In the discussion and sitting around afterward we were eating snacks of peanut butter and crackers, grapes, and sliced oranges. Again, it had a familial social interest and caring kind of chit-chat about kids, about families, about things they were doing that played in and out of the program. The image I had is that the mothers enjoyed being out, they enjoyed each other, and that the program was an easy vehicle for that. Some of the mothers, although I don't know about this group, live close enough and Judy, one of the mothers, was telling me that these women tend to walk their kids in strollers up to the activities at the center.

Also these are all first time mothers with children who vary from I think about 5 or 7 months to about a year. Two boys and one little girl. One more vote for the hypothesis that first time mothers are your best candidates. We'll see how that develops. (3/3/88)

The researcher's background and inclinations, and his view of the nature of the setting, prompted his playing out a particular role that evening, a role that would carry through in other parts of the program throughout the research process.

My role in all of this was kind of a little bit of an outsider and a little bit of a grandparent. I played with a couple of the kids as they were wandering around on the carpet, held them and switched them around, and pointed them back on the rug toward the center of activities. When one active little boy came crawling and began to climb all over the 7-month-old girl, who wasn't really moving but just holding herself up with her back arched strongly and her head high, I thought she was going to lose an eye or head, so I separated them and held the one and let the other one move on back elsewhere. No big problems but mostly indicating that I tried to play some kind of an interested and mildly or casually involved outsider.

The investigator's moving in and out of the program speaks clearly to program dimensions such as informality, acceptance, and facilitating interaction with the parents and children. Events such as these also help build further relationships with the staff.

With the parent educator Abbie Thompson, who gives a quick one-liner and is very quick generally, we got into some banter back and forth that I enjoyed and I think she enjoyed also.

When I left I had the feeling that as they said good-bye and thanked me for coming that they were really very pleased that I had gotten out on such a night and had come to see what was going on and had a view of their part in it, and was willing to listen and talk about what they were up to. So it was another good night. (3/3/88)

The reflections continued in several additional but important ways. Partly, moves toward theoretical abstractions appeared; partly, thoughts about specific strategies and tactics occurred; and partly, controversial value and political issues flowed into the discussion.

One other item has to do again with that issue of the nature of organizations that Etzioni (1961, 1966) sometimes talks about. It has to do with the normative, remunerative, and coercive kinds of organizations and kinds of control structures. In some fundamental sense, with these volunteers in terms of the parents, and the participants, and with the underpaid staff members you have to go for people who are normatively oriented. Essentially they engage in activities because they like it, they think it's good, they think it's important, and not because of either what they are paid or what they are fearful of. So even though you try to pay them, and from my point of view ought to pay them much better than they are paid, you still want people who are basically involved because they are in agreement that it is a good and important idea. What other conditions make it possible for them to do that—in terms of spouses, second salaries, other resources, I don't have any notion at the moment. (3/3/88)

The notes veered to another issue, specific techniques in the maintaining of individuals in the program. In a sense, we are pursuing antecedents of attendance at group meetings, in the complex context of an urban program.

We talked a bit about some of the parents who have been urging her to have night meetings, but who didn't show. She called them on Monday and Tuesday but not last night. In some ways that's probably a mistake, that she should have called them again. But in two-job families there's pressure to have night meetings as well as the day meetings because they can't get to the day meetings. But then when it comes

*off there are other problems and priorities that come up. Some
of them might have made it in terms of the snow and the ice
and the miserable night, but they didn't. Again, more of that
will come out later I suppose.*

*The geography and proximity again its seems to me are
variables that are worth exploring in the same context. I feel
like I'm beginning an argument of a neighborhood school kind
of position. (3/3/88)*

No simple answers appear to questions of attendance and maintaining
individuals in the parent education program. Simple devices of calling
and reminding both work and don't work. More complex techniques,
shifting meeting schedules from the daytime to nighttime, create both
opportunities and other obstacles. Moving toward more immediate
neighborhood centers evokes images of neighborhood schools and more
intimate community buildings.

Several additional large issues arose in the notes from that significant parent group meeting. "Motivation of participants," "meanings
of the experiences," and "program potency" are the more general and
abstract conceptions. The particulars were these.

*It's now 8:51 p.m., and I am almost home. . . . Some of the dis-
cussion, though, that was triggered off by the peanut butter
snacks is that one of the women grinds her own peanuts and
makes her own nonadditive peanut butter. They compared
notes on doing it in a blender and doing it in a vegetable
chopper. Also, the notions of where the ideas came from and
why they were doing it worked in and out of the discussion. So
there's lots of little exchange of information that seems to
occur in all of this.*

*The image I have is that someone like our daughter-in-law,
Sandy, would just revel in being a part of that and having her
kids a part of that and being involved. (3/3/88)*

As particular meetings are observed, and the particulars always carry
their own idiosyncratic content and events, images of the program
appear, and conjectures, if not generalizations, about this parent education program and other possible ones follow soon after.

Items in the notes reveal that one's thinking never quite stops
about program events. A day later a few more thoughts occurred.

*Another item which I don't think I really commented on
enough was the three mothers and their babies. The mothers
all seemed to be pleased and happy about being parents*

and pleased and happy with their kids and pleased and
happy about being a part of the program and seeing each
other and having the time out, so to speak. There was an
open, friendly, outgoing quality about their interaction with
each other, with the parent educator and the coordinator,
the people from the nutrition program, and even with me. The
image I have is that they were all from working-class families.
The one commented about the small house she had. Another
one commented about growing up in the neighborhood. I
don't know all the ins and outs of all of that. (3/4/88)

In a simple sense, that is a small but powerful evaluative statement
about an event in the program.

Further Complexities of the Group Meetings

Group meetings of parents with PAT staff and outside experts is
a major and continuing part of the parents as teachers program.
Videotapes of early meetings held by White and his associates in New
England present an almost idealized view of this aspect of parent education, at least from our perspective. The views from urban centers give a
much more varied set of images. These images provide the concrete
illustrations and instances that give meaning to the general subtitle of
our earlier report, "Dilemmas and Resolutions." Nothing seems simple
as the parent educators struggle with their "situations of practice" as
Schon (1983) conceptualized the world of the educational practitioner. In
his words, situations of practice are characterized by "complexity,
uncertainty, instability, uniqueness, and value conflicts" (p. 14). That
seems a powerful way to think about the PAT group meetings, for those
meetings were complicated, not so predictable, full of value conflicts
and yet idiosyncratic. And, as Schon argued eloquently, very large consequences follow from this conception of practice. Technological solutions seem less relevant than reflection on actions-in-context and considered judgment.

Sometimes the innocence or naiveté of an individual new to a
program is instructive for what he or she sees in his or her first visits.
Then gradually the individual moves toward understanding how a program functions. Observations blend with recollections and merge into
preliminary interpretations. The "summary observation and interpretation" notes dictated immediately after being in the setting have a unique
kind of power for producing this blend toward both particular and general understanding. Such seemed to be the case in early March 1988 as
Smith returned to the university from the Attucks School.

*Presumably because of the transportation problems, Wilma
has cut back their heavier schedule at Attucks to having one
group meeting per month. This is on the first Wednesday, at
10:30. All that's constant. It reminded me of Geoffrey's straight-
line scheduling of every morning at 8:45, for example, you'd
have spelling and at 9:30 you'd have reading and at 10:15
recess, etc. It made for a clarity in the day for him and for his
kids, and it makes for clarity in the program for her and the
parents. I would guess that's important. (3/2/88)*

The two key ideas, reduce the schedule and make it consistent and predictable drew the observer's attention back to an early experience and
study (Smith & Geoffrey, 1968) of an urban class and the teacher
Geoffrey's attempt to order the days for his pupils. Now we are reaching
for a generalization across the urban community, and probably more
broadly. Later discussions confirmed the importance of the idea.

*But seven parents, one set a husband and wife pair, seem to
be an awfully small number, for numbers that might run to
something like 60 families per parent educator and 12 parent
educators is into the seven hundreds of possibilities. Explaining
that it seems to me is a major, major problem and issue. That
one is hugely bigger than just transportation so it seems.
(3/2/88)*

The observer was extrapolating rapidly and perhaps over generalizing
as he was learning another piece of the realities of the complexities of
difficult to reach, maintain, and help urban families. Further reference to
the Smith and Geoffrey book, *The Complexities of an Urban Classroom*, and
to the open house at the Washington School and parent teacher association meetings might have been made, for the same attendance problems
occurred there—at a different time and place, with a different ethnic
group. Concepts and images of Oscar Lewis' (1961) "culture of poverty"
extend our thinking even farther and suggest the difficulties of resolving
our inquiry problem. Vis-a-vis these cultural variables and context, the
PAT program, and others like it, seem to be small and possibly weak
innovations. But we are wandering far from our concerns of the
moment, the group meeting part of PAT.

But the PAT program in the form of a group meeting was working along, in its own way that morning in early March. The notes caught
more of the particulars of setting and activity.

*The space that they are in is really jammed. In what amounts
to a regular size elementary classroom they've got one area*

> *by the entrance which is the desk of the secretary who's a youngish to middle-aged Black woman. There's an area next to that that is essentially the discussion group area and with a half dozen or 10 chairs pulled up around that. Over in the other area there was a rug with play activities and another area with a little slide that also could be used for play activities. This is where the parent educators kept the kids while the mothers and the one father were in the discussion. None of the kids this particular morning was crying or screaming or yelling or running around. That made the din and the noise at a relatively low level but it was constant all the time. But at the same time people could hear and see and it seemed to work out all right. (3/2/88)*

One forgets that schools lag far behind business and professional offices and work space. Limited space and limited privacy are part of the PAT program. Yet staff and parents make do, and the program operates.

The observer began again to reach for broader interpretations as he observed and reflected on his observations.

> *The potential of viable group meetings and the continuing development of the group into a reference group for the parents it seems to me is hugely important. The seeds of that are here but the reality it seems to me is a long way away. (3/2/88)*

Hypotheses coming out of the observations and prior experiences lean toward the possibility and the power of group influences on the array of issues in childrearing in urban communities. Can the group meeting component of the PAT program become significant enough to influence individual parents? And are these influences more significant than the lessons per se and the kind of information being communicated? How do the group meetings fit into the larger family and kin structures? What is the community and the sense of community that the program is fitting into or elaborating? These become elements in our reconstrual of the PAT program for urban families. The notes continued to pick up on specific possibilities.

> *How to keep bringing new parents in and keeping some of the old ones tied up and coming, and how to get people to know each other and to respond to each other is all part of that. I suppose if there were a recommendation these days, I'm now up to maybe two. The first is to provide transportation and the second is to put some additional creative thought into the parent group as a reference group. How that mixes with Black*

working-class parents is another question. It seems as though some of the women are really parts of these larger extended families and much of their needs of that sort are met and taken care of that way. Don't know for sure. And how the gentrified West End of the city relates to the rest of the midtown community is another question.

The problems and issues keep moving toward contextual and larger community domains. Some of these are beyond the PAT program per se.

In a way not realized at the time, the very next paragraph in the notes seemed to provide one partial answer to the question of how to develop the center's group meetings into a reference group. The parent educators were busy.

In terms of activities going on at the same time as the parent meeting, the parent educators were helping the one set of twins and their older brother on a slide and playing back and forth on that. That's a small wooden indoor slide. Another parent educator was giving one of the babies a bottle. She seemed to be enjoying that, and we talked about, reminiscing back in her case 20 years and in my case 35 years to when our kids were that age. Another parent educator was playing on the floor with a young infant of 3 or 4 months. The baby was lying on her back and the parent educator was moving her hands and her arms and her legs and feet. It was a very quiet, easy kind of relationship. She sat on the floor while she worked with that child. Another couple of parent educators were working and helping the kids play with toy cars or toy airplanes which were part of the equipment in the place. (3/2/88)

Be it demonstrating or modeling, the parent educators were exhibiting a joyous, nonpunitive, involved connection with the children. The parents were pleased to have their children in the center.

The lesson of the morning produced some contrary images and further initial thoughts toward recommendations. The world keeps pushing into one's thoughts.

Another suggestion, based now on two group meetings, one with the woman with the film from a week ago at Wellesley and now at the Attucks, as I met the two pharmacists, Pete and Evan, resides in the need to some kind of training of the trainers and speakers. (3/2/88)

The notes specified the perceived problems.

Somehow the speakers just seemed to miss both groups. I think I have some notes on that from the other meeting. In this one, they really don't have any knowledge of how to present a lesson. This was a team affair where the older man was just sort of instructing a senior student at the pharmacy. He tended to butt in and take over and the young man didn't seem to know what to do, both when he tried it and then when the other guy was chiming in and sort of taking over. It's incredible what potency a teacher education program can have. You learn how to do some of those things. Most particularly they seemed to focus, again, too much on the content and seemed to miss the reactions of the mothers who were the students in the program. Somehow they weren't able to involve them, get them going, and enter them into the discussion. From some of the glazed looks, which are not atypical from some of my classes either, it seemed as though the material was just passing them by. (3/2/88)

On a more positive note, the observer's reactions picked up on another aspect of the lesson.

They did come back to a couple of key lessons: (1) being very attentive to reading labels, (2) finding out what to do, (3) calling the Poison Control Center or the pharmacy for more specific instructions, and (4) safe-proofing the house to some degree. (3/2/88)

In retrospect, the final sentence or two of the paragraph lays the basis for an important recommendations.

In a sense, Wilma seemed to be a better discussion leader and contributor than some of the other parent educators. Don't know quite why this is except there's an overall difference in poise and bearing and being in control of the situation. (3/2/88)

The ability of key staff to pick up a stumbling learning situation and make it more relevant and involving is important. Whether that is a simple training and experience issue or whether some larger and more central personality attributes are involved(e.g., "poise and bearing"), is another important set of issues. At a minimum, the long-term selection of outsiders as speakers, the long-term development of PAT staff as "teachers" of small groups of adults needs attention, if the program is to have the immediate benefits desired for the parents and the longer term benefits for the children. For Smith, visions arose of his colleagues Marilyn Cohn and Vivian Gellman who have developed and carried out the Washington University preservice teacher education program for many years. The involved, difficult, and time-consuming task engaging the creativity of these women provides concrete images of how parent educators could be made into effective teachers. Immediately, concerns arise over time and financial resources, that would make such development more possible. Equally important is the need for an imaginative concept of teacher education, a much maligned field and intellectual topic.

But pieces of the "realities" of PAT group meetings were beginning to arise and to fall into place, in a way helpful for thinking about the dissemination of the program to other urban areas. Such adoptions and adaptations, when viewed at this concrete level and when interpreted at a much more general and abstract level, are not simple one off additions to overall programs. Our reconstrual of the program continues.

Parent Reactions, "Good" Clients, and Urban Complexity

Qualitative inquiry has a way of breaking down stereotypes, seeing other perspectives, and suggesting ways of reconstruing and improving educational programs. Serendipity seems always just a breath away—even with very brief conversations. After one parent education group meeting the following notes were recorded.

I talked with several of the parents and the parent educators very briefly. One of the parents, a White woman who lives over on the south side, and is one of Wilma's clients, invited me to come on any visit that Wilma made to her home. She's mid-30s, a physical therapist, and has a little boy who they didn't think they were going to have. He is 18 months, "a real miracle." Apropos of the project, she raised a couple of key items. One is she's Catholic and this is a free educational program, that is, one supported by state tax dollars and one of the few educational benefits that accrue to some of the Catholic families. Just on the surface, that seems to be an important selling point in terms of the program generally and perhaps also for some of the difficult to reach and hard to maintain families. She raised a second point about coming to the Attucks Center as opposed to Hawthorne. And it sounded as though she didn't really know much about Hawthorne and what the possibilities were there. But she was quite clear that she wanted her child to experience some of the contacts with the Black families and the Black community. This was connected with her value system as an important ingredient of solving those problems. She volunteered this without push or probe from me. I

was a little dumbfounded. I'd assumed she was from the west-
end, but not so. The geography of this project is one that's a
little bit more complicated than I guess I had originally imag-
ined or thought.

This reporting and these musings led then to some broader thoughts
about the program that we have woven into several parts of the book.

One of the real important generalizations is the diversity of the
urban community. There are lots and lots of kinds of people on
almost any set of dimensions that you could envision from eco-
nomics to race to religion to social motivation. Forgetting that
puts you in great peril. And to make some generalizations
about all of the city or all of urban areas or all of disadvan-
taged is a real unfortunate stereotyping.

The abstracting and generalizing, at least in the form of questioning,
seemed not to want to stop. The next paragraph of notes furthered several central ideas in the overall perspective we were developing.

Another aspect of the draw of people into the program for
these group meetings is what might be labeled quality of per-
sonnel. It seems to me that Wilma becomes an excellent illus-
tration, and this young mother becomes the coordinate part
of that illustration. Although we didn't talk specifically about
that, the image I have from the way she mentioned Wilma
and her name and her willingness to have me come is that she
thinks very highly and positively of Wilma. The real trick is identi-
fying what it is that makes up "a quality parent educator."
Fathoming that one and then being able to identify or select
on the one hand, not to mention train and develop on the
other hand, it seems to me is a huge big issue for the program
in general and right at the core of getting people to attend on
the other hand. I had some of the same feeling about Abbie,
the parent educator at Hawthorne.

The final sentence of the paragraph moved directly to another level of
specificity about those characteristics.

There's a kind of good cheer, common sense, interest in kids
and parents and child development, competence, easy rap-
port, all of which seem to come together. (4/20/88)

Thinking about that last sentence immediately moved us to consider the kind of performance test in a real setting that would enable one to select individuals who would have some idiosyncratic but effective blend of the characteristics. Such thoughts also led to a concern about which parts of the pattern would be teachable, even in an effective teacher training program. In our recommendations we raise some of the kind of continuing inquiry that will lead to ways of thinking about and acting on the ideas.

Group Meetings: Summary Interpretations

In the late spring and early summer of the first year of the PAT project, Smith wrote an interim report for the foundation that had supported the inquiry. In a sense, it was one of the first of the memos that he later developed to facilitate his own developing interpretations of the urban PAT program, his desire to communicate with the multiple individuals involved in the program, and his need to keep the foundation informed. For our purposes now it serves as a fitting summary of this part of our description and analysis. In addition, the writing style continues our attempt to involve the reader in our "discovery" style, that is our perceptions and reflections as we came to know, understand, and make suggestions for program improvement. Hopefully, our readers are increasing their competence as reflective practitioners of parent education.

I have attended group meetings with as few as 2 or 3 parents and as many as 40 to 50 parents. The average would be a half dozen parents per meeting. Some meetings were canceled when weather was severe during part of the winter and spring. I was surprised at those attendance numbers for each center has between 600 and 900 families. Reports from other PAT centers across the state indicate these are not atypical figures. The program mandates that each parent receive five contacts in the academic year, three of these must be individual visits and the remainder may be individual or group meetings. Further, in regard to my surprise, I had developed expectations out of the training sessions, the reading of White's work, and some of my own beliefs about change in social behavior that the groups would be "reference groups" and "support groups," to use some of the old and new jargon from the group dynamics field. Some individuals raised the question of the parents' perception of the relevance of the group meetings. So the surprise may be more my problem than the program's problem. Nonetheless I spent a good bit of time this spring talking with people and thinking about the issues of group meetings in the overall PAT program and with the special focus of the research projects brief of "difficult to reach and maintain families."

Figure 5.1 is an attempt to develop an initial summary model of possible antecedents of these events and to represent them sort of "iconicly," to use one of Jerome Bruner's labels of ways of representing reality. I find such models helpful in seeing the overall pattern of relationships under discussion, while I trace out the implications in more extended prose.

Topics. *It is a common belief among most of the staff that different topics will draw different numbers of parents to the meetings. Toilet training and discipline are thought to be the most heavily attended. The one meeting with the 40 to 50 parents which I observed was on toilet training. It was also one of the most "vigorous" meetings as parents had a wide range of particular questions on their minds. The questions ranged from when to start, how to know if the child is ready, what to do about siblings, the use of potty chairs, and so forth.*

The array of topics of meetings I attended included nutrition, safety, poisons, sexual development, immunization, intellectual development, language development, literature and libraries, and so forth. Each of these warrants fuller discussion in the final report.

I am still trying to make sense of the significance of the relation between topics and attendance. Should the program have more of one kind and less of another kind of meetings? Do some topics overlap with topics in the one on one private visits?

Transportation. *Only one of the centers seems to approach being a neighborhood center where a number of the mothers walk their children in strollers to the center. This raised in my head a number of old arguments regarding the debates over neighborhood schools and their pros and cons. Some of this appears in our book,* The Fate of an Innovative School *(Smith et al., 1987). I have not heard much discussion of this, nor have I raised it with the PAT staff as yet.*

But transportation becomes exceedingly important when families have limited income, no car or only one car, and public transportation is limited. The program has used special funds from the desegregation program and from the incentive grants to pay for taxis to bring mothers to the meetings. Attendance was lower during the period when funds from the one program ran out and the arrangements for the other funds still were being made. At some meetings it seemed that one third to two thirds of the attendance depended on the taxi vouchers. All this is one piece of the larger issue of financial resources for the PAT program. At this point, acknowledg-

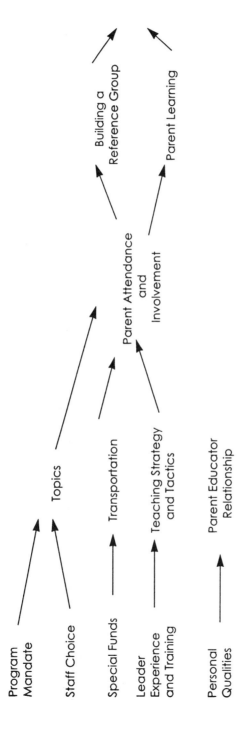

Figure 5.1. Hypothesized antecedents of attendance and involvement in group meetings

ing my own limited knowledge and understanding of the details, it seems particularly critical for the "hard to reach and maintain" families.

Teaching Strategies and Tactics. In my view, one of the most productive ways of looking at the group meetings is from the perspective of teaching and learning. The general hypothesis is that "good" teaching will interest and help the parents and they will want to return for more of the program. The subhypothesis is that this is even more true of the hard to reach and maintain families. The meetings were quite variable. The best ones, again from my point of view, seemed to have several characteristics. These characteristics might become an agenda for the continuing education of the parent educators, another part of the program that I know little about at this point.

I was struck with the opening tactic of having the parents say one or two things about their child that had occurred in recent days or weeks. Sometimes this was done by the leader of the day's program and some times, especially when there was an outside speaker, by the coordinator or by one of the parent educators. Some of the parents are very reluctant to speak in the meeting. This opening tactic seemed to give them opportunity and practice in a simple, warm, pleasant way. It is a simple, but in my eyes, a very powerful tactic. Except for the few very large group meetings it is feasible with almost all of the other meetings.

Some of the outside speakers and some of the parent educators have been trained as teachers. As the people had some conception and experience with what a "lesson" is they seemed to move more easily in the group leader role. And within this group, the leaders with the most involvement and participation of the parents were those that moved from a more textbook kind of lesson to a more experiential, hands-on kind of lesson. Still more difficult is the skill of improvising to the comments and questions of the moment. One of the best moments of this occurred when one of the children wandered from the play area to his mother and had the beginnings of a temper tantrum. The child's behavior, the mother's behavior, and the alternatives and the possibilities opened into a vivid, vigorous discussion of all of the participants. It was an unplanned but powerful event.

As one who has faced years of classes of all kinds, and seen rows of passive faces, and has had lessons that didn't work as I had hoped, I know both the sinking feeling, and the what-can-I-do-about-this feeling. Teaching is not a simple task, nor is it one that any of us do well all the time, but it is a central part of the program and a part that can be worked on by all of us. Again, I know little about how this currently is being handled.

For instance, only one of the meetings I have attended has been videotaped for later discussion of strengths and weaknesses. I don't even know whether the program has such equipment as part of its resources. Over the long haul, I believe that these are issues important for our focal group of difficult to reach and maintain families. The final report should speak more definitively to issues such as these.

Conclusion. *In short, the group meetings in my view are important and open for interesting and I presume controversial discussion as alternative views of their nature and place in the overall program is debated.*

A Thought or Two More

Early on in the inquiry, Smith entered the PAT program through the group meetings, as he thought that that would be a simple and easy way of getting acquainted with people and events and, in turn, the people would get to know a little of him. And now, even though our intent is to present items for discussion of the curriculum, we find ourselves struck that it is "curriculum-in-action" that keeps coming up in the initial notes he made. The attendance issues linked into the dismal weather of late winter and early spring in St. Louis. The special problems outside speakers and presenters had in relating to the special audience of families difficult to reach, maintain, and help seemed everywhere. Not insurmountable, and not totally different from teaching in other settings with other age groups of students and adults, yet different enough to call forth ideas of how to understand and improve parts of the program. The ever present resource problem—money, inadequate or unreliable equipment, limited space—seemed another kind of reality to be thought about, creatively handled, and coped with. These perceptions and reactions, as Smith tried to get his footing, are probably not too different from what other "outsiders" will have in other urban communities as they try to adopt and adapt a program such as PAT. Each item we raise should provide important content for small and large conversations as educators and citizens plan and implement a PAT program. In a sense we have enlarged on the usual discussion of "curriculum." That, too, is an important lesson from our perspective.

CURRICULUM: TOPICS AND SUBSTANCE

The range of questions asked and information presented regarding child development seem unending in the PAT program. The observer, thinking back to his graduate school days in the early 1950s, had reappearing anxieties, concerns, and images of the need to have Leonard Carmichael's old *Handbook of Child Development* (1946), Leo Kanner's old *Child Psychiatry* (1949), and Arnold Gesell's (1928) *Infancy and Human Growth* not to mention their more recent counterparts, in his hip pocket if he were to deal adequately with the topics under consideration. Normal child development and all the variations off of that, even short of the severe psychiatric diagnostic categories and cases, is a huge intellectual agenda. Furthermore, aspects of social psychology appeared as topics such as modeling in group meetings arose in our discussions. In this section, we raise some observations, interpretations, and recommendations regarding the curricular content of the PAT program as we saw it in action. Once again we have a potpourri of important ideas.

Modeling Parent–Child Interaction

On occasion, educators present or imply that the one-on-one "tutoring" type relationship is the ideal type of education. When one's goals are social, as in the interactive relationship between a mother and her child, group settings carry an important set of qualities beyond the possibilities of the tutorial. One of these qualities arose in a conversation about a parent perceiving, reflecting, and changing the quality of her interactions with her child. *Modeling* was the label we gave this part of the curriculum of PAT.

LS: Can we . . . ? Just in reflecting on that, and it seems to me
        that she made a comment yesterday, Wednesday, the
        fact—is her son's name's Russell?
WW: Hm-hmm.
LS: That he is better now and so on. And . . . I guess I want to tie
        her into that . . . hard to reach or difficult to maintain. Does
        she fit that category or . . . ? She's obviously got some differ-
        ences about her.
WW: Hm-hmm. I . . . I really don't perceive her as being . . . either
        hard to reach or difficult to maintain in terms of her openness
        to the program.

[Note: Cassie is actually in the hard-to-help category, but we had not conceived that label at the time of this interview.]

*So she's actually looking for some outlet for herself
because I would imagine that her life with Russell . . . up until
she started coming to the group meetings was not fun,
because, as I said, the relationship was so—they seemed to
always be at odds. I think she wanted an outlet—a way to get
away. I think that she's not difficult to maintain because we
have the cab service to get her out to those group meetings. I
think that that's an essential component for her, because it
gets Russell in touch with other children. It lets her see other
children's behaviors right next to his so that she can see that
he's not really that awful. He's not doing anything any different than most other children do. We see her two to three
times a month. She's at the center or we're at her house two
to three times a month. So she's able to get some reinforcement and some positive feedback from us, with regard to
how things are going. And I think that's important for her.*

LS: *So in a sense it's one of the strongest reasons for the group
meetings of anything that we've talked about?*

WW: *Hm-hmm [yes].*

Next, the parent educator made a causal analysis of the relationship between Cassie's attendance at group meetings, and changes in her
interaction with Russell.

WW: *. . . I think that seeing other parents at the group meetings
interact with their children, seeing how he could get into a
group and with the right—with the right kind of structure get
along with that group. I think that all of that has been very
helpful in her movement towards a more—a more pleasant
relationship with her child. One of the most . . . one of the
most compelling reasons for having group meetings as far as
I'm concerned is that parents get to see their children in different situations, but the other thing is that for those folks who
are having a difficult time, they get to see other reactions.
They get to see other ways of handling the problem without
anybody ever having to tell them anything. I think that we
often don't give enough—we don't give enough credit to
the role of modeling.*

The phrasing "they seemed to always be at odds" captures in
easy colloquial language a major kind of parent–child relationship, one
of continuing discomfort. Although group meetings are seldom spoken
of in this fashion, the idea that parents might be unobtrusive role models
for each other raises an important mode of teaching and learning in the
parents as teachers' group meetings. Other children "model" similar
behavior and actions that demonstrate that one's own child might not be

as atypical, "bad" as it might be felt, and other mothers have ways of
dealing with the behavior that one had not thought about. At the time
and later in individual home visits the parent educator can refer back to
the earlier episodes and help specify and generalize the significance of
the behavior and actions of the child and the mother, further enhancing
the meanings of the action and the interaction. Implicitly, we are reconstruing another part of the program's curriculum and structure.

Emotional Development and Learning: The Variety Continues in Group Meetings

The variety of group meetings, in content, presentation, and parental
reaction continued to appear as we tried to make sense of the overall
PAT program. The close description and interpretation present images
that anyone wanting to adapt or adopt the program, or develop a related
parent educational effort, might find numerous suggestions for practice
and policy. The lesson of the day concerned emotional development,
and the notes developed the day's events and interpretations this way.

> *I'm on my way down to the Hawthorne School to check into
> the group meeting this morning. I believe it's on emotional
> development, and I believe it's being run by one of the parent
> educators. It was just a week ago that I was down there with
> the snowstorm and the nutrition program. It seems like a centu-
> ry ago with all of the ins and outs of other things I've been
> doing the last week. (3/10/88)*

A context always exists for one's learning and understanding. In addition a series of conjectures also always accompanies one's observations
and helps put meaning into the observations.

> *In terms of weather-type hypotheses, today's a good day to
> check that out. It's a lovely, cool spring morning. the sun's shin-
> ing, there's hardly a cloud in the sky. If people are able to walk
> their youngsters in strollers up to the meeting place at
> Hawthorne they'll be able to do it today. It's at 11 o'clock in
> the morning so that none of the complications of evening and
> family responsibilities of that sort are present. Who knows?*

In an important sense, the observer has set himself for the morning and
what he might see and hear. Some small but specific "foreshadowed
problems" are present, but they are not "preconceived solutions" as the
concluding question indicated—"Who knows?" Two hours later the
notes continued.

It's now 12:15 and I'm on my way home.

And then.

In a sense I had the feeling that this meeting was what meetings are supposed to be all about. There must have been, finally, about 16 mothers at the meeting. Some of them had their kids in the room where the meeting was held, maybe five or six, and most of the other children seemed to be down in the playroom being attended to by other parent educators and aides of one kind or another. You could hear them down there from time to time. The field notes are full of the particulars of the meeting.

Without going into detail, the group leader, Abbie Thompson, raised ideas in a simple three-phased outline: feelings, emotional development, and ways to help with emotional development. Questions were raised and taken from the mothers and responded to by the parent educators. For instance, they included disciplining with a sibling, dealing with a scared child, having an outgoing child versus a shy one, how to teach children to express feelings rather than hitting out. A number of handouts helped clarify and extend the discussion, for example "It's helpful if you can relate feelings to actions and to thoughts and to think about them and control them." Everyone smiled when a mother raised the issues of "negativism, stubbornness, and defiance." The parent educators, now three who were working together as a team, made a series of comments, starting with "It's normal behavior." The discussion included a variety of other comments and suggestions: be constant in one's love, maintain a calm attitude, view incident from the child's point of view, give choice if possible, avoid threats, deal with undesirable behavior immediately, and let children know you are in control, but allow some latitude. As one might imagine, the discussion between the parents and the parent educators—and between and among the parents themselves—was vigorous.

The summary observation notes continued.

Basically a few summary general observations that seem significant come to mind.

First, I was struck by the teaming of the three parent educators. They easily went back and forth with each other as they each had special assignments within the overall discussion of emotional development.

Susan and Nancy, two of the parent educators, engaged in a role-play between a parent and a child who were in a kind of "you will" and "I won't" struggle, with the "parent" saying things like, "pick up your toys", "sit there", "I'll tell your daddy", and the "child" interspersing a "No!" between each parent directive. The parent audience howled with laughter. The discussion went on.

> Second, I was struck, too, with the discussion finally occurring with the parents speaking out. Again the feeling I have is that this is a more working-class neighborhood and the levels of education and sophistication weren't what one might expect out of West County, but the parent spoke quite directly and quite vividly to a variety of issues in raising kids. The emotional aspects seemed to run in and out of most of that but not totally.
>
> The third item that really hit me as being the most poignant, were the issues around the three generations. A couple of the mothers raised issues about their own mothers or about their mothers-in-law who were either living in the same household or living in the flat upstairs or living fairly close by. These third-generation or older generation of parents were doing things that the mothers of the young children here didn't like, essentially telling the young children things like "you're a bad child" or being, if not quite abusive, very abrupt and harsh with the kids. The mothers didn't like their own mothers doing that. Then the question became how they dealt with that. Also, the question came in terms of them still being caught in their own mother–child relationships. It was very difficult for some of them to be assertive and to be able to somehow indicate to their mothers that they don't want them to do that. I found all that discussion to be very powerful in terms of getting into significant issues. Not really solving them in any fundamental sense, but at the same time continually talking about them and working on them in fairly common sense terms and helping the parents get some perspective on them. (3/10/88)

The generational problem in multiple forms appeared and reappeared in our observations, interviews, and discussions. It is a major item in an urban parent education program.

> The notes captured further aspects of the very productive morning meeting.
>
> Another item that I was struck with was the ability of the parent educators, and particularly Abbie on this one, to convert the discussion into very specific, very concrete, very practical kinds of activities. For instance, she had paper bag pup-

pets, she had books, she had illustrations, she had comments about doing a temper tantrum routine with a doll at a later time. I had the feeling I was in the middle of one of my creativity lessons as people thought up options as to how to handle things. This occurred within the group and with a couple of the mothers in particular leading the way. The feeling I have is there's a lot of creativity that one might not tap into in some other ways, that gets tapped here and that goes into being a parent and a parent educator. How one finds those people or works with them is another question, especially regarding the parent educators, the working with the mothers as is occurring in this meeting today. (3/10/88)

Creativity in teaching and in interpersonal relationships as a selection criterion for parent educators and as a goal of inservice education of the parent educators is a major generalization coming out of our observations. This one meeting captured some of the best of our insight.

But other things happened that morning that deserve some comment because they focus on related emotional events, and they suggest the kind of integration between the curriculum and teaching in home visits and the events in the group meetings.

Another point that seemed to be happening with each of these three parent educators who are leading the meeting, and maybe a little bit with one or two others whom I didn't meet, was the follow-up of more specific detailed conversation with their individual clients. All of them got involved in quite intense conversations that way. The blending back and forth of the individual conversations and the group meetings seems to me to be the kind of thing that is useful and helpful as the program runs its course. I need to find out who attended this meeting and how many of them belong to Abbie, Susan, and Nancy, the three parent educators who are leading the meeting. It's a question as to what draws the parents in and how much that kind of personal identification would. There were two from the several last week and Abbie is the parent educator for both. (3/10/88)

Implicitly, another potential set of hypotheses emerged in the next short paragraph in the notes.

I keep hearing lots of discussion of Catholic churches and people at different places, etc. The religious background and who is being served it seems to me is another key issue. (3/10/88)

The centers located in different parts of the city appealed to varied audiences and integrated differentially with subgroups of families. The ideas
explicitly suggested further places to recruit and implicitly suggested
ideas on maintaining and helping urban families.

During the breaks in the group meeting, the conversations
swirled around other topics. Important conjectures of several sorts arose
easily and informally.

> I chatted briefly with one of the mothers who I had met briefly
> a week ago. She's the one with the little redheaded boy. She
> was talking about her own mother-in-law living upstairs in the
> flat above. She commented that she's raising three children:
> her son, her husband, and her mother-in-law. Some of that
> had to do with how each of them tended to be more infantile
> or needed to be the center of attention and the kind of prob-
> lems that creates for her. She also indicated that there's
> another set of problems with her husband on his attitudes
> toward women. She saw this as negative in effect. I didn't real-
> ly push that one very hard. It grew out of an earlier kind of role
> modeling where the husband apparently swears and uses fair-
> ly foul language, and she's concerned about the kid learning
> that and popping out with it in front of a nun one day. This
> woman looks—seems—close to Abigail. It seems as though the
> kinds of things they were talking about really involve a much
> broader agenda of the kind of personhood of this woman,
> which would be my phrase and I'm not sure how well it fits,
> and the role of the parent educator. And particularly some-
> one like Abbie Thompson who is bright and well-trained and
> generally knowledgeable and on top of things.

The paragraph in the notes would not quit. The conjectures continued in
ways that would recur throughout the study of the program.

> In a sense, it's almost as though the parent educator role mod-
> eling is part of a much larger need for some women to have
> people they can talk to, people they can do things with, peo-
> ple who can in effect acquaint them with a huge variety of
> alternative lifestyles. Lots of that is speculative and yet that's
> the sort of image that went through my head. (3/10/88)

The observer/interpreter had some reservations about the mix of what
he was seeing and what he was bringing to the situation. Later, and
based on observations and interviews with other parent educators, the
ideas would move toward a reconstrual of the role of the parent educator, one of the most important ideas developed in the inquiry. But the
conjectures continued on this day in early March.

*In a sense, it's very difficult for me to jump from my own univer-
sity world, and my own kind of upper middle-class suburban
neighborhood, plus cosmopolitan England, plus whatever,
and somehow grab hold of where these people are and what
kinds of things are going on in their lives, and what kind of
background and experience, both in their own childhood and
adolescence and now in their marriages, is happening. A person like this woman with the redheaded youngster may well
be looking for and wanting a whole variety of different kinds of
things. It's as though she knows that it's out there, and she
knows that she's not satisfied with the way things are, and the
question is how to somehow obtain or get more of another
kind of life. Again, I've got to emphasize that this is all specula-
tive and that it just seems to fit, but I don't really have any
hard data, so I'm working it out. Muted cues is Andrew Halpin's
(1966) old notion for some of that. But if any of that's true, then
one other aspect of the high attendees or the ones who are
involved in the program is that ability to relate to their parent
educator in some of these very broad ways that are based on
some very deep-seated needs and depend on some kind of
clicking of personalities in the relationship. When you get a mix
of some of that it seems to me that change and the possibility
of change is very great and the subsidiary business of coming
to meetings and being involved is solved. (3/10/88)*

A major methodological idea followed. It was one that we implemented
only briefly and episodically.

*In a sense I guess I'm finding the possibility of an interview with
some of the parents and a question of the order of what are
you enjoying about the program, the meetings, the one on
one, and where does it fit into you life, and were you surprised
about anything, and what seems to make you want to be a
part of the whole affair? (3/10/88)*

A final paragraph from the summary notes tied down another series of
hypotheses related to the group meeting on "emotional development."
Some seem more related to the context, the antecedent, and consequences of general program effectiveness. The dictating continued.

*I'm getting close to home and just a couple of other items. On
the way in I noticed one mother who drove in and another
who had her toddler walking with her. I noticed another mother who had a stroller and was walking down the busy main
street and coming across from the other side of the street. The*

weather hypothesis was helpful at one level. Another item that needs to be mentioned is that in the hallway outside the room there's a bulletin board and someone has set up or has put the pictures up that were taken last Thursday. They even had a couple of the relaxed ethnographer as well as pictures of the mothers, the people in the program presentation, and the parent educators. A third point, the coordinator has some kind of an Apple computer and a program for doing graphics and letterhead, and she made up the announcements and did all of the little stuff that gives a little flair to things that are sent out, or identify what's on the bulletin board, etc. Another, fourth point that needs to be emphasized, too, is that Hawthorne has the best space of any of the four centers. They've got one regular sized classroom that they hold their meetings in, and then one regular sized classroom which is really a glorified preschool room, with toys and rugs and dolls and different kinds of things that the kids can play with. Further, they have an attendant who handles all of that and maybe a couple of more people. I'm not sure. There's also a big spacious hallway connecting the two rooms where the bulletin boards are and that, in effect, gives a flow of space and room between the two rooms. It really feels like it's a small wing of the building. Which in a sense I guess it really is.

The last sentence gives a general conclusion.

In brief one has the image that the program is really up and running today. (3/10/88)

The meeting topic was emotional development, and it was, but it was also considerably more than that. It was about the child's emotional development, that of the siblings, and of the mother as well. Shortly it became the emotional development of all three "children"— the child, the father, and the mother-in-law living upstairs, downstairs, or nearby. Continuously, it took on a social interactional flavor—what is going on, what can I do about it, and how does it relate to all of the other aspects of our home and life.

The topic(s) was approached with lecture, role-play, handouts, total group discussion, and smaller dyads and triads of parents or parent educators in intense conversation, and formal and informal team teaching. Creativity, humor, and common sense seemed blended with more formal materials.

The longer reach of parent needs, hopes, and aspirations—ideas, models, and life style possibilities—kept appearing subtly and on the fringes of the discussions and conversations. This latent agenda seemed always to be edging toward the surface. Individual parent educators varied in how much they wanted to enter this part of the domain of "emotions, feelings, and parenting." The formal documents of the program tend not to address the issue. In an urban community such as this one, it seems present and important.

Parties as Curriculum

Cassie appeared in an interview again as another major aspect of curriculum was raised, one we came to call "Parties as Curriculum." We felt it raised a simple but extremely important practical principle about empowering parents. Actually it has been a part of our intellectual agenda for many years (Smith & Geoffrey, 1968).

WW: *We had a little Christmas party for the kids. A nonreimbursable activity. It was something that parents just said they wanted to do. And I think it's really wonderful that the group of parents who took the lead in that enterprise would traditionally be thought of as hard to reach and maintain. Cassie is one of them. Frances and Rowena are both on Aid to Dependent Children. Frances in particular is having a difficult time—and I'm positive she is one of those people in the group who said they were having difficulties with—with their own mothers . . . in giving unwanted advice as to how to rear their children. But all of these—all of these women are women who have really taken advantage of our cab service and who come to our group meetings. We gave them a list of moms' names and said, "OK, go home and call them and tell them that we're getting ready for the Christmas activity." I met with them twice and said, "What plans do you have? What are you going to do? What kinds of activities? What do you need us to do for you?" They wanted to have refreshments, they coordinated all of that, and you know, everybody brought something. The center provided paper products and that kind of thing, but they provided the food. This—this set of moms came early to help set up so that, you know, things would be right. I was really impressed with the fact that it was this particular group of mothers who followed through with everything. It was a very successful activity.*

LS: *Do you have anything for Valentine's Day or for Easter?*

WW: *I let them decide what they wanted to do. So the next one is Easter. It worked out very well.*

LS: *How many parents did you have in for that?*

WW: *We had about . . . I think there were about 23 moms.*

Curriculum comes in many forms. It serves multiple purposes. It even involves activities that are nonreimbursable. Some of the difficult to maintain and help families are responding to the variety of possibilities within the program.

Discipline

Perhaps as much or more than any topic in the personal visits and the group meetings, the issue of "discipline" was on everyone's agenda. Images from earlier years appeared in the form of Sheviakov, and Redl, & Richardson's (1956) *Discipline for Today's Children and Youth,* a popular manual for parents and teachers three decades ago. Parents want their children to listen, obey, and behave in general agreement with their own family values and practices. Our notes and conversations are full of images and problems. We present two items to suggest the array of ideas and complications in this area, one from our memo's and one from our conversations.

Social Reality and the Setting of Limits

One of the important ideas from general social psychology is that "social reality" is not a god given or natural law, but rather the construction of a group of people. Families and communities create views of what is right and wrong, what is appropriate or inappropriate, out of their religious and cultural traditions. Children learn these as the parents have clear expectations and views, as these are communicated to the child, and as parents follow up on their views. One memo recounted a particular incident and an interpretation.

> *Sometimes an old idea (e.g., the setting of limits) appears in such graphic form that it is worth presenting the illustration and trying to put it into a slightly larger rationale. Once again the data come from a parent educator conversation and a parent's observation. The parent educator and parent have been working on "setting limits," a task particularly difficult for this parent. Part of the rationale has been, in my words, making social reality appear as regular and as immutable as much of physical reality. The sun comes up every morning regardless of your wishes or mine, as parent or as child. Some parts of social reality, so I am arguing here, should be of the same order.*
> *The parent reported on an episode in a drug store where they had gone to buy the 30-month-old child some crayons because the child "likes to color." While at the store, the child entered into a rather familiar routine of wanting some candy*

and wanting a number of brightly colored and packaged toys, many of which were age inappropriate, and which provided the parent with an opportunity and reason for saying no. The problem was in the child's running about and picking up the toys at high speed. Eventually, the parent picked up the child and indicated that the child wouldn't be put down unless he held the parent's hand and carried the crayons to the check-out counter. The usual whining and twisting began, but this time the parent kept insisting that the child could not have anything else and would be carried to the counter unless he did what he was told. Social reality became like physical reality. There was no problem, according to the parent's observation, in the child's understanding of what was being said and insisted upon. Surprisingly, a full-fledged tantrum did not occur. The child acquiesced, if that is the right word, and he was put down. They walked hand in hand to the counter without further difficulty. When they got home the child colored for over a half hour. He has an incredible attention span for some activities, which may or may not be a part of setting the limits. (Memo 12)

Responses from parent educators indicated comments of the order, "these methods are generally accepted practice in PAT." The difficulties lay in the special circumstances of each family and child. In this instance, the parent's insistence did not provoke a temper tantrum in the store. If that happens, then one has another kind of problem. And that interacts, as we indicated in an earlier chapter, with the parents own needs and his or her ability to let the child "perform" in public and for him or her to tolerate the "embarrassment." Furthermore, if one's spouse agrees or disagrees, it turns "the problem" into a new and different issue. As strands of problems in action and interaction spin out in this form, possibilities increase for "significant conversations" in the personal visits and "significant discussions" in the group meetings. Social behavior has many facets—negativism, tantrums, hitting, biting, not sharing—and many settings—dinner table, bathroom, stores, play yards, and neighbors' houses. The illustration suggests where some of those conversations and discussions went in our observations of the PAT program.

Contextual Issues in Discipline

Observations and interpretations, being true to both the first and the second record, as the historian Hexter (1971) phrase the external and the internal worlds of the inquirer, run in multiple strands. A group meeting was the setting, discipline was the topic. Some 20 parents, all but 1 were mothers, was the audience. Greta was leading the discussion. The summary observations and interpretations were recorded this way.

Perhaps more this time than with any of the meetings so far, I had the impression that everything was really working as it was supposed to work. The speaker, Greta, is a very experienced woman who's run a daycare center for a half dozen years and taught several years in a couple of local school districts. She in a sense knows how to teach and how to present and does it with some drama and some change of voice and some excitement and some old shoe comments as well as other kinds of things. I think I would have lingered on some illustrations and got the people to come out with some more items, but then maybe I do too much of that anyhow. The point about the business working this time that struck me so forcibly was that the mothers from time to time would break in on an issue or on a discussion and present a related but extended illustration of some facet of discipline or some complication and then they would then talk about their situation. The most dramatic one of these perhaps was of a young mother who had been quite talkative all through, and was one of the big participants in that sense, finally commented very late in the meeting about how her 4-year-old spends most of the time living with her father and then comes on every other weekend to live with her and her husband and new child or two. She raised the kind of problems that that creates in terms of the child "giving her a lot of lip," which is close to a direct quote, and being difficult to live with. These kinds of complications it seemed to me were significant additions and enabled the people to talk and think a bit about what they're doing beyond the kind of guidelines or truisms or general common sense rules that were being presented and raised. (3/31/88)

Discipline always has a context, and the divorce and remarriage seemed an important one for this parent and her new family.

At a kind of "meta-level" the very way in which parent educators and parents think about their discipline problems became a "problem" as well. It became something that needed further thought.

All of that suggests another notion about the relationship of common sense and general principles to more abstract or scientifically based concepts and principles. The continuity between these levels and the complications with the different situation are amazing to behold. We ought to be able to get a huge number of illustrations to make some of those points.

And then.

I was struck, too, by another illustration of the complications that occur when grandparents get involved in the situation and what one does when they do or don't do things the same way that parents do. And then this is further complicated in that some of the grandparents do it differently between themselves, much less between themselves and the parents. And around and around it goes.

And then.

I'm struck also that there is an array of specific problems around sleeping which came up and around sibling relationships.

Finally.

One other quick comment. Some parents were talking about a TV show on child care which they had seen. Apparently these outside influences will creep in from time to time. I didn't really get any clarity about it. (3/31/88)

The topic was discipline. The discussion in the group meeting was open. The mothers raised major complications about discipline as they played out in their lives. The group leader entertained those examples and interpolated her own ideas and reflections. The variations in specificity and abstraction level were apparent as meaningful attempts were made by everyone. Parental participation was vigorous and thoughtful.

Multiple Settings, Learnings, and Transfer?: Parental Beliefs and Community Realities

The complexities of discipline as an issue for parents who are difficult to reach, maintain, and help appeared in one of our long interview/discussions. Parental beliefs about "toughness" was the initial issue, but "mutual change" in both the parent and the parent educator became the latent and important idea we want to communicate. Initially, we phrased the parent educator's dilemma as mediating among her personal viewpoint and the community realities faced by parents and their young children. A particular resolution occurred as we talked about Laurie, one of the mothers in the program.

WW: *I think I've been able to modify her views somewhat in the area of corporal punishment and discipline. But she still believes in the value of swatting if it is necessary. And she*

LS: *doesn't overdo it but I think that sometimes her expectations are a little bit high for the children in terms of—*

LS: *Their social behavior?*

WW: *Their social behavior. The other thing that's interesting about her is that from the beginning—her first child was a boy—and she has some very strong feelings about socializing boys to be independent. At a very, very early age she consciously began—and we discussed this many times—but she consciously made a decision not to pick him up a lot. And not to cuddle, because she said that just made him soft. He had to be tough, you know, because those people out in the neighborhood were going to demand that of him. So we've been discussing that back and forth . . . that kind of an issue really makes—it really makes me as a parent educator coming in and talking about "You don't want—you don't want your children to hit. You don't want—"The real life situation is often a little bit different and it makes you step back and think about some of these assumptions that I've made and how do I make a real good case for my point of view when the real facts are that he is called upon to defend himself sometimes and if everybody in the neighborhood doesn't share Laurie's view of the world [if Laurie accepts the PE's views regarding hitting, etc.]— does that mean that we're setting her son up to be the neighborhood punching bag? [laughs] It takes a lot of talking through to try to get to something that she's happy with. So I think she—she picked him up a little bit more but not as much as I would have picked up a baby that age had he been mine, but more than she would have if—if I had not been there to discuss with her a baby's need for affection, a baby's need for cuddling.*

LS: *Does that dilemma come up in other conversations, that I've got to make my son, and my daughter, tough so that they can survive outside? Or is this more classically illustrated here than elsewhere?*

WW: *I think that the ability to verbalize it is something that Laurie does well. But I think that the dilemma is present and you can see—you can see the results of that thinking in—in multiple cases.*

The parent and parent educator relationship is dynamic and the influences are bi-directional as illustrated by subsequent comments.

WW: *It's—it's really interesting to go out into the real world with a set of theories about what's optimal child development and optimal rearing conditions, and then to go out and see how people adapt to that in the real context of their lives. It's caused me to—to think a great deal about what is really*

> *adaptive behavior. What is the—what's the most adaptive response in a given circumstance? And I'm going to be quite frank with you, all of what I read in the child development book, or even what I experienced myself growing up, that's not always the most adaptive—the response that would have come to my mind if you had asked me a question about it before I was in the situation, is not always the most adaptive when you consider the real world.*
>
> LS: *So in a sense, your idealism gets bent in terms of specific cases of realities presented by the parents and the kids?*
>
> WW: *Yes, I think that—that I've become more grounded in reality. I've become more grounded in what it actually takes to get from day to day. And these specifics really do change my overall view . . .*

We do not want to move to some easy and facile generalization about or conclusion from this conversation. One's own experience growing up, one's general professional training (i.e., the child development book) not to mention the specific PAT preservice and inservice training, are now tempered by one's day to day experience with the clients and their situations. Altered expectations, compromises, integrative solutions to problems, long-and short-term goals all become a part of the rationale one needs to think through the adoption and adaptation of a PAT program for one's own school district and community. In the Missouri program, these discussions are occurring in the local school settings and in the district and statewide inservice meetings. A formidable agenda! We believe that the education of parent educators must continue to incorporate cases and issues represented by "Laurie" and her beliefs.

Language and Thinking

Within PAT, in general across the state of Missouri, in the urban community at large, and especially in the sample of families that are difficult to reach, maintain, and help, language development is a major part of the PAT curriculum. From our notes and conversations we picked a half dozen vignettes and interpretations to suggest the kind of ideas and issues that require exploration on the teaching and learning of language for families like the ones we have worked with and studied.

Standard English

In a perhaps overly simple memo (#14) Smith began a discussion of the broader reaches of language development within the PAT program. The memo provoked considerable discussion.

Considerable debate exists within American society regarding the need and desirability for accenting languages and dialects of indigenous groups of peoples who make up the overall population. Currently much of that discussion occurs regarding the place of Spanish in Hispanic communities and within the general school curriculum.

Over the last couple of decades controversy existed regarding the place of Black dialect within educational programs. At one extreme the argument stated that Black dialect was an important language and should be honored and taught to Black children as part of their culture. At a more moderate position, some educators thought that Black language should be used early in the child's formal education in literacy and that gradually the child should be moved toward full understanding and use of standard English as his or her central language. Third and fourth grade would be the major time of this transition. Ultimately, the child would become "bilingual." At the other end of the continuum, while recognizing and honoring the Black dialect as a second language, the child should be introduced immediately to standard English, and taught to speak, read, and write in the standard language. Although seldom phrased as "mainstreaming," one might well apply such a title to this emphasis, for the basic rationale was the opening of mainstream culture and opportunities to Black minority children.

The PAT program's perspective supports the latter option. Language development is one of the central goals of the program and language activities are among the most widely used and accented parts of the day-to-day aspects of the program. That language is standard English. This emphasis in the first 3 years is felt to be a major means of improving the probability of initial school success, of social acceptance in the wider community, and eventually integration into mainstream American society. I have not heard much debate on the more abstract issues of assimilation, fusion, or pluralism as social and educational ideals which have been under discussion over the last couple of decades here and abroad. (Memo 14)

One parent educator commented, "May we discuss the use of the term *Black dialect*. My position is that there is no such thing. There are some nonstandard dialects that Black people speak, but they are no more Black than an Appalachian dialect is White." We were reminded of the subtleties of this point in the phrasing of a fellow Missourian a century ago. In an explanatory note at the beginning of *The Adventures of Huckleberry Finn*, Mark Twain (1955) commented, as if to respond to our memo:

In this book a number of dialects are used, to wit: the Missouri Negro dialect: the extremest form of the backwoods Southwestern dialect; the ordinary "Pike County" dialect; and four modified varieties of this last. The shadings have not been done in a haphazard fashion, or by guesswork; but painstakingly, and with the trustworthy guidance and support of personal familiarity with these several forms of speech.

I make this explanation for the reason that without it many readers would suppose that all these characters were trying to talk alike and not succeeding. (p. iii)

If we had the ear and eye of Twain we would have written a better account of these issues. Then, too, he might have discriminated, better than we, dialects among a number of groups in late 20th-century urban St. Louis. In one of our long conversation/interviews, our discussion flowed this way regarding the educational implications of standard English and "Black dialect."

LS: *Has there been any discussion of standard English either with or from out of the National Center or early childhood unit in the city itself?*

WW: *I don't know that there's been a great deal of formal discussion although within our unit, for example, the recognition that we've got to instill in our children this knowledge of standard English and the ability to use it and to use it comfortably, permeates the philosophy of our program.*

The rationale appeared in further comments.

LS: *And the issue that's under discussion is standard English and the PAT position on some of that.*

WW: *And I'm not real sure if this is the official PAT position or my interpretation of the PAT position, but I do feel that we do very strongly suggest that we recognize varying cultures, we honor them, we recognize that we're talking about culturally different, not better or worse. But we can't get away from the inescapable recognition that there is a culture of business, so to speak. That culture demands at some level that you be able to use standard English. Most people recognize that most folks really have two languages—the language that they use at home when they're relaxed and in informal situations with friends, and the language that they use on the job. One of the things that we stress is that you have got to be aware of that job, the language that you're going to use to compete. It is all right to talk the dialects, to talk the pop whatever kind of language when you're at home and among friends but you must—must pass on to your children a*

*knowledge of standard English. So that they'll be in a position
to compete because people judge you, right or wrong, first
on your appearance, and next on what comes out of your
mouth . . . sometimes the obstacles that we place in our own
way become almost insurmountable, no matter how good
our ideas are, how much we can say or offer. People can't
get past those initial impressions. So to that extent, we do
strongly support looking at the world through middle-class
eyes.*

Although cultural differences of many forms are respected, and
especially in home and family situations, the position is clear that children, if they are to move easily in the wider U.S. society must be able to
speak and write standard English with clarity and facility. It is clear also
that the PAT program, working with children in the first 3 years of life is
to contribute to that goal. The schools' major objectives tilt toward
assimilation.

Elaborated Language and Thinking

The parent educators in the St. Louis program, as elsewhere,
blend the work in language with the development of children's thinking.
The possibilities occur everywhere. Part of the task is to make the parent
aware, to model, and to develop informal commitments for following
through. We raised that in Memo 15.

*Interrelated with a conversation on standard English was a dis-
cussion of a particular parent–child visit involving language
development. This involved a mother who had been in the
program for a couple of years with an older child and a father
who was now living in the home. The visit occurred at 8 a.m.
because of the mother's variable workshift in a fast food
restaurant. Also part of the context were a variety of problems—an earlier miscarriage, depression, no job until recently,
minimal education, apprehension over taking the GED, and a
general dissatisfaction with her life and her ability to cope. The
visit occurred in early December before Christmas.*

*The personal relationship between the parent and the par-
ent educator (Memo 2a) becomes the sine qua non for working with such a parent. The specific skills in talking about these
large "life problems" kind of issues and moving on to "the lesson" of the morning demand discussion in their own right.*

*But the lesson itself is the point of focus here. Reading a sto-
rybook together was the specific goal. The parent educator
was emphasizing this, "getting her plug in," in some of her visits*

because she hoped that the parents would spend some of their Christmas present money for books for the children. She had selected Peggy's Good Food partly because it was sturdy, colorful, and available at a local store. But mostly she had selected it because each page asked a question—why did this happen, what was the reason for that, what would happen next, etc. "It gets the parents past the naming stage and into thinking." The parent educator talked a little about the book, modeled it briefly by reading and talking to the child, and then had the mother read it to the several children who were home at the time. Discussion with the father centered on his commitment to read to the children a little each day when he was home as primary caregiver.

The major point, buried in the long account, is that "elaborated language," to use B. Bernstein's (1971) label, opens up the move, in rudimentary form, to the very important more complex intellectual skills. Beginning to have the child "dialogue" with the material is part of this. (Memo 15)

It goes without saying, that we feel that such questions as "Why did this happen?" and "What was the reason for that?" and "What would happen next?" are hugely significant parts of the child's intellectual environment. One doesn't have to invoke references to experts and their ideas like Torrance's (1965) "ask and guess test" and the encouragement and development of creative thinking to make one's point. Nor do we need to appeal to Bruner's (1960, 1986) many essays on the nature of intuitive thinking and his hypothesis that one can teach anything to anyone regardless of age, if one sets the conditions right. We found the roots of much of these higher order intellectual objectives in the PAT attempts to teach language and thinking. The parent educator was particularly pleased with the father's involvement. As indicated in the memo itself, the kind of personal relationship established here seems part of the larger dynamics of the long-term and strong personal relationships, significant conversations, and informed decisions. We have not accented the long-term issues as much as we might have, partly because the program is only a few years old and the frequency of these long-term relationships is only now appearing. But that seems a most important set of issues in both the development of parenting skills and in the development of the child's language and thinking skills.

Multiple Dimensions of Language Development

One of our later conversations played back into the situation raised in the memo on elaborated language and thinking. We captured more of the context and the reasoning lurking behind the activity itself.

LS: Did you go in to expressly talk about language development and that sort of thing or did it come spontaneously out of this conversation?

WW: You know, my—my express purpose was to read a storybook together. So language was a central focus. I wanted to focus in on the books and reading, and I especially do that in the month of November with a number of parents because they're going out to buy Christmas [gifts]—[laughs]

LS: Go buy the kid a book or two.

WW: Yes, to buy for Christmas. And with very young parents and with some of us older ones, too, there is this real strong tendency to go out and buy all of these glitzy, battery-operated, computerized toys. I like to get my plug in for while you're out there and in the buying mood, please, a couple of books. [laughs]

LS: What book did you take over?

WW: I took along a little—it was this Piggy's Good Food. I picked this one especially for her because I bought it at a store that's right down the street from her house and it was on sale. I wanted her to know that you don't have to spend $5 or $10 to buy a book that's good. I also picked it because it has—one of the things that it does on each page is that it asks a question, to try to get her involved. Sometimes it's difficult for parents to get past the naming stage. "What's that? What's that?" This book gives a real nice example that she can just have right there in front of her. I pointed out to her how on each page, there's a question that's asked that will cause the child to really think a little bit and answer in a sentence and not just give a one word response.

LS: Did you read part of it to the child or did—

WW: Well, I started it off and I'd talk to the mom and dad about the book and the features in it that were appealing to me and that I thought were important for them to look at as they choose a book. And then I—I asked the mother to read it to him.

LS: Can she read well enough to—

WW: Oh, yes. She can read well enough to handle this book without any problem.

LS: Did the father read any at all or did you ask him—?

WW: He did not read this particular book. The mom did most of the reading today. He cares for the children during the day. The focus of the visit turned to involving the father in reading activities. We were talking about cartoons and animation [the father had read the comic book versions of some of the books]. We were talking about how it was important to read to the kids. We have this—we have this agreement going that he's going to try to read to them once a day between

now and when I come back and let me know how that
goes. We talked about the benefits of it for him, too.
LS: *Had he done much of that as far as you could tell?*
WW: *He said that he didn't read to them a whole lot, but he saw*
to it that they could look at Sesame Street. We talked about
the importance of having adults around to talk with children
about things they're looking at on TV. And he said that some-
times he asks questions. But he admitted that most of the
time he was in another room. And so we talked about that—
the importance of his role in that whole process. The mother
knows this, but he's new to the family structure. So we talked
about that a bit. And he seemed to be amenable to trying.
And so I . . .
LS: *It sounds like one of those centimeter moves that may really*
turn out to be a—with a little bit of luck, and a little push and
pull—a major one over the long run.

In short, language development has a number of facets—reading storybooks together, holidays and presents, and concepts and thinking skills. Affective elements such as cuddling and personal closeness
receive a strong stress here. Blending occurs with TV watching and
question asking. Significant also, is the father's only recent appearance
as a regular member of the family and his need to learn that role and
their need to develop a workable family living structure.

The last comment to "one of those centimeter moves," is part of
one of our standing jokes and commentary about the slowness of
progress, centimeter by centimeter and inch by inch, in many of the parent educator's attempts to influence the family, both parents and children. Immensely rewarding as it occurs, it also is very difficult as well!

Pretend Play

Language and thinking extend into the longer reaches of imagi-
nation. As observations piled on other observations the nature of the
PAT "curriculum" continued to expand. "Pretend play" is a widely
accepted activity for young children. Part of the dynamics in one home
visit surrounded the three children in the home during the lesson. A
memo stated it this way.

Each visit to a home with a parent educator takes on its own
kind of charm and fascination. Nothing varies more than the
activities brought by the parent educators. Recently, I had the
occasion to see a lesson built around "pretend play." The par-
ent educator had brought several cups, saucers, glasses, and
plastic "cookies." It took the year and a half-year-old little girl

some time before she really entered into the activity. However her 3-and five-year-old brothers found it to be fun and entertaining. As they drank their coffee and ate their cookies, she edged into the activities. The older youngsters had the language skills to carry the activity. The "edging into" the activity was not an isolated social response, for the younger sister also did this as the parent educator was reading a book to the 3-year-old.

This memo started out with a concern for "pretend play" and I wanted to raise a reference to Sara Smilansky's The Effects of Sociodramatic Play on Disadvantaged Preschool Children (1968), an intriguing account of the intellectual and social development of disadvantaged young Israeli children. Some of that seems applicable to disadvantaged urban children. Along the way I have been fascinated with the importance of social behavior which might be called edging into a social activity. (Memo 40)

But these issues regarding the underlying conceptual structure of the program were germinating throughout our study. After a group lesson on language development, the speculations moved dramatically in another direction, yet one important for concerns regarding the broader context of the relationships between language development and cognitive development.

Another issue that seems part of the entire set of circumstances is the amount and kind of reading I need to do related to what is going on. For other purposes, teaching the educational psychology course, I have been reading some of Margaret Donaldson's (1978) book, Children's Minds. *She has developed what seems to me to be a powerful almost neoBrunerian statement of Piagetian theory. Apparently, she's been running a very imaginative experimental program at Edinburgh. What she has done is to mount what seems to be a very successful critique of Piaget on the basis of the need for a contextualist understanding of what is going on in many of the kinds of tests that Piaget has set up. She and her students will change some of the class, subclass, kinds of problems into ones that are "more understandable to the children," and the children can then solve some of those problems than when you leave the problems in their more formal arrangements and instructions as Piaget has done. In a sense it is almost as though she is building a child development that is a little more close to the realities of children's lives and sort of in between Piaget on the one hand and Bud White on the other hand.*

The conjectures in this set of notes returned a bit closer to the day-to-day aspects of the parents as teachers group meetings and the individual personal visits.

> *She is very much into the development of ideas regarding children's language and intellectual development. In this sense, she is on many of the same targets as White is and the program is. Part of my question is how much of that is to be read on company time and how much of it then to incorporate into whatever kind of report we work out. In a similar vein, how much should one include exercises and activities that the parents might do, particularly as the children are toward the upper age range of the ones included and give them some feeling for thinking about what their kids are doing? Many items of the reading and what that puppet lady of yesterday was doing seem to be organizable into a little more coherent framework in terms of these ideas. Whether they would be more meaningful to parents is another question and whether, by the very formulations of them, new ideas about what one might do with parents could be raised is a second important counterargument. (4/21/88)*

In short, the PAT program had some important things to say about this part of parent education and child development. The ramifications into the education and training of parent educators seem equally obvious and important. Furthermore, the need for a continuing broad-based inquiry program connected with the PAT program seems another possible implication. Practice-based inquiry can be a powerful component to maintaining a viable and vital practical program of educational curriculum and teaching. Pretend play seems to have taken on further and more metaphorical meanings.

A Word of Caution

Language development is related to the larger issues of intellectual development. The observer found himself in the middle of these issues on one visit with a boy named Frank. "He Doesn't Seem to Understand" was the title given to the memo describing the events and the interpretation.

> *On occasion, I have had a slight mix up in schedules and found myself "sort of being a parent educator." With a little trepidation, both because of the neighborhood which was a northside area of boarded up houses and cleared lots*

between houses and because of not knowing the family, I knocked on the door 10 minutes after what I thought was the meeting time. The mother knew I was coming and indicated that the parent educator was due a half hour later. So there I was. But that isn't what I want to raise. Rather, her son Frank, a 2 1/2-year-old, is the focus.

In the course of talking with the mother and playing with Frank, I found that she was concerned with his lack of talking. His same age cousin jabbers on and on, in contrast to Frank. The only two distinguishable words I could make out were "ball" and "bus." The latter go by frequently on the street out-side a front window where he sits and watches a good bit of the day. As we played with a ball and he put it through an indoor net, I tried to "teach" him to sit across the room and roll the ball back and forth. When "sit" was used, and sometimes with his mother's help, Frank would go occasionally to his chair and sit facing the TV set. He would sort of turn toward me. I would roll the ball to him and ask him to roll it back. Initially I assumed that this would be a relatively simple activity. He didn't understand. At best, he would take the ball to the net and put it through. Then, off and on over a full half hour, in between looking at picture books and a coloring book, I tried to teach him what I meant. It wasn't that he could not hear for he would attend to me or his mother. And it wasn't that he did not know what a ball was, and its proper place through the net. Rather it seemed that the words, "sit," "roll the ball," and "to me" were beyond his understanding. Later, in trying out other activities, the picture book and the coloring book, the toy truck on the table, and having him point to various parts of the body did the magnitude and generality of the receptive language disability appear.

Several images ran through my mind. One had to do with the preschool teacher this next fall trying to work with him as one member of a group of children. Second, and far be it for me to want to label children as young as 2 1/2, but I have been struck with the little discussion of individual differences that I have heard in the program. Never have I heard the term mental retardation used. Occasionally someone will use the term developmentally delayed, which seems to me to carry the connotation that the child will catch up. Nor have I heard anyone use Florence Goodenough's term of mental adequa-cy and inadequacy for different types of activities. How does one use a test, for example, the Denver, to talk with the parent about a child who scores low on the test? What is the role of PAT and parent educator in developing parental expectations for a child? (Memo 37)

Later discussion revealed several additional aspects. The parent educator and the mother had discussed the child's delayed development at some length. The mother still believes that the child will outgrow the problem. Referrals to physicians have occurred to rule out any medical problems. PAT's screening program is under way with all children. General policy, and common sense as well, argue for not labeling children without a more formal testing and diagnosis by a competent certified psychologist. Most parent educators are wary of labeling a child in general and in particular with a too early and a too informal diagnosis. They perceive their job is to help the child and the mother to maximize the child's opportunity to learn. Too frequently, the hard to reach, maintain, and help families have not had those opportunities.

IDIOSYNCRATIC MAJOR PROBLEMS AS CURRICULUM

Gradually emerging out of our thinking about PAT curriculum ideas and practices, came the idea that we have come to call "idiosyncratic major problems as curriculum." When all was said and done about specific lessons about child development, a large untouched problem remained in our view of many difficult to reach, maintain, and help families. For some it was temper tantrums, for others it was getting the child to bed, and for others it was dealing with in-laws residing a few blocks away or extended families living in the same house or apartment. Some of the observer's initial musings appeared in a memo that started out talking about the use of videotapes of child development as part of a home visit.

A Child Development Videotape and the Problems
of Young Mothers
Recently, I had my first experience observing a parent education visit where the basic content of the visit was a videotape on child management and discipline. Dick Van Patton, the actor, did a professional narration of the content, which was a mix, in my view, of common sense principles, of modeling, of positive reinforcement, and ultimately a brief illustration of a token economy. The tape was long and contained a huge amount of information. The parent educator elected not to stop occasionally and break in on the video presentation for discussion and commentary. The discussion afterward picked up on only a few of the points made in the video as the ideas related to the child's, Suzie's temper tantrums, sleeping behavior, the relative merits of touching versus verbal reassurance and so forth. The tape was left with the mother for the father to watch in an evening.

I was struck by the rich environment of toys, games, and books in the child's room in a nicely decorated and well-kept small single-family dwelling, a two-bedroom bungalow. The mother reported a round of "cabin fever" and a need to get out of the house on occasion. She found the group meetings and play group meetings an opportunity for this. I was struck that the mother seemed to be reading all kinds of child development articles and books, seemed to have a way of observing and thinking about her 18-month-old, (e.g., using the phrase "need to understand where Suzie is coming from)", and seemed to be able to talk "the child development game." All this seemed appropriate.

Yet lurking behind these positive views was some feeling on my part that the mother's personal concerns and worries were where the "parent-child action and relationship really was." Some of this arose in the way she talked about the family, some of her statements regarding having a second child, and my thought that that would increase the stress level substantially. The parent educator indicated some mixed messages from the mother.

I began to wonder about the wide range of reasons that induce families to join the PAT program and what that has then to say about how the program is tailored to each of the mothers and their child. This pushes me toward thoughts well beyond "the informational content" of the one on one meetings. Further, I am struck by the side conversations I have observed that go on between and among the mothers at the group meeting independent of the particular content of the meeting.

Somewhere in our report we need to talk about the "problems" of young mothers for that seems to be a latent agenda for many. (Memo 28)

The third paragraph of the memo raises "the mother's personal concerns and worries were where the "parent–child action and relationship really was.'" In our prior discussion of "difficult to help mothers," similar illustrations appear, and perhaps we are restating, from a curricular perspective, some of the items raised there. A mother's only partially verbalized, underlying concerns make it difficult to help her and also make the concerns a curriculum problem. At least, so go our conjectures.

Having Enough to Do

As we detail elsewhere, as parent educators leave the program, the families are transferred to other parent educators or, in some cases, the coordinator becomes the parent educator. Reflection at such a time produces thumbnail sketches of the mother, the child, and the interaction between the two. On occasion, the idiosyncratic major problem sets the curriculum agenda.

WW: *I begin seeing them in the middle of next week. But . . . but at any event, I know Cassie because Cassie comes to meetings regularly.*

LS: *Yeah, I think she was there that first time—when you were divvying them up and I had a group of . . .*
I didn't notice him during the meeting, but at the close of the meeting, when she and I were talking, he was quite content to be working with a coloring book.

WW: *Yeah, see, one of the things he's discovering is he really likes to color. He loves to color. And he'll probably ask you to color a picture. An observation that I made is that one of the things that contributes to many of the discipline problems that young moms have is that their children are not involved in anything.*

LS: *They don't have enough to do.*

WW: *That they're not doing anything. And when you don't give kids things—when you don't provide things for them to do, they find things to do. And usually the things they find are things that parents don't want them doing. And it's just very difficult for us to get that notion across, that you have to structure your child's environment. That you have to do things with him—you have to provide things for him to do. But once you get that notion across and parents see the difference in the way their life goes throughout the day; that they don't have a headache at the end of every day—they're not yelling at the kid all day—well, then the benefits begin to become more obvious to them. At first, I don't think the benefits are really that obvious to very young mothers. It all takes a lot of time—a lot of effort.*

In a quick, almost intuitive comment, a "major problem" has been characterized as the child not having enough to do. The consequences came to dominate the relationship. The time and effort required to get a parent to see such a "simple" point is often great, which, in turn, suggests it may not be so simple from her point of view.

Bigger Problems, Encouragement, and Helping to Cope

The formal doctrine or philosophy of the PAT program focuses on "lessons in child development." Much of the reality of the parent educators' daily work activity especially with difficult to reach, maintain, and help families carries a different flavor. Words and phrases such as "bigger problems," "encouragement," and "helping to cope" seem to capture the part of our experience with the program. Wells, as parent educator, is talking about a client named Rose who has a son named Carl.

WW: Carl. Rose is . . . about—let me see, Rose is 19 years old now, I think. She enrolled in the program when her son was first born. And Carl is now 2 years old. She was still in high school when I enrolled her. She graduated from City High.

LS: After the birth . . .?

WW: After the birth of the baby and after she enrolled in the program, she graduated from City High.

LS: Tell me how you got her and then a little bit about how she got through school.

WW: I got Rose through the baby's father's sister who is in the program. Rose got through school because Brenda and Brenda's mother and another aunt babysat for her when she needed a babysitter while she was in school. And luckily, Rose had access to a car. So she was able to get around to drop the baby off in the morning. When I first met Rose, one of the things that impressed me about her and one of the really strong impressions I got about this household was that Rose really was the central figure in that household. That she was the one who saw that the younger brothers and sisters went to school, did their homework.

        She told me something that I'm really kind of worried about. She said that she has to go into the hospital for a test. She was supposed to go in this month but somehow the appointment got messed up. But she says that she has to have some test. When I talked to her yesterday, she said that they wanted to look to see if she had some kind of a cancerous growth or something. So she wasn't too clear on it.

LS: Uterine or breast cancer or . . .?

WW: Uterine cancer of some sort. You know, she said, "Down there." So I mean . . . so I'm not really sure because she's not—she wasn't very sure. I said, "Well, what are they going to do? " thinking that if she could tell me what they were going to do, I could—I could get some notion of it. And it looks as if they're going to do an exploratory operation.

LS: Do a biopsy of some kind?

WW: And look. She wasn't sure of that. I have—I have suggested to her that she call the doctor back and ask him to tell her exactly what they're going to do. She said because they kept using a lot of big words that she didn't understand. I suggested to her that when that happens, just say to her doctor to "tell me exactly what you'll do so I'll know what to expect." And when they say a word you don't understand, say, "I

*don't understand that word. Say it so I can understand it." I'll
be getting back in touch with her later on next week, to see if
she was able to get any better understanding of exactly what
it is. I'll be keeping in close touch with her, with regard to that.
But she seems—she seems to have a lot of potential. And it's .
. . it's very important to me that I keep in touch with her so
that . . . so that when she needs some encouragement and . .
. to get on back in school—that at least some—I'll be there to
say, "Try to keep that up, keep going."*

LS: *Does she get that anywhere else? That encouragement?*

WW: *I think she might get some from . . . an uncle that she spoke
of at one point who said that he would be willing to help her
with her expenses. And the fact that . . . she has people who
are willing to watch the kids for her. That's a big source of
support right there. So she's getting some support there, but I
think that it's probably not enough to see her through when
times look really, really rough. I've been trying to help her
identify some of the possible sources of aid.*

Our "interview/discussion" began as many did with a brief
account of the client and her child and when and how she got into the
program. The family and friends' referral continues to be a major
resource for urban family recruitment. In retrospect, the fact that the
mother finished high school after the birth of her baby seems a major
accomplishment. Family support and the availability of transportation
seem like major factors as well. Perhaps most of all is the impression of
Rose as a "central figure in that household."

But the point we want to emphasize mostly is the health problem, "down there" with which she is trying to cope. The clinic doctors,
presumably trying to do their best, speak in a language, "big words that
she didn't understand" that makes planning and coping difficult. The
parent educator moves in directly—and forcibly—with comments of the
order "I don't understand that word. Say it so I can understand it."
Follow-up with her is part of the parent educator's efforts.

Helping a talented young mother solve immediate problems and
think about further educational and career opportunities is part of the
context of helping her child's immediate and long-term development. Part
of this is the worrisome issue of "when times look really, really rough."

We have posed all this as a "curriculum problem" for the urban
parent as teachers program. It seems an issue about which productive discussion and planning might engage. Staff development never quite ends.

A Basic Principle? "If It Means More To You . . ."

A final illustration of our concerns for idiosyncratic major problems appeared in the following short memo:

Some years ago, when my wife and I were raising our two chil-
dren, we came to the generalization, "If it means more to you
than it does to your child, then you have a problem."
Recently, in a discussion of toilet training with a parent educa-
tor it seemed as if she was making a similar point. One of her
statements involved the similarities among eating, sleeping,
and toilet training. Each provides the child with an arena for
exerting his or her independence. The parent educator's posi-
tion emphasized, the more you can make the toilet training
"the child's problem," the better off you are as a parent. As I
heard this, I was reminded of our old principle, "If it means
more to you than to him or her, you have a problem."
Underlying this is the further principle that one has already
begun training the child to eventually be an independent,
responsible, and autonomous adult at 18 or 21 years.
Does this then eventuate in the generalization, that ulti-
mately (at 21 years?) the child's life belongs to the child.
A further implication follows: the parent's day-to-day deci-
sion and action always have both short-term and long-term
entanglements. That back and forth changing of perspectives,
"dialectic" to use one of my colleagues favorite words, is
exceedingly important also. (Memo 24)

The idea presented here, if it means more to you as parent educator than it means to the parent, or, if it means more to you as parent
than it means to the child, then the relevant "you" has a real problem.
For the parent educator, the recruitment of difficult to reach parents
often puts the parent educator in this difficult position. We have raised a
number of ideas regarding this in earlier chapters. In the present context,
the concern is with a parent who has a similar problem with her child.
The kind of discussion needed is raised in the memo. A clear view of
where you want the child to be at 18 or 20 (e.g., fully independent and
responsible) an agenda for getting the child there, and finally seeing the
implications in the infant and toddler's behavior in eating, sleeping, toilet training. That kind of concept is a large and difficult curriculum and
teaching problem for the PAT program. But, in our view, important.

Reconstruing Curriculum: Latent Meanings of Appointments, Scheduling, and Lesson Plans

An Intuitive Hunch

In one of our long interviews, really discussions between ourselves, the latent meanings of scheduling, making and keeping appointments and lesson plans became the focus of a series of hypotheses. The

broader implications of caring and educational and social service programs arose as well. These conjectures added new dimensions to our
reconstruing curriculum and the role of the parent educator.

WW: *I was talking to someone the other day and she said that she
was going to have to miss work today. And I said, "Oh." And
she said, "Yeah. I have to go to the doctor." And I said, "Oh,
so you're going to have to miss the whole day." She said,
"Well, you know, I'm going to Regional." And, you know, I
thought when you go to Regional Hospital, you do have to sit
there the whole day a lot of times. Poor people go to a clinic
with a 9 o'clock appointment that they share with 50 other
folks. And so you go to the doctor at 9 o'clock in the morning
with no idea of when you're going to get out. So what is a 9
o'clock appointment? You go to the—you go to pick up
your—to the Division of Family Services or whatever, and you
can sit around in that lobby for half a day. So what is an
appointment? And I thought about that. And I said, "Well,
maybe these folks miss appointments with me because this is
the only. . . ." [laughs] No, this is one where an agency of society is coming in and they can miss an appointment with me.
But I was just thinking about it. I said, "Because just about every
other organization treats them as if their time is not worth anything." And I don't even know if that means anything or not.*
LS: *One other is that in school we talk about the hidden curriculum kind of thing. And in a sense one of the hidden curricula
of not only ADC but of government agencies is that your
time isn't really very important and you don't have to . . .*
WW: *Yeah, but I was thinking about that and I said, "Maybe—
maybe we're agents of helping them feel a little bit more
control." And that's why they miss my appointments. [laughs]*
LS: *I have a little bit of a feeling that there may be a hint of
rationalization in that, Wilma.*
WW: *No.*
LS: *That the only agency that they have control over.*
WW: *No. But really I do think that that's one reason why it's so
important for us to keep our commitments, our appointments
with our families. Even when you have a parent who's—you
go and they're not there—if you make the appointment, you
have a commitment to keep it, because by doing that, we
say to them how important we think it is that they keep
appointments. And I think that if we're persistent in that,
sometimes over the long haul it does help our parents commit to the appointment.*
LS: *In the same way.*
WW: *Uh-huh. But anyway, I was just—*
LS: *That is a nice bit of irony.*

WW: *It ran through my mind, you know, as I was . . . as I was being*
      late this morning.
LS: *Now you said that, I didn't. Okay. No, that . . . that back and*
      forth though within a culture of the . . . a little bit of non car-
      ing on the part of the person and then an institution that
      doesn't care in the same way and it just feeds back and
      forth, it seems to me. And breaking those cycles . . . well, I
      guess in some sense that's a part of what we're about.
WW: *Yes.*

Agendas always have a long-term as well as a short-term dimension.

But it is not our intention to think our way through a long-term
overhaul of the various welfare and aid programs for urban families.
Rather, as we confronted some of the particulars of the PAT program in
the urban community, we couldn't help slipping over into larger and
larger social issues. If our specific conjectures of the nature of time in
social service organizational structures and processes have any truth at
all, then they suggest actions that need to be taken that will reduce some
of the self-defeating aspects. Studying health clinics and tax-supported
city hospitals is not on our agenda, but if ill citizens have to wait for
hours for medical services then questions arise regarding possible caus-
es that can be altered. Some of these presumably filter back to the broad
category of limited resources. And these provoke the difficult discussions, debates, and decisions as to how our communities at the local,
state, and federal level want to live—especially in a climate of waning
resources in general.

Missing appointments, the place these thoughts began, seem a
long reach in the causal chain we have tentatively constructed.

Ground Rules: The Curriculum in Action

A number of issues arise in the first appointment when the
enrolling is carried out. At that time the experienced and skilled parent
educator conveys her expectations and needs for the long-term relationship. She tries to establish what might be called the "livable and workable conditions" for the relationship.

LS: *What's your feeling at this point in time that . . . ?*
WW: *My feeling at this point in time is that when you enroll a fami-*
      ly, the enrollment visit is just critical. You lay out the ground
      rules at that visit. And one of the things that you say—and it's
      written up in our mutual agreement—is that you devote the
      time to me, you and the child. But I think that needs some
      further explanation and that you should just get very specific
      and say, for example, "It's important that the TV not be on.

It's important that it be at a time when you're not trying to get dinner ready or you're going to have to leave in 10 minutes to go pick up your other children. So let's try to figure out the best time to try to set the visit so that it fits in with your schedule so that we can do this." And then you explain to the parent why it's important that you have that time. The next thing is that when you come the first time and the TV is on, it's important that you ask if you can turn it off. If the mom doesn't make a move, to turn it off, it's important that as a parent educator, you make that request. There are several ways you can do that without offending the mother. The thing that I found most helpful is to just say, "I know some people can concentrate with the television on, but for myself, I can't do it. I find that it's very distracting to me. So would it be all right with you if we turn it off?" And then I haven't put any of the blame on her really, it's all, "Do me a favor." And I find that that works very well. Sometimes it's best, for example, if someone else is at the house or whatever, or the mom is on the telephone and she's trying to talk, sometimes I find it helpful if I just say to her, "Why don't you just finish that up? And then we can get started." Rather than trying to talk over it. It's very important to just be straightforward and honest. Say what your needs are.

In our experience, curriculum structure and process seldom if ever are conceptualized as expectations for "livable and workable conditions." Yet that seems precisely the agenda for initial meetings with parents. The specifics vary from turning off the ubiquitous TV to cutting through telephone conversations. Uniformly, parent educators try to solve these small but ever present constraints on parent attention to the issues of the visit. Crowded quarters and other family members add to the difficulties. But having reasonable "ground rules" for home visits generally are accepted by parents. Sensitivity to scheduling the visit becomes part of this when there are "must-see" TV programs that one works around. And gentle ways of phrasing one's desires as the parent educator also are part of this. We find these aspects to be an interesting kind of concrete and situationally specific creativity. Discussions among parent educators of the order of "How do you handle this . . . ?" and "What works for you in this kind of situation . . . ?" become part of the professional folklore of parent educating. Ideas like ground rules become embedded in the overall aspects of the program.

With experience comes a more sophisticated view of lesson plans and the realities of the personal visit. The subtlety and latent meaning in issues of establishing rapport and being tested appeared and reappeared in our discussions.

WW: *And by that I mean . . . you can come in and you look at the curriculum, and as a novice parent educator, you might think, "OK, I'm going to go in and do it, boom-boom-boom-boom-boom." But as every good teacher knows, some days you go in with your lesson plans and what you come out with at the end of the day . . . well, you hope there's some semblance to the original plan. But the plan is just that. It is a guide. It is not set in concrete. You use it to keep you from veering too far off the path, knowing full well that your . . . your approach to the parent is not always going to be straight, but you're going to zig-zag. And you use that plan to give you some reference point that you don't get too far off the mark. And that's what we're coming to realize with our Parents as Teachers curriculum is that it's—it's our reference point but that we do have to veer off the mark sometimes but it keeps us from getting too far astray. In our lesson plans, it says, "Establish rapport." And you have about 5 minutes for that. We know very well that the development and the establishment and the maintenance of rapport goes on throughout. In the very beginning, that might be the major thing that's going on. That as a matter of fact that probably is the major thing that's going on. And that you don't get to the point where you're really engaged in substantive discussions of child development most of the time until well into the program year with people who are just starting out in the program.*

      There are some families that I go to see, who seem very unresponsive and uninterested. But then I said, "Can we make another appointment?" "Oh, yeah!" We make another appointment. But I wonder am I getting through to them? And I think I referenced it before when Brazelton was here, and he talked about those slitted eyes. When he said that, I said, "Oh, the man knows exactly what I'm talking about." [laughs] He knows exactly. And I had come to the conclusion that what was happening was that I was being measured. I was being measured that first year to see if I was for real, if I would keep coming back. Once I got a handle on it, I said, "My goodness, it's the same thing my 16-year-olds did to me when I first started teaching." You know, they were testing me to see if I was going to give up on them.

In this discussion that we labeled "timing in the curriculum process," a number of issues are in the air. Wells' "zig-zagging" in reaching her objectives intertwines with issues of "rapport" necessary for the presentation and discussion of the scheduled curriculum content of the day. The substantive agenda must be worked in and out as one goes along. But rapport is not a simple one-off or 5 minute exercise. Difficult to reach, maintain, and help urban families raise particular aspects of the rapport phenomenon. The "slitted eyes" comment seems relevant to any teacher who has had an initially skeptical pupil or class, as Wells generalized the experience. The "testing" is not simple as Wells indicates, almost as a throwaway line in the conversation, "to see if I was going to give up on them." For a teacher, having faith in "one's students," and for a parent educator in one's clients seems a vastly understated part of curriculum and teaching. Earlier we argued that the parent educator needs to keep trying, not give up on one's clients. Now we accent this slightly different vantage point, the client almost waiting to see if the parent educator will not give up on me, the client. Subtleties beyond belief.

The Lesson Plan as Implemented Curriculum

Our discussion moved to immediate situational factors that influence the turn of the personal visit. Current problems of health and current home activities are two of these situational factors. But the "lesson" flowed in and out of the visit.

LS: *Regarding Rose yesterday. Tell me if you can explicitly what you thought you were going to do with that when you went into that visit yesterday. What was your "lesson plan" looking like? And then what happened and how did it diverge or whatever?*

WW: *Both children are in the program now. Betsy is 3 months old. And Carl is 2. And with Carl, the particular focus of our discussion was supposed to be on self-help skills, how they are emerging, and things that Rose can do to help him.*

LS: *Now this is putting his socks on?*

WW: *Putting his socks on, washing and drying his hands, beginning to let him make—make some of his own sandwiches, pour milk into—that kind of a thing. For Betsy, I was going to talk with her about the increasing coordination of her behaviors and ... the ability to use two—two sensory inputs at once, you know, the fact that she's able to bring things to her face, look at them, grasp them, and how important it is to start giving her things to grasp and practice that skill. One of the things that Rose had been concerned about is that she said, "This baby just does not smile a whole lot, she doesn't laugh." She said, Carl, when he was little, he would just laugh—he came here laughing. Well, Betsy is a much more contemplative baby. She just kind of looks around. I had practically promised Rose last month that if she just gave it a little while, I said, "I bet you by the time I come back, she's going to have started smiling, and just become a lot more sociable." As I was talking I was crossing my fingers that it would actually come to pass. [laughter] But those are the things that I was going to talk with her about. I was going to check with her on how her job was coming. That was part of my agenda, to touch base with her on that. When I got to the house, they were in the middle of a massive remodeling. They're putting up dry wall. [laughs]*

LS: *All over her house, huh?*

WW: *Everywhere. And so a good part of our discussion centered on, "Do you have someplace else that you can go? Because I'm not real sure that it's the most healthy thing for the kids to be with all the dust that was being generated by the dry wall." And so she said, yeah, she was going to take them over to her mother's. So that took up a good part of our discussion. And then the other thing that took up a . . . a larger part of discussion than I had anticipated was when I asked her how things were going with her, she shared with me that she's going into the hospital. So we spent some time—*

LS: *Oh, this was on the possibility of the cancer?*

WW: *Yes, on the possibility of cancer. And so we spent time talking about that because . . . she was obviously concerned about it. She didn't seem to be as concerned as I probably would be. But she was concerned about it and I wanted to give her a chance to talk about it and to find out exactly where she was going, when she was going, so that I can keep in touch with her. I made my next appointment for a few days before she's scheduled to go into the hospital so that I can check with her and make sure it's still on and then I'll know exactly where she is and I can go to check up on her. Then we did talk about, after we had talked about all of those things, I . . . I told her that one of the other things that I really wanted to talk about was the self-help skills. And we got into a real nice discussion about Carl's self-help skills. And then when I asked her about Betsy, and had she—had she started smiling for her yet? She said, "Oh, yeah, I was planning to tell you." And I said, "When did it happen?" One of the real neat things about being a parent educator is when she says, "Betsy's not smiling." And I could say to her, "I want you to really watch her because when I come back I want to know exactly when she started." And when you come back, they can tell you everything from "Well, she spit up at 2 o'clock on Tuesday." But she said, "Well, actually, it was about 2 weeks ago, she just started smiling." And she was just so overjoyed. And of course I was able to say, "Didn't I tell you?" [laughs]*

But we need to use language to help him figure out how to do it rather than showing him all the time. Helping Rose to use language. So we talked through that. And the last part of the—of the puzzle activity, I just gave the puzzle to them and they played with the puzzle while I played with Betsy for a while, but I kept looking over to see what was going on. I really wanted her to work at it with him. So I played with Betsy for a while. And then we got back to talking specifically. When Gary was able to handle it pretty well, we let him work on it, while I talked with her about how Betsy was coming along and she gave me all the latest developments and we talked about ... ways to support Betsy's development.

So in terms of what my original plan had been, I think I got most of what I had originally planned to do. But I spent time talking about things that I had not originally planned to talk about. And the visit went a little bit longer than planned.

The longer term issues of dependency and responsibility became a part of our discussion. Bringing the large and abstract back to concrete choices and actions remains a major part of the long-term resolution.

WW: *I think that we do have to maintain a clear sense of what we're about when we go in.*

LS: *That you're a parent educator?*

WW: *That we're parent educators. And in that capacity, one of our roles is to help parents hook up with the different agencies. And at all times, with this notion of empowering families . . . I think it's important that we not go in and do everything for a family, but that we give parents the tools to do for themselves. It's important that when we go in and a family needs food or clothing or whatever, that we give them the agency, we can give them a number, we tell them who to talk to, but we don't actually do that calling for them, in most instances. Now there are going to be a few cases where the best thing to do is to do the calling, when you're working with developmentally delayed parents or whatever. But for the most part I think it's very important that the parent actually do that calling. But we point them in the direction and try to see that they follow through on it. If they have difficulty with that, we can even role play that out. We can script it for them. We can help them with the script of what do you say next? If he says this, then you say this. We can do that. But I think it's important that the parent actually do it.*

LS: *What about—I can see that on . . . easily and clearly on material things as we were just talking. What about when you ask your question, "How are things going? " and the sort of parade of what might be called psychological problems comes up? And they give you a little talk about themselves and the children and the difficulties in the family and so on. Where do you go with that, I guess?*

WW: *Well, with that, I think that you listen to it. And I think then the next question has to be, "Okay, so what now?" You have to get to the so what question? "What can we do right now in this place? Now if we can actually provide some instrumental help, we do that. Okay, let's line those up and let's do those. If it's a matter of I'm feeling stressed out and pressured, Okay, let's get you in touch with the Annie Malone Crisis Center. Come out to the next group meeting. Come back for Stay and Play. We can get you up to the center if that's what you need." We have to stop and say, "Okay, so what are we going to do?" And then I think it's really important that you do something. I don't care how small, but you do something. You don't just continue the litany.*

LS: *In the difficult situation . . . or when that's very present and you're trying to utilize this strategy, does it take 15 minutes of the hour? Can it take up to 30 minutes of the hour? Or have any feel for the ebb and flow of that time?*

WW: *I'm going to tell you, sometimes it takes the whole hour. I'm just going to be very frank with you, sometimes it just does, and you can't get past it.*

In this section we raised some of the realities of the PAT program in action with families that are hard to reach, maintain, and help. These "realities" pushed us toward what we have called "reconstruing the role of parent educator." We see these as an interconnected part of the continuing adaptation of the curriculum program as it evolves in ways that are meaningful to parents and parent educators who retain a strong concern for empowering parents to facilitate the development of their children.

SUMMARY AND CONCLUSION

This chapter has been more illustrative than definitive. *The Program Planning and Implementation Guide* lists and develops a huge array of further substantive topics.

We chose to present brief views of the dilemmas in goals and objectives. Preparation for school success vies with children's quality of life at the moment. And even here, within the dominant preparation for school success perspective, the emphasis on more immediate skill training vies with those longer range goals of curiosity, confidence, and risk taking. Most parent educators blend, alternate, and interweave among these nested, complementing, and competing objectives. The rules and strategies, beyond common sense, for this integration are not spelled out in the program literature.

We indicated briefly some of the similarities and differences in personal visits and group meetings. And, mainly from field notes, interviews, summary observations and interpretations, and an interim report, we posed some of the issues in the latter, while emphasizing the curricular elements. "Teaching" small groups of parents in the group meetings is a fascinating exercise requiring a special set of teaching skills. Didactic lessons vie with more discovery approaches and with "group discussions." Simple opening techniques involving parents saying something "good" about their babies and toddlers vied with complex theoretical knowledge of child development and child problems and with practical knowledge and techniques for handling specific and particular problems of individual mothers in their particular family situations. The variations and complications around toilet training, feeding, sibling rivalry, sleeping, fears, as found in individual families, are legion.

Our discussion of topics and substance tried to indicate the breadth of curricular items appearing in the program from modeling and parties as curriculum to idiosyncratic major problems as curriculum. Discipline and the multiple facets of language development became our chief illustrations.

As important as these curricular issues are, and especially with the detailed *Program Planning and Implementation Guide* in hand, we found, for our targeted audience, the curricular issues secondary to concerns over the nature of the population of families in our special sample, the complex role of the parent educator, and the organizational issues in an urban PAT program. A fuller, book length monograph on "curriculum adaptations for the difficult to reach, maintain, and help families" still resides in our observational data and interviews. We believe such materials would make excellent additions to the teacher education curriculum for preservice and inservice parent educators.

section
three

PAT as an Educational System:
A Macro View

We believe that all educational programs, as they become parts of schools and school districts, take on the properties of systems and organizations. Although this belief is neither original nor perhaps earthshaking, we think the realities and implications of such a belief are often overlooked by educational innovators, reformers, and utopians, to use a set of distinctions raised by House (1979), Bestor (1970), and Smith et al. (1986). An ethnographic "manual" needs to speak to these organizational issues if success is to be more than personal intuition and blind luck, as important as these may be, and if success is to imply institutionalization of innovation, a kind of permanence to the changes.

In one long chapter we develop two basic sets of ideas: (a) organizational structure, analyzed into positions and roles; and (b) organizational process, events over time. These distinctions enable us to describe and analyze where the PAT program fits and how it works within the St. Louis Public School District, a school system involved with massive community change, limited and declining resources, a major metropolitan school desegregation program, and 50,000 pupils, a decline from 115,000 pupils two decades ago.

Within the PAT structure are the positions of director, coordinator, and parent educator. We draw composite pictures from our interviews and observations of incumbents to describe and interpret the roles of each of these positions. As we spell out what people do, we are able to look at practices that might be transferred to other communities wishing to adopt or adapt a parent education program similar to PAT. Organizational processes include such items as the rhythm of the year for the schools and the program, coping with school and program flux and change, administering and supervising, cooperating with other schools and agencies, and organizational monitoring and record keeping.

Planning, organizing, implementing, and institutionalizing a PAT program within a large city school system is a challenging but fascinating set of issues and practices. We believe that a number of our observations and interpretations should be useful to teachers and administrators in other districts.

chapter
six

Organizational Structures and Processes: Toward a Systemic View of PAT

A PRELUDE TO THE ORGANIZATIONAL
AND SYSTEMIC CONTEXT

Early on, as the outside observer was getting acquainted with the PAT coordinators, he kept running into the "realities" of the PAT program and its context. A meeting and interview with Helen, the fourth coordinator he visited, provoked a number of observations and interpretations. The notes facilitate our introduction to aspects of the organizational and systemic aspects of the program.

> *It's now 2:50 and I'm on my way from the Branch School and back to the university. Once again I had another good meeting with a coordinator. Helen's an interesting individual. In some ways she is more reserved and wary of me and what I'm trying to do, or at least so it seems, but in another way she's also quite substantive and gets started and talks a blue streak on all kinds of items about what she does and how she does it. In that sense the whole business moved along very nicely, and I felt like I was in a mid-semester or end of semester interview. So it looks now like all four of the centers are going to work very well.*
> *Just as I was leaving, Helen introduced me to her assistant principal who smiled when she heard about the difficult to*

reach families. I joked with her a bit about that in terms of get-
ting more information later and talking with her. She's a tall
interesting looking combination of a schoolmarm and a
sophisticated woman—sophisticated lady. Again, I can't get
over the variation in people that I keep running into and the
interesting differences in terms of who they are and what they
do and their points of view. I took several pages of field notes
with Helen and will have more to say about a lot of that after
a bit. I'm in some hurry to get back to the university for an
appointment at 3.

    As I drive around I'm struck with the real variations in the
neighborhoods as well. Some fairly near the school are quite
well kept and quite well together. Others are burned out and
closed up and that kind of thing. The variability is a huge and
interesting subproblem.

A comment then appeared regarding research strategies in the larger
context of PAT.

The Branch School setting is a sample of the problems in
research methods of a more formal pre-set type. I would find
that kind of experimentation to be overwhelmingly difficult in
this kind of a program.

Program evaluation presented continuing dilemmas to the PAT leadership. Summative data on children's growth were in constant demand,
but, as the note indicated, they were extremely difficult to obtain within
the complexities of an urban population and program.

    A series of administrative issues relevant to the hard to reach
and maintain families followed in the notes. These issues elaborated on
the difficulties in both program development and evaluation.

As I listened to Helen talk about her various recruitment strate-
gies, what she called "stable families," her own policies as to
when to terminate some of the families and get other people
on the case loads who can make the five meetings [necessary
for reimbursement], the problems of the interplay of policy and
practices of multiple sorts, back and forth on the recruitment
and attrition problems, it seems to me are there in all their glory.

The complexities of that long last sentence in the notes provoked a major
summary conclusion.

I've got to get the kind of social systemic nature of things out with some clarity and care, if I'm going to be able to really handle that one. No simple model and set of suggestions are going to be defined, except in those more systemic terms. (2/16/88)

For an administrator from another community to adopt or adapt the PAT program some idea of the "reality" as Helen was presenting it seems very important. Similarly, if one is to summatively evaluate the program, attention must be paid to the same "realities" of the organizational structures and processes.

POLITICS, POLICIES, AND PAT PRACTICES

Any time public monies are allocated or denied to a particular educational or social program, politics and the making of policy are involved. As Eliot (1959) and others have long argued, that is what politics is all about in schooling and in other institutions and programs. If that be true, then all of the kinds of program activities—innovation, administration, evaluation, and even the recruitment and maintenance of urban parents and children in a program—have political implications. School districts wishing to adopt or adapt a program like PAT must come to know and deal as well with these "realities" as part of the overall effort. In urban schooling some of these issues and dilemmas are acute. And some of them appeared in our observations, discussions, and interviews. This is part of what we mean by developing and having a "systemic view" of the PAT program.

In the notes an aspect of the political implications floated through Smith's mind.

Although it didn't come up in this context, another item that seems to me to be very significant is the fact that the program is getting shifted in slight but potentially very important ways. For instance, instead of taking the parent in the last trimester of the first pregnancy, they're accepting parents with multiple kids and kids who may be 7 months to a year, year and a half old. Again there's the push from the public school orientation of working with everyone. If White's argument, as I understand it from scanning his book, that the third trimester of the first pregnancy is the optimal place to do parent education, then you're violating one of the central tenets of what he's trying to do. That's an interesting one to think about both theoretically and practically.

The magnitude of that shift in time of admission to the program gradually assumed increasing importance in our views of the adaptation of
the program to the urban community.

From our perspective, the issues in early childhood and parent
education contain important value stances about which men and women
of good intention will disagree. Part of the struggle goes on among academics who are close to powerful individuals in government who are
making policy and part of the struggle goes on with individuals who are
trying to make parent education programs work in local communities.
The PAT program in St. Louis is one of these local communities. Our
data and reflections enter us in the several levels of debate.

Politics at the Local Level

As indicated, one of our major generalizations concerns "politics"—the
development of policies in school districts, the give and take of negotiations when conflicts occur, and the underlying differences in values that
appear in U.S. society today. In our view, the United States is in contentious times. In an early conversation during the training workshop,
Smith ran into a set of issues that would return later in multiple forms.
The conversation, and the tentative interpretations, set the stage for later
political interpretations.

> *Another item that came up, both in that conversation and an
> earlier one, concerns the mix of different rules and policies held
> by different school districts and the mix of different services pro-
> vided for teenagers who become pregnant. How all that
> weaves in and out of things I'm not really sure at this point. How
> it relates to what the parent education program can do is
> another issue as well. Finally the array of different local services
> that are provided in terms of other schooling experiences, in
> terms of special skills for kids to finish their high school diploma
> or get a GED credential or whatever seems to be part and par-
> cel of the whole enterprise. Somewhere along the way in one
> of our conversations somebody was commenting about using
> some of the young mothers to talk to junior and senior high
> school classes and tell the people the real difficulties in having
> a baby that young and what it does to the rest of one's life.
> Again I don't know—remember—where that was from but I
> think it was somebody besides these three. (1/21/88)*

This workshop, early in the project, triggered further observations and
conversations, that, in turn, led to further interpretations. Parents,
patrons, school boards, school administrators, and PAT personnel are

not of one mind concerning adolescent pregnancy and mothering and how much pregnancy and mothering should appear in public schools and classrooms. Our view, in the short term, leans toward helping these adolescents solve their problems and plan toward the future. For the long term, we believe that adolescents should come to know the consequences of their immediate actions and be able to think their way through those issues and the multiple and conflicting pressures under which they live. Such views are political ones and are open to debate as policy is formulated and as day to day actions are undertaken.

Summary and Conclusions:The Larger "Macro" Context—Again

Fitting a new educational program into a larger context poses major and continuing dilemmas for policymakers and program implementors at all levels of new programs such as PAT. Partly we brought such concerns to our mostly "microanalysis" of the PAT program, but partly we ran into the issues as we tried continuously to ground ourselves in the more general discussion of urban families. Early on, the notes recorded these initial interpretations.

> I'm on my way into the university and have spent the morning reading a good bit of Wilson's (1987) new book, **The Truly Disadvantaged**. It pertains quite well to some issues in PAT. . . .

The notes continued.

> Just a quick comment about the Wilson book on the underclass or as he calls them, the truly disadvantaged. It looks like a liberal response to some of the neo-conservative critique of the last decade. He's a Black man, chair of the sociology department at the University of Chicago who has written a couple of books now which I've not seen or actually know anything about. He's a MacArthur Prize Fellow as well. The book reads along very tightly and very analytically. Presents lots of larger social statistics type data undergirding much of what he wants to say. His central argument is that much of what has happened in the development of the truly disadvantaged group, what he calls "the inner-city underclass," is the result of economic changes. Partly it's the slowdown of the economy since 1960 and partly it's the basic change in American industry where lots of manufacturing jobs in steel and rubber and autos have left the country and this has impacted more dramatically on blacks and particularly young

*Black males. This has caused a huge dissolution of the Black
family and the social disorganization in the inner city. Along
with this have been the more generally judged positive
aspects of both freedom to move and freedom to change
locales of many advantaged Blacks. It results partly in a growing social class split within the Black community among the
haves and the have-nots. It also argues in his view for the kind
of social pathology that exists in the black community that has
risen dramatically since about 1960. This set of issues has not
been handled well by the liberal political or social analysts
who can't cope with the fact that the Voting Rights Act got
passed, that Affirmative Action programs have appeared,
and lots of things that were quite successful, but the plight of
poor Blacks has gotten worse. Joblessness, migration, isolation
loom large as the key explanatory concepts that drive his
analysis. More on that later. His discussion seems relevant to
the general reconceptualization of what the PAT program is
about and where it fits in the current scene. (1/28/94)*

Among the number of ideas touched on in those notes, Wilson's subtitle
to his book focuses our interpretation: *The Inner City, the Underclass, and
Public Policy.* The PAT program is a Missouri statewide policy initiative.
If Wilson is in some sense right, is PAT by-the-mark of the big issues of
inner-city life? Or does the program, intentionally or unintentionally,
have an important role to play? The program per se, insofar as it was
successful, created strengths in families, which in turn, so we argue elsewhere in the book, enhanced the development of the children. These are
the kinds of data-gathering, hypothesis-generating, and theorizing that
we are about. "Joblessness, migration, isolation" appear at multiple
points in our descriptions and interpretations. Parent educators and
local coordinators coped with these phenomena on an hourly, daily,
weekly, and yearly basis.

ORGANIZATIONAL STRUCTURES AND PROCESSES: POSITIONS, ACTIVITIES, AND DILEMMAS

The broader issues of politics and policies flow easily—or uneasily on
occasion—into the internal structures and processes of organizations
and programs. For us, the data and ideas suggested several large themes
within this larger view. We found the position and role of the PAT coordinator to be a significant element in our attempt to speak to the issues
of difficult to recruit, maintain, and help urban families. School districts
that intend to adopt or adapt a program such as PAT need to think carefully about this position and the potential incumbents of the position.

Another cluster of issues focused on the problems in the selection and training of parent educators. Our data, interpretations, and recommendations flowed together and apart in highly significant ways as
we tried to put some general intellectual order in this large domain of
particulars.

Finally, we brought together a number of ideas under the general rubric "dilemmas of organizational structure and process." Trade-offs
seemed everywhere and we tried to explore those in ways that would be
helpful to school districts and their officials thinking about instituting a
parent education program.

Through all this, flowed images of Schon's (1983) "reflective
practitioner" working on "messy" problems filled with complexity, idiosyncratic elements, uncertainty, ambiguity, and conflicting value claims.
In his eyes, "situations of practice" are only partially susceptible to technical rationality. We feel that this is what we are about in our inquiry—
both methodologically and substantively. This section accents much of
this even though the entire book takes on the same general flavor.

The Coordinator's Position and Role

In chapter 1 we raised brief comments about the position, role, and
incumbent of the director of the PAT program in the city. Now, our
focus on difficult to reach and maintain families, rather than the PAT
program in general leads us to concentrate now on the key position of
coordinator. Coordination, like leadership, is one of those concepts that
seems to defy simple characterization into patterns that are generalizable across groups and organizations. Our gambit lies in presenting concrete illustrations for interpretations, occasionally by us and necessarily
by the reader, who hopes to implement PAT in his or her district.

First, a quick contemporaneous glance indicates there are four
coordinators in the program. More specifically, our interviews and
observations have produced a number of images and ideas toward a
conceptualization of the coordinator's role. These include a concern with
prioritizing one's time, coming to know one's clients, matching clients
and parent educators, fiscal management, and supervising a staff of secretary, aide, and a dozen parent educators.

As the program has moved beyond its first few years of operation, the coordinators have had lightened caseloads and have increased
the amount of time spent supervising. Although each coordinator has
her own style, issues arise that permit a more general set of reflections
on the task of supervision. We integrate a number of conversations and
a several hour group interview/discussion with all of the coordinators
into a "generalized coordinator," whom we identify in the discussion as

"Coord." Although our focus remains with the difficult to reach, maintain, and help, the comments often broaden to problems in general and with all clients.

The Coordinator in Action: Defining the Role

Elements of the process of coordination begin to enter our pictures. Our images set the occasion for interpretation—by the reader, and, on occasion, by us. The illustrations arise not only from our observations and our one-on-one interview/discussions but also from a long group interview and discussion with all the coordinators. That broadened our perspective another degree or two.

Coming to know one's clients. The acquisition of key information about a client is a delicate process in itself. Coordinators have a major responsibility in this regard. Such information is a key antecedent to matching client and parent educator.

Coord: *But again we have the case of Sharon who we first met at a shelter. As a matter of fact, you met her at the group meeting.*

LS: *Ah! She was kind of laid-back—was it her kid I was holding?*

Coord: *Hm-hmm. Yeah.*

LS: *Let's divert for a minute. Tell me about her.*

Coord: *Sharon's interesting. She was originally enrolled in the program by Marilyn. I first met her when she came to a group meeting on discipline and I will never forget. . . [laughs] . . . during the group meeting she was just so disbelieving. "[She said things like] Oh, this is just so stupid. I don't understand what you're talking about." She was not very friendly toward the group. After the meeting I talked with her and she said that she wasn't going to come back anymore. I said, "I'm really sorry to hear that. We really would like you to come back. And if—if you come back often enough and you have things to say, you can just say them to the group—talk to us rather than mumbling and making those noises." I said, "I'm sure that we can have some really good conversations. And you can help us and we can help you." Well, she did come back to another group.*

The coordinator went on to explain that Sharon's former parent educator described her as alternately dependent and belligerent. When the parent educator visited at the shelter, Sharon tried to monopolize her attention. When the parent educator left the program to go back to school, the coordinator talked to her about assigning her a new parent educator. During that conversation, Sharon provided insight into her own life, which she said had been filled with abuse. She was abandoned by her mother and placed in foster care after her father left the family. She said she was abused in the foster home.

> *Coord: Sharon needs somebody to hug her . . . and to pat her face and to complement her when she does well. She also needs someone who will call her when she spins these wild, weird tales.. . . I think she'll get that from Janie, her new parent educator.*

Matching parents and parent educators. Knowing one's clients facilitates all sorts of activities of the coordinator, one of which is matching parents and parent educators. The subtlety of this arose in a discussion of the "temperament of families." The thought processes of a coordinator in action are exhilarating to observe.

> *LS:* You mentioned earlier, if I got the phrase correctly, the temperament of the family. And that was part of that matching business. What do you mean by temperament of the family?
>
> *Coord:* That may have been the wrong word—but it takes into account . . . [such things as] . . . is this a mom who really knows a whole lot about child development, is really on top of it, knows all the basics and essentially what we really have to give her is an enrichment experience. Then I'll want to choose a parent educator that I think has that background. Some parents are young . . . and they want somebody they can relate to. Some of the parents are a little more flighty than others and I have parent educators who are better at dealing with that than others. And I think I know pretty well the [parent educators] who can work well with each kind of family.
>
> *LS:* So there's a big matching hypothesis in back of your head?
>
> *Coord:* When I talk about the families, yes. For example, one of the things I try to match—if we're talking about an extra caseload—is geographical location. If the parent educator lives north I try to give her extra families who live over that way. It just makes it easier when you're trying to schedule an early evening visit. I think parent educators feel a lot more comfortable going out closer to home in the early evening simply because we all feel more comfortable in familiar surroundings.
>
> *LS:* Other things on the temperament?
>
> *Coord:* Ah, if it's a family where there seem to be a lot of problems and a need for extra services—that's something you want to take into consideration. I would try to avoid reassigning such

a family to a parent educator who herself had a lot going on in her life and thus may not have the time to devote to pursuing the extra services this family may need.

LS: *Another element of the matching hypothesis centered on another aspect of "more difficult" families? That word—the more difficult one's obviously pertinent to some of our more general interests. Talk a little bit for the moment about what makes them more difficult at this point or who made that—put that label on, whether you did or Helen did.*

Coord: *Well, when a parent educator is slated to leave the program, I try to sit down with her and go over the caseload, case by case. One of the reasons for doing this is to get a feel for what the family is like and [to find out] if there are things the parent educator can tell me about working effectively with this family. For example, things like "Well, she never likes to be seen before 11 o'clock. As a matter of fact, she doesn't even like being called before 11 o'clock." Knowing that kind of thing can be very helpful when we make the first contact to keep us from getting off on the wrong foot. Also, the parent educator knows the remaining staff. So I ask if there's anything about a particular family that would preclude me from just randomly assigning them to another parent educator? Or if there's a certain match that would facilitate the changeover. I've had a couple of instances where Helen said that she thought a family would be more comfortable with a Black or White parent educator. If that's the case . . . I need to know that. I don't make promises as to what the assignment's going to end up being, but I need to know that kind of thing going in. I also determine which parents are particularly difficult to schedule. As I said, when we redistribute families, we're really asking parent educators to take on an overload and . . . I try not to overload any one parent educator with a lot of difficult to schedule families.*

LS: *So the key criterion there is that the difficulty is just the scheduling business?*

Coord: *There's the business of scheduling which is one criterion. Also if there are a particular constellation of problems that beset this family.*

LS: *What would a constellation of problems be?*

Coord: *Well, one is that—for example, we have a family where, say, the mom is developmentally delayed or the baby has—has serious health problems or something like that. And during the ordinary assignment of cases, I try to see that everybody gets an equal mix of that because it's—working with that family takes more time and effort than working with a family where things are going along relatively smoothly. But especially when it comes to the case where I'm redistributing a case load and putting an extra workload on parent educators, I don't want to give them additional difficult cases if I can help it. So I try—I try to take the ones that are going to take extra time and effort.*

Listening to a supervisor think and talk her way through a practical task in the general run of tasks is informative. The array of detailed information entering into the thinking and deciding is very large. The facility of shifting categories and items, the intellectual processes, as the match is sought is equally intriguing.

Supervision

Coord: *Oh, this week I'm doing—as this week and next week I'm doing basically supervision kinds of things, because of we're coming up on the end of the first half of the program. . . .*
LS: *You have to make some kind of formal statements to people about the staff and that sort of thing?*
Coord: *I like to make a formal statement to the staff about what I think about their performance. It's very important that we not go on what we think are shared assumptions but that in reality might be very different. It's important that I actually say to them the things that I think they are doing well and the things that I think need to be improved—that I say that to them explicitly, so that we both have an understanding. Earlier you commented that we [parent educators and coordinator] meet a lot. We do.*

The word *support* is used frequently in the PAT program. During an extended interview, one coordinator spoke of "supporting parent educators" as one of the key aspects of her job.

Coord: *My most important function as a supervisor is, as parent educators are supportive of the parent, then I should be supportive of my parent educators. My job is to make their job easier. In order to do that I have to keep tabs on how things are going with them. I want our relationship for the most part to be very nonthreatening. I hate the notion of a supervisor who's there to catch you doing wrong. A supervisor is there to help.*

Throughout our observations we saw support operationalized in both formal and informal ways. As parent educators prepared to go into the field each morning, they talked among themselves about the families with whom they worked. Frequently, these discussions focused on difficult family situations and included the giving and taking of advice about how to approach a specific dilemma. We think that opportunities for this kind of informal give and take are important to parent educators who work with hard to reach, maintain, and help families. The organizational structure of the St. Louis program that calls for all staff to report to a common location each day supports this kind of opportunity by assuring that staff come into contact with each other daily.

More formal support was provided through planned activities during staff meetings. Some coordinators allocated a portion of the staff meeting to allow parent educators to discuss cases, share ideas, and vent frustrations. Sometimes this took the form of reviewing cases that quickly drew comparisons to other families with whom parent educators currently were working. Other times, the discussions resulted from an invitation to share a concern or frustration in order to get input from the entire staff. Still another strategy was to focus on a family that was initially hard to reach, maintain, or help, but was no longer considered so, trying to determine what specific strategies brought about the change in the hopes that they would be transferable to other families in similar situations. We recommend that others seeking to implement the PAT program with families similar to our target population build these kinds of activities into their program staff meetings.

During a later interview, the conversation shifted to a recounting of the "lessons" learned about supervising a PAT program. Essentially, the discussion centered on "things I didn't know but would now like to pass on to anyone else thinking of starting a program." We think this is an important issue.

LS: *What about other elements of supervision that come to mind? The things you do that you're really pleased about or . . . the thing that you still find problematic or . . .?*
Coord: *Much of it I don't find as a problem—and I think this year I grew a lot more than I had before. I mean, just the sternness in which I could say it—some things. As I say, coming from a teaching background, I knew the way to communicate and get my thoughts across to children, but I was always in fear of hurting someone's feelings in dealing with adults.*

Although we do not wish to overinterpret a particular comment made by a coordinator, a general point does exist that we don't wish to pass by. The kind of learning occurring in the life of a professional may be highly idiosyncratic and very important. The move from direct work with children to direct work with adults sometimes raises significant shifts in "mindsets" and habitual ways of interpersonal acting and behaving. A mindset, in this illustration, seems a complex set of beliefs and assumptions that guide one's own individual behavior and is presumed to guide the behavior of other adults, in contrast to children. Then one is faced with the "fact" that one's construal of the world doesn't quite fit. Words like *sternness* entered into thinking about and talking with one's adult "peers," in this instance parent educators about how things needed to be done to accomplish the larger goals of the program. The position, in this instance that of coordinator, begins to shape the beliefs, feelings, and activities of the individual holding the position. One not so small item and a very broad, and we believe very generalizable, interpretation.

Other items appeared.

LS: *Extending some of this kind of discussion, it seems to me that much of this falls into the role of the coordinator or aspects of supervision. And again I have these images of the four of you talking to your groups at the beginning and so on. And then the kind of monitoring along the way and so on. Are there other elements of supervision that stand out as, "My God, that's a lesson I have learned that I want to tell anybody who starts the program." What other kinds of things exist about supervision that you've learned over the last three or four years that somehow ought to be a part of . . .?*

Coord: *One is if . . . if there's only one coordinator, you've got to find someone within that district that you can rely on that you can go to for advice and have that person act as a listening post for you. We do it with each other. When I have problems, I don't hesitate to pick up the phone and call one of the other coordinators and say, "This is happening. How can we solve it?" Usually it's happening everywhere. So then we get together. So we're sounding boards for each other. So, as I said, when we speak, we speak basically as one person. Forming that kind of bond with some other administrative person really has helped me.*

Although the discussion moved with the particulars of "who do you talk with," the implications reach out in much larger directions. As we have thought about the coordinator's comment, she seems to be arguing implicitly for a kind of organizational structure that involves elements of trust, openness, sharing with peers, and bringing of rationality of multiple intelligences to bear on the problem. Explicit also is the belief that many of the problems are general, "it's happening everywhere," and implicitly the belief that the solutions have some generalizability. "Sounding boards" is a well used—and respected—colloquial way of summarizing the relationship. All of this seems very important for coordinators and parent educators who are working with difficult to reach, maintain, and help families.

One final item, really a further implication of the relationship among the coordinators, appeared: "When we speak, we speak basically as one person." That, too, seems an item of major organizational structure. It is not clear who the object of the consensus is toward—higher administrative personnel, difficult parents, or others. But, to us, speaking in one voice does convey a mobilization of power among a group of individuals.

The interview twisted and elaborated another idea or two.

LS: Is there anyone outside of the program that you talk to heavily?
Coord: Yes, I talk to my sisters a lot. Number one because I know that
        they don't know anybody that's in the program. I have one
        sister in particular who is just really quite skilled at getting to the
        heart of things. She's had supervisory experience. She's very in
        touch with reality and—and she's a real good people person.
        She's very good with that. Probably a lot better at it than I am.
LS: Yeah, part of—my curiosity is beyond the immediate
        instance. In that ethics business, when I get those tough
        problems, one of the people I try to talk to is my brother, who
        has nothing to do with academia, and—but has kind of a—
        he's a—sells insurance, that kind of thing. But he's knocked
        around for a long time. And what seems so complicated
        sometimes, when you pose it to him, he kind of shrugs and
        goes, "It's obvious." That kind of thing.
Coord: Well, I guess it's the same kind of role my sister plays for me
        because sometimes things that I'm so caught up in, she just
        seems to be able to cut right through them, saying, "Well, it
        seems to me this is what's going on." And . . . when I have
        difficult decisions, I kind of play them off of her to see how
        it—how they run at her end of town. [laughs]
LS: What about the parent educators? Who would they talk to,
        besides each of you? . . . And each other?
Coord: They have the option of calling in outside people. They call in
        the trainers from other districts, which gives them a whole dif-
        ferent perspective.
LS: Other aspects of that?
Coord: Oh, gosh. There are so many things. And you almost see it on
        a daily basis. The one thing that I've liked about this is watch-
        ing people grow. Watching people who I thought in the
        beginning were never going to make it, never going to
        amount to anything, who really turned out—well, seeing
        them evolve into just a whole different kind of person. A per-
        son who is really committed and a person who is willing to
        put forth more than their expectations. And having that
        same person come back and say, "Well, I did it because I
        got the direction from you. I picked up on what you were
        about. And you seemed to help me."

LS: *What I'm hearing is "Once a teacher, always a teacher."*

Coord: *Yeah, it really is. And I do.*

LS: *Except it's with adults rather than with the kids, in that sense? Do you agree?*

Coord: *And it is really important when you're working with a group of people who are coming with a bunch of different backgrounds and who are looking at the world through different eyes, that you state explicitly what your shared assumptions have to be about working together in this program. A supervisor has to take the initiative and know that it is . . . it's a supervisor's responsibility to set the frame of reference. Now it will be adjusted by the parent educators but we set the initial frame of reference. And the ground rules for operating harmoniously. I think that that's one of the things that we're articulating here. In the beginning, we assumed certain things and assumed that people were going to know what we were assuming. And we were all trying to read each other's minds. As it turned out, that doesn't work as smoothly as when you just come right out and say what the ground rules are and how things are to operate. And . . . and also build into that a system for positive feedback.*

LS: *But part of that is almost needing to be a coordinator a while, just as being a teacher, so that you know what it is that you really want of your expectations?*

Coord: *Exactly.*

Coord: *Yes. Well, yeah, I think that there are books on leadership that you can read. And they will tell you all those things. But you don't internalize them until you do them.*

Coord: *Yeah, exactly. The way we're doing with parents. They can pick up the baby books and read all this information, but until they actually see their babies doing it, then they don't picture it as well.*

We don't believe that we were "forcing" the discussion, although that might be a plausible interpretation of the interaction, but the comments made by the coordinators did resonate with a point of view, an educational teaching/learning perspective, that we strongly endorse. The experience of seeing other individuals "grow" in the course of their activities is a major value held by most teachers. Coordinators who see the world this way and act on it have part of a belief and action system that is very powerful. The "different backgrounds" also sounds like many teachers talking about their students— at almost any age from kindergarten to graduate school—or in this instance with adult parent educators. Furthermore, the need to help establish a "frame of reference" and set of "ground rules" is another teacher conception with both power and merit. Finally, the problem of "internalizing" ideas links with "doing it" at some quite concrete and particular level. We believe that these are important and generalizable beliefs of a general stance on teaching. Approaching problems and dilemmas with such an orientation is a major asset to one who wants to coordinate in a program such as PAT.

The conversation then turned to the monitoring component of supervision and some of the possible problems. Although not typical of the large majority of parent educators, occasional problems occurred with job performance and record keeping.

> *Coord: I think one of the other lessons we learned is . . . well, early on, we thought that some parent educators really require much less supervision than they actually do. To keep close documentation of each and every visit that you make with that. . . . And then just the idea that maybe they didn't hire the most responsible people. And sometimes we've found the same thing. You know, people who say they've done one thing and haven't actually done it. I think they run a greater risk than we as coordinators would.*
>
> *Coord: I think each center probably has at least one, sometimes two, maybe even three, who don't fall within the realm of getting work or whatever done in a timely fashion. And the monitoring we do, we do individual conferences with them. At some times the Unit Director was called in for a conference and even at other times it got up to the director's level. And when it got up to his level, it's about the time for walking papers and that kind of thing. But I think each year we've had maybe one person. And I think part of that is that some people come into the program not really understanding the importance of portions of it.*

Coordinators identified several procedures for monitoring service delivery.

> *LS: How do you monitor that? The occasional calls you make, I guess. Are there other procedures that you use?*
>
> *Coord: Just drop by when they're scheduled for visits in the home. You know, unannounced observations of them.*
>
> *LS: To see if they're really there?*
>
> *Coord: Yeah, one thing one other coordinator told me, and I've started doing, is just driving through the neighborhood to see if I see a car. I recognize everybody's car in my center. So if I drive through and I see the car in the neighborhood that it's supposed to be, I'm assuming that that visit has taken place at that particular time. Random telephone surveys, spot checks of records. Parents will let us know readily if they're scheduled.*

Coord: *Another way is if you just look at records. I would be. . . . I don't want to say this 100%, but I would look with some skepticism at a parent educator who has—we keep what's called a time and effort log, and it's just a recapitulation of your activities during the day, not very detailed. And one of the things that you document in there is when you attempt home visits and they don't make for whatever reason. I look with a good deal of skepticism on someone who has a time and effort log and all it says is, "Completed home visit. Completed home visit. Completed home visit." But there are never any cancellations. That is not normal. [laughs]*

LS: *It doesn't sound real, in that sense?*

Coord: *It's not for real. And you can . . . there are things . . . I mean, there are subtle kinds of things when you—you have to look at lesson write-ups. And when the write-ups seem that they came out of a textbook, you know that that is not—*

LS: *Rather than some event that happened with a particular—*

Coord: *You have to pick up idiosyncratic concerns of families within those write-ups. And if they don't occur with some degree of regularity, that is cause for you to say, "Well, things don't look quite right here." And those are just some things that we've picked up on as we have done this that will help us to key in on—*

LS: *So you can monitor sort of softly or a little heavily depending on how it looks that way.*

Summary. Although much is written about educational supervision, much of what the PAT coordinators learned about the supervision role came from trial and error. In fact, none of the PAT coordinators came to the position with a background in supervision, rather they are essentially early childhood and child development specialists. We believe that this lack of formal training in administration probably is not uncommon in many supervisory positions. It may be especially true among PAT programs that are likely to be implemented by women who closely resemble the coordinator who previously described herself thusly:

> *Coming from a teaching background, I knew the way to communicate and get my thoughts across to children, but I was always in fear of hurting someone's feelings in dealing with adults. And I came from a mind set that if you're an adult and you're told what you're supposed to do and you know what your job requires of you, then you go out and do it because that's the way I do my job. And I learned through this position that [although most parent educators share that perspective] everybody doesn't feel that way. That was the biggest thing [that I had to learn].*

We think that the lessons learned by the St. Louis coordinators are generalizable beyond programs working with families in difficult situations. We think that they are applicable to any and all PAT programs. Figure 6.1 presents the overall framework.

Selection, Inservice Training, and Continuing Development of Parent Educators

The longer reach of coordinators' responsibilities extend into the selection, training, and continuing development of parent educators, although others share in these responsibilities. We continue to present materials from our group interview/discussion. Along the way, we insert some comments from parent educators. The latter is in the form of a critical minority report on some of the issues. The coordinators argued about the generality of this particular parent educator's views. These discussions make the case for continuing and further research and inquiry into the program.

As context for this discussion, one of the major "lessons learned" by coordinators was "Do not go out and hire people that you think you are going to be able to train on the job while they deliver the service." It is not possible in their view to both train and deliver service at the same time. Coordinators uniformly felt that parent educators had to come to the position with a certain mix of adequate knowledge base, an ability to relate to a wide range of personality types, and a nonjudgmental attitude toward nontraditional lifestyles and family structures. Our comments on backgrounds, training, and continuing development of parent educators, and the coordinator's role in all this, must keep in mind these broad parameters. Much of their views had grown out of early experiences when the program had first started, and when they were in the midst of the sorting through complex problems of "competence, class, and race."

Competence, Class, and Race

One of the farther reaches of the professional versus semiprofessional aspects of the parent educator background and training occurs in the complications of competence, race, and social class. We believe that this is a phenomenon of all urban communities. The coordinators in the St. Louis program have clear and strongly held views of this part of a successful program. An initial view of the competence issue arose in a long discussion among the several coordinators.

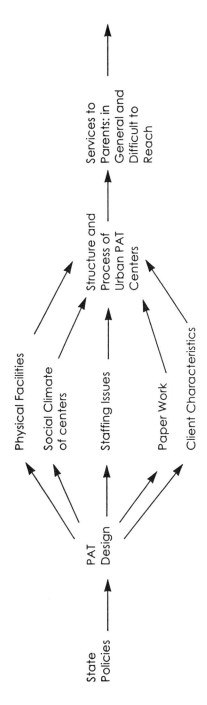

Figure 6.1. Organizational implications of PAT project

Coord 1: *Yeah, she was at the south side center. And I visited with families. I will admit I was a little bit concerned because we were way over in southwest St. Louis for a number of them. And the other, we were in southeast St. Louis where there is a lot of racial prejudice. I found that as long as parents perceived me as competent and concerned, that I didn't have a problem. The problem comes when a parent perceives that they know more than a parent educator knows.*

Coord 2: *That's exactly what I—that's a 100% true. Like at one center, they thought, oh, South St. Louis, no, you cannot have any black parent educators. That was not true. The first year I was shaky because everybody told me in South St. Louis they are so prejudiced. But they told me mostly toward Blacks, and be careful with parent educators, to which house you send them to. I said, "How could I have control over who is going where? They are recruiting families and they are going on home visits." But that's very true. That if my competent parent educator's knowledgeable, those who dress up nicely and can communicate with parents and have a good knowledge, I have never had any problems with them. I have had problems with white parent educators who had no knowledge and the parent called me saying, "I don't know if I want somebody who is coming talking about my child and child development to me and doesn't know how to talk or spell things." I have had problems with the Black parent educators who do not have the knowledge. I haven't had any racial problems.*

Coord 3: *It's either social or educational.*

Coord 2: *Education, I would say.*

Coord 1: *Those are most of the problems. Yeah.*

LS: *So it's race, class, and the competence you're talking about is educational, in that sense?*

The complications of competence and expertness with race and class appeared later in the interview. Some of the job parameters and the selection procedures can mitigate indirectly against well-qualified Blacks and single parents becoming parent educators. These issues then entangle all of the educational and organizational processes in PAT from recruitment to service delivery.

LS: *Is it possible to escalate yourself out of business in the sense of having standards so high that people that you would really like to have either don't want to work parttime or don't want to work for the salary that you can provide or the ...?*

Coord 1: *I was going to say on the issue of race. But this is my perception of it. I think that the fact that this is a part-time job, has no benefits, and that we require—we need to have a certain level of expertise in terms of education and the ability to work with families, I think that in some respects that mitigates against getting good—forgive me, Lord, please—but getting well qualified Black parent educators. And I think that the way it does that is because with the economic situation the way it is, most Black people who have that kind of background are looking for a full-time job. Wives are working not to have spending money, but to form the economic base that the family is operating from. The economic condition of Black people at this point in time does not allow us the luxury of having large groups of well-qualified Black folks who can have a job and a half in the household. We need two full-time jobs to acquire middle class status and to maintain that status.*

LS: *What's the solution to that prob—or do each of you agree with that?*

Coord 2: *Yes.*

LS: *Do you agree essentially to . . .?*

Coord 3: *Oh, yes.*

LS: *Then what's the solution to that kind of a—*

Coord 1: *I think it needs to be a full-time job.*

Coord 2: *We have many parent educators who are competent, and every year, we go through this frustration of we're going to really lose the people because of that. We've got a number of single parents who are heads of households. They have the abilities. But because the job doesn't offer enough for them to sustain their families, we know we're going to lose them.*

Coord 1: *Yeah, the one thing that we get in terms of most of our—our well-qualified Black parent educators, I think, are people who are not looking forward to scaling down their participation in the work force. We're looking at people who are working this job and trying to go to school. And once they finish school, we can look forward to losing them altogether.*

LS: *So you're a way-station toward the place they're going?*

Coord 3: *Hm-hmm. In some sense. And the only way to address that inequity is to recognize parent education as a part of the entire educational system with fulltime status.*

Most urban communities have been in high transition over the last couple of decades. The populations are increasingly aging, containing higher percentages of African-American populations, and often larger and larger areas of poverty and underclass residents. Within those changes, considerable variety exists, as our introductory vignettes in chapter 1 indicate. Now as we listened and participated in the discussion with the several PAT coordinators we turned directly to the issues of competence, class, and race. The very way in which the several coordinators phrased their comments indicates the background of concern, attempts to use intelligence and rationality in planning and policymaking, and tentative steps in implementation. Competence of the parent educators became the crucial bridging conception. But it was a two-edged sword, for the program had limits in remuneration, benefits, and part-time employment. Some of the most capable of the parent educators used the program, and we don't mean that pejoratively, as a stepping stone toward better paying full-time jobs, a process often mediated by further training in finishing AB degrees or in obtaining teaching credentials. Our observations and theorizing took us back into the "macro" issues, the larger community context of the program, and the latent constraints and resolutions of those larger issues. In this regard, conceptions of the "success" of the program took on a wider scope and vision. Intended or unintended by the policymakers, we saw this as an important part of the experience of the PAT program in this urban community.

Implications for Training Parent Educators: The Coordinator Perspective

The coordinators discussed some of their own experiences as parent educators. From these come some of their concerns for translating ideas and practices into inservice training for their parent educators.

Coord: *I think, in particular, the parents that have problems and those so-called hard to reach, those parents would like somebody to understand their problems first before they come to Parents as Teachers, the schedules and lesson plans and going through child development. I think if we can get their attention based on "We care about what's going on with you," we will be more able to focus on child development.*

LS: *Does a particular parent or session come to mind when you say, you know, somebody that you've really spent time working on to get that rapport, that later then led into the . . . ?*

Coord: *Um, I had a family that was not that hard to reach family, yet with lots of problems. Each time I had to go there, we started with the program and how the baby is doing and starting with whatever I had to do, but the minute you talk about some kind of behavior of the child, then you'd see that parent jump in and talk about her husband and the problems that exist in their family. And on those situations, I just turn the whole visit to what she wanted to know and what she was looking for, information how she can deal with her husband first in order to be able to get to the child. So a parent educator should be able to handle those kinds of family situations. And then it would be helpful for parent educators to also be familiar with family problems as a whole.*

Coord: One of the things that parent educators have talked about is that when you go into a family that has this kind of a situation, where you do have to work through the presenting problem, as it were, the family situation, to get to the child development, that there is a difficulty for the parent educators in determining how far do you go with addressing the presenting problem. At what point have you done all that you can? Or at what point must you—must you begin to focus on the child's development? It's a clinical decision, that I don't think anyone can tell you case by case, do you put in so many minutes? But as competent practitioners, each one of us has to make that decision. But where do you draw the line? I mean, do you go for the whole year discussing the women's marital problems, as it were?

Coord: No. No, in my case, I mean that particular case, what I did I focused on her problem for a while. And then I switched it to what I was trying to say, if this is the kind of behavior that, for example, a four year old was so upset. And when she explained this to me, I was able to understand because of family problems, this four year old was having problems. And then she was going to say that this four year old was jealous of my new baby, therefore she picks her up and picks the baby up and throws her here and there. You need to be able to come around the whole problem and then focus on what you want to talk about to the parents. The parent educator should have the ability of being considerate of their problems, yet to focus on what you have to do.

LS: It just goes on forever.

Coord: Hm-hmm [yes].

The discussion here might have been phrased as "which problem when?" as the coordinators reflected on their experience and what they needed to teach their parent educators. They would have their agendas and their lesson plans and hit some higher priority problem of the parent, for example difficulties between the mother and the father. The coordinators seemed to have the ability to respond to the mother's immediate concerns then to "switch" back to the agenda of the day, but with the added interdependency of the broader and usually interrelated problem. Technical knowledge and skill seems to blend with common sense knowledge and skill. It sounds simple, but, obviously, it is not. The training program that handles that is even more problematic. And we are back to the kinds of discussions that go on among peer professional practitioners and on some occasions the parent educators and their supervisors. Once again we see ourselves building a file of specific problem situations that might serve as a curriculum for inservice training.

Coord: And they look on you as experts, that "You can tell me." And then we may create family problems as well. That's what I was trying not to do. You have to really know the family and you have to know what you're saying.

LS: Did I hear you correctly? You said "that creates family problems, too"?

Coord: Yes. Sometimes. But what we're saying really is that parent educators have a need to be trained in that kind of an approach, where you serve as a sounding board for parents to straighten out their own perceptions of the problem, but then you don't offer solutions to them. And then the other thing is that a parent educator has to be skillful at recognizing when you have in a sense—like when you're beating a dead horse you discuss the presenting problem and elaborate on it. And you have to recognize the point at which you have to start redirecting the focus of the visit from the mother's primary concern with her marital relationship in this instance to the more global concerns of how that is effecting the child's development. Parent educators also need to recognize when the appropriate response is to refer parents to another agency — for example, a marital counselor.

Coord: I don't think I'm just sitting waiting for the moment to hop in because I think that at a certain level, once—once you get into a problem, you have to kind of let—you have to let the parent get a certain amount of it out.

The discussion seemed to be moving along very productively. Smith intervened one more time in a significant way, reflecting important emotional and intellectual content and making an interpretation. In effect he was trying to understand what was being said and to push the limits of that understanding. His underlying assumptions seemed to be that they were accomplished professional clinicians on the one hand, teacher educators on the other hand, and supervisors on the third hand. That's a pretty complex role. The discussion continued to elaborate on the subtleties of the issues involved.

LS: And get around it, in a sense? As I hear the two of you talk, handling the parent interview and the discussion, that's a very sophisticated set of skills. And I guess the question that comes to my mind is how generalizable or how general are those skills among your groups of parent educators on the one hand? And then on the other hand, where does one learn how to do that and how does one teach somebody else how to do that? So we're talking about a complicated, I think, clinical skill, if you like. And where do the skills come from? And then how do you teach other people about them? Thoughts on that or . . . ?

Coord: Well, I do believe that there—there may be some innate component, I mean, something that people have learned, I'm not saying that they're born with but that they bring to the situation. A generalized ability to relate to people well. Although I do think that a good part of it is teachable. And one of—one of the things that it's just real important to do at the very beginning—I think she referred to it earlier—is that we have to give parent educators a clear conception of what it is that they're going to be doing. The other thing that has been helpful for me in working with the staff that I work with is going on observation visits.

Coord: As a rule, they do not go with me to one of my families. They go with an experienced parent educator. And my point in saying that is that in order to learn to do this job well, you have to be willing to give yourself the latitude to maybe make a couple of mistakes. To maybe ask a question that you think is really stupid. This is the time to learn what it is that we're about. So ask anything, ask for any help that you need, ask to go and see and do anything that you think is going to be helpful to you. And the other thing is that on the first visit that I go on as an observation, I make it very clear that this visit is not going to result in any evaluation. If you feel yourself getting stuck in the visit, turn to me and bring me into it, because I will use that opportunity to try to model for you the way to do it. And I have had parent educators say to me that that has been very helpful to them, when they get stuck.

LS: So in a sense, it's almost as though they were going with you with one of your families, it's that if they get stuck, you assume part of the role and in effect they see how you do it.

Coord: Yes. If parent educators have a difficult case and want some consultation on it, I'll make it a point to go out with them when they go to that particular family's house. And one of the things that I think is real critical is that when you're going out on a visit with a parent educator, you talk about that family before you go. We talk about them in depth. Tell me about the kids. What are they doing? What's the mom concerned with? What do you see? Do you have any particular areas you want me to look at? Is there something you want some feedback on? But you talk about that family so that when I walk in, I feel that I have a feel for what's going on. And particularly if you think it's a difficult—there's a problem there for you as a parent educator.

Coord: Yes, one advantage of sending them with the seasoned parent educators is that they don't feel like, "Oh, my coordinator is watching me." And they get to try to actually try. And it's hard for them to just demonstrate what their abilities are. And I've heard them saying that, "Oh, by going with so-and-so, I think that I wasn't that scared of what I'm doing."

LS: You take the authority part out of the relationship?

Coord: Yes. Right. And I think that is very helpful to parent educators.

LS: Now that's when they go with the kind of a senior parent educator to watch that person do it, or do some of the parent educators go on visits with them when they have their own families also?

Coord: We can do that. The first visit with—new parent educators going with the old parent educators.

LS: I would come along with you and observe how you do it, as a parent educator.

The conversation turned to a discussion of feedback from parents and parent educators.

LS: Regarding the frustrations and comments from parents, the image I have is that this is one instance of either phone calls, letters and so on, that have tremendous impact on you as practicing parent educators, where some parent tells you something or how much either the conversation or the program has meant and so on. Is that so or is that . . . ?

Coord: It really is very helpful to me. I mean, at least the — we always talk about this with parent educators, they also get letters, they also get things from parents. And they say no matter how many problems, how many times we go and they are not home, or they get frustrated, one word or one sentence, it will make their day, or it will just make up for a lot of frustrations.

Coord: I can agree with you.
        [laughter]

By way of summary, burn out, the gradual development of fatigue, loss of interest, and loss of faith in one's ability to work meaningfully and effectively with clients appears in all service professions. The other end of the burn out continuum is professional growth of the parent educator. Our experience with the program suggested several "natural" and "planned" resolutions. Earlier, the observer had caught a glimpse of one item and wrote the memo, "on being supportive."

As I move toward the end of the observational part of the project and begin to reflect on key elements, one of the words I have heard most frequently, in multiple parts of the project is "supportive." Initially, it was an accolade of parents toward parent educators. I can still remember and visualize a parent commenting to me at a group meeting, that it was not the information, nor even the discussions, but it was the supportiveness of the parent educator which was so important to her.

But the point I want to make here is relating "being support-
ive" of the parent educator to the "continued trying" of the
parent educator with difficult and hard to reach families. I am
not sure what "being supportive" really means. For instance is
it similar to or identical with "caring," a word that has almost
become a cliché in sociology and psychology these days, for
example in the writing of Nell Noddings (1984) Caring. Most of
us in varying jobs in education see ourselves as being support-
ive with people we work with. Perhaps not so frequently do stu-
dents, clients, and subordinates perceive the same degree of
supportiveness. In my view, an urban PAT program with its quo-
tas, with its limited supplies and facilities, with its instability in the
school system, and with its difficult to reach and sometimes
minimally responsive families is a situation which demands an
unusual degree of supportiveness for its staff.

How all that works its way down from the National Center
and from the Central offices of the school system to the day-
to-day lives of the parent educators is a problem I would like
to brainstorm with each of you. For the moment I believe it is
very important. (Memo 45)

A coordinator raised much the same point, one that we labeled "talking PAT," as she described her learning and action about difficult cases.

LS: *Now how is that done? Or how was it done in your own*
case? Was it you talking with your other parent educators in
the first year or two? Or was it —

Coord: *Much of it was a feeling that I brought because of my own*
experience. It's very helpful to me that I don't come from a
middle class background because . . . I think I have a pretty
wide view of the world and a pretty realistic one. It became
more cemented as I talked with more and more parent edu-
cators who were having experiences that were both similar
and different from my own. It seems very obvious, but what
parent educators come away from those discussions realiz-
ing is that no one approach works for everybody. That—that
we have to be flexible. We have to go in with an open mind
and say, "Okay, let's assess the situation. Let's see what
resources we have at hand? And how can we best use
those resources, as I said, to meet our mutually established
goals. In this instance "our" refers to parents and parent edu-
cators. This program will not work if parent educators go in
with inflexible goals and methods. We cannot begin without
asking the parents, "What are your goals, for your child? And
what do you think is important? And how can we work
together to do that?" We're there to support parents, not to
come in and impose our set of values on them.

LS: *When do those discussions with the parent educators occur? When you say it becomes cemented, as you talked with other parent educators?*

Coord: *It takes place in an institute sometimes, in training sessions, it takes place at meetings with other parent educators in the St. Louis district—it takes place at staff meetings at my own center—just wherever parent educators all get together and meet and talk about—naturally whenever we get together, that's what we talk about. [laughs]*

LS: *Are there key people in your own personal experience within the parent educating group that you talk issues like this over with? I guess I'm curious as to who are the people you argue your tough cases with?*

Coord: *My really tough cases I talk with—sometimes I talk with my supervisor. And I also talk with my coworkers about it. I think you can learn from each other.*

LS: *Yeah. So it almost plays into a kind of supervisory role as well as "Help me clarify my own thing."*

Coord: *I think that in real tough cases, often one mind can't come up with a solution—you need to have more divergent views, if only because as the person with the tough case, I'm so caught up in it that sometimes I can't see everything and someone else who's less involved can—sometimes can tell me where I may even be contributing to the problem. That's difficult for the person right in the midst of it sometimes.*

Trying to comment on or summarize the poignancy and power of that group meeting with the several coordinators seems almost a fool's errand, but several items seem worthy of a brief noting or an exclamation point. The idea that the parent's well being is on the parent educator's agenda seems fundamental to rapport with the parents. But, such a gambit moves the parent into discussion of their personal and family problems. Being able to listen, make a comment or suggestion or two, and then move the discussion on to the child's development in that context approaches the skill of an art form. The limits of these discussions is a difficult judgment call.

The possibility of suggestions contributing to or creating further family problems is one of the hazards of any interpersonal work of this kind. Issues of selection of parent educators and the multiple modes of working with them in these kinds of situations is part of the agenda of the coordinators. Discussions, going with the parent educators, and making referrals blend in many forms. The problems of authority appear, and resolutions, in the form of having other more experienced parent educators go with each other, appear as additional alternatives. The idiosyncratic backgrounds of the coordinators, their autobiographies, as it were, flow in and out of their approach to these problems. And people continue to talk with each other, bringing two or more minds to the problem.

The coordinator perspectives are a major part of organizational structure and process.

Outside Experts, Staff Development, and Inquiry

One part of the PAT project is continuing education by outside experts who are brought in to meet in various ways with different groups of staff in the parent education program. Sally Provence from Yale University's program was one of these individuals. A January 1988 workshop was part of her schedule. Several of us from the city PAT program attended a smaller special meeting with her as well as the larger meeting for experienced parent educators. Among others, Smith found it quite provocative. If stirring one's thinking was a goal, the meeting certainly succeeded, perhaps in ways surprising.

Antecedents of Reconstruals

Lurking in the background, always seemingly, are questions that arise from immediate experience coming into contact with prior experiences that leave discrepancies. One of these arose in the very planning of the research project. The early notes phrased it this way.

> *Wilma also talked a little bit about the program being transformed from essentially a program that should work reasonably well with relatively stable, intact families and circumstances to becoming a program that is supposed to impact on disadvantaged kids and families in some way. She had some question about that transformation and the realism in it and also some question about whether there was enough impact in the program. I shared my feeling about whether there was enough "clout" in the experimental treatment to make the kind of differences that they want made. She agreed. There are a number of major, practical, conceptual, policy issues that run all through that transformation, if it really be that. On the surface it seems like it is. Much of that might well be phrased in the old cliché of sending a boy to do a man's job. I'm not sure the program is man-size enough to carry that out. (1/18/88)*

Multiple tentative hypotheses seem to be running loose in this brief comment. First, the idea of the shift to the urban community amounted to a "transformation" in the program. Things could be very different. Second, a kind of "realism" ran through Wells' orientation and approach. Implicitly, a contrast with "idealism" and perhaps "true belief" among program staff seems a tenable hypothesis. Third, a concern for enough potency or "clout" in the program to reach the goals that existed seemed in the air as well. Observers and evaluators seem to carry into the setting what Malinowski (1922) called "foreshadowed problems" and what Hexter (1971) called "the second record." The intellectual work of observation, interpretation, and evaluation begins "before the beginning" of any qualitative inquiry project. The shaking of the intellectual framework of an educational program always seems to be one possible option in the inquiry.

Early Thoughts on "Outreach"

In qualitative ethnography and action research inquiry one has goals toward new ways of solving difficult and continuing problems. Creation of such alternatives is an important intellectual exercise, and one that often is not confronted directly in traditional quantitative verificational research and evaluation. The inservice program led by Sally Provence had other important elements toward enhancing one's thinking.

> *Another idea that arose came from the outreach aspects of the program that Sally Provence runs or has run in New Haven, Connecticut. This program, both in her book and in her lecture, talks about people going out of their way to help reach these disadvantaged families. In the course of that it struck me that if the parent educators would not only help set up appointments but actually take people to where they had to go that that might get over some of the initial hurdles. When I raised that with Wilma she countered with all of the kinds of accident, insurance, lawsuit types of problems.*

Often that kind of reaction indicates where thinking has gone before, the limitations of new proposals, and difficulty in changing practices. In this instance the notes carried several important continuing thoughts.

> *If all of that's really so, and I don't have any real doubts about it, then it seems to me that one way that you tinker with the program is that you add resources to cover insurance costs for that kind of thing. That would be a bit expensive I assume on a $170 per year cost as it currently is budgeted, if I have the right figure on that from the brochure. The kind of pragmatic theorizing and practice I guess I'm arguing for is that each reason-*

*able item then proposes some reasonable reasons that you
can't do it, then you've got to counter with some reasonable
proposal to meet the reasonable objections. Then one keeps
finding what those chains are and keeps stretching them out
and building in possibilities. Ultimately they get integrated into
some of the kinds of patterns I presume.*

Elsewhere our observations and interpretations will raise the program's
very successful use of cabs to bring parents to group meetings, an
improbable idea with improbable funding from another program in the
schools. Yet it seems very effective. Creativity in ideas and practices?

Idiosyncratic Arrangements

The kind of model for educational programs we are working
toward tends to be less doctrinaire, less formalized, and less systematic
than some. Opportunistic, idiosyncratic, and improbable are adjectives
we hold in high esteem. Ideas come from everywhere. Provence continued to be stimulating in this regard.

*Another item arose about a more formidable carrot and goal
process. The Yale program was hooked up with the pediatrics
department. A very real lure in that program was that the parents got special medical help and treatment for their children.
This seems to me to be such a major item that it's going to
draw people and keep them in the program even when they
might not otherwise be interested. It also enables them to
require the parents to be in every month or two for developmental examinations and it also enables them to maintain
some kind of continuity of the parents with the same physician.
That is so different from the usual lower social class medical
relationships as I understand them to be, than from the middle-
class situation where you pick your private physician and you
stay with him or her and they know you and you know them
and you develop a long confident relationship.*

The extrapolation to aspects of the urban situation followed in the form
of a set of hypotheses, several of which seem highly relevant to the goals
and strategies of the PAT program.

*Part of the problem in the urban settings is that often you don't
have these kinds of contacts and continuity with good medical care and it's part of the-you-can't-count-on-anything, a
continuing pattern of activities. I really need to check that out*

*with the medical histories of some of the people. Having some
kind of continuity in the medical care program and having it
relatively available and having it relatively cheap would seem
to make a lot of difference in all of this. It seemed important in
the Yale program.*

In PAT, medical referral processes, and other social services as well,
were both developed and utilized as a functional equivalent, of sorts, to
this part of the Yale program. Knowing the particular local resources
became an agenda item for all new parent educators.

Dilemmas of Innovative and Ongoing Programs

Issues of competence, training, and maintaining morale and
focus in innovative and ongoing programs arose in the talk and conversations with the outside experts. Early on, questions and hypotheses
were the agenda rather than the realities of the program per se.

*The whole issue of the competence of the various people in
the program also comes to mind. In the Yale situation they
had these high level professionals who were in and out of all
phases of the program. That's just not going to happen in
some other kinds of settings with other kinds of facilities.*

At this point, no reference was made directly to PAT in general and PAT
in the particular St. Louis urban environment. That would work itself out
in time through our observations and interviews, although the possible
contrasts with the first PAT pilot project and evaluation (Pfannensteil &
Seltzer, 1985) were already on our minds. The notes continued.

*It is striking again as to how the pilot projects have their own
kind of rationale and their own kind of facilities and support and
these vanish partly with the winds of federal and other kinds of
monies and partly with the ending of the new idea and the
new experience that attracts people into them as intellectual
puzzles and problems. When one reverts back to the normal
day care, the normal educational, and the normal medical situation then one has a very different kind of set-up. I guess the
big generalization is how to keep that initial excitement and
competence going in a long term project or organization.*

Those issues and dilemmas were to return throughout our experiences
in the urban PAT program. Early items that were more in the form of
questions, hunches, and hypotheses, as data and evidence entered were

tightened, reformulated, and retold—as confidence appeared in the patterns we generated.

Life History and Biography

In recent years, much of the discussion of "personality" of teachers, social workers, and counselors has been subsumed and transformed by discussions of life history and biography of individuals. During an early training session the issue arose in several ways. First came the methodological point then a more substantive one in the summary notes.

I've lost my train of thought. I was on to something of the order of doing mini-cases of parent educators who are very good at reaching the difficult and the hard to reach cases. That will be interesting as it sorts out in the wash and as people talk about who their best educators are. At that point, too, I'll be able to get some subcriteria as to why these are better than others and the way in which people think about that problem. (1/19/88)

Implicit in those thoughts are conceptions of "good" parent educators, the criteria that individuals in the program use for making their judgments, and the use of biographical mini-cases as means of organizing and reporting on the findings. Endpoints in the recruiting, training, and selecting parent educators become visible and thereby guide inquiry and thought about the program.

The blend of background and training arose in the next item in the summary notes dictated during the workshop training.

Another idea that I don't think I got into the notes relates to biographical aspects of the people's backgrounds as it relates to becoming a parent educator and then success as a parent educator. It arose in one of the discussions that in 1 week's training you can't really turn out instant experts. The people who do it well have got to come out of other backgrounds. In the case of the current group there are an awful lot of people with teacher training and with social skills and counseling, social service skills and counseling skills, that seem to tie into what the program is trying to do. Other individuals are parents and grandparents and have gone through that particular kind of fire. Others I assume have done everything from camp counseling to babysitting to raising their nieces and nephews. I would guess there's a tidal wave of that kind of experience, all of which sharpens and focuses and points toward the kind of thing to be done in the parent education program. In a sense the training program gives some definition to all this. (1/19/88)

As those observations imply, much of the education of parent educators fell on the local district coordinators and supervisors in the program. In effect, among other aspects of their role, they become teacher educators of the parent educators. We found that educational process to be continuing and never ending. But the important point here lies in the strengths and weaknesses that appear in the life histories and biographies of the parent educators.

The notes from the Provence meeting had one other major concluding thought that seemed important early on and also now in longer retrospect in our view of the PAT program.

> To this point Mildred Winter seems to be very good at all of this with her outside experts coming in to infuse the project with some new ideas and part of the vigor of the national scene, with her ability to infuse more and more resources both public and private into the program and with her ability to attract interesting people to work on different activities.

Part of the admonition lay with our urban project as well.

> Another huge moral of all this is the need to think systemically about these issues. There's always another piece in the system that hooks into it, whether it be leadership on the one hand, as with Mildred here, or whether it be blocks and barriers of another kind elsewhere. (1/18/88)

The early staff development sessions had an obvious provocative quality in our thinking that day in late January. It helped formulate questions and suggested creative alternative to explore in our documents, observations, and interview data. We were a very small and perhaps special part of the overall PAT program, but a part we were. The inservice program was helpful.

Dilemmas in Organizational Structure and Process

Dilemmas is one of our favorite concepts in thinking about educational programs and activities. It implies that there are no simple right or wrong answers or unvarying rules to be applied to "which action is to be taken." Rather, multiple alternatives usually exist, trade-offs in the form of some pluses and some minuses exist for any alternative action, and choices must be made. Furthermore, the structures and processes in place are not writ in stone, rather they are constructions that people have made through prior decisions. Although some may be very resistant to change, and often necessarily so, changes are possible. Indeed, the very functioning of the organization often creates the upward or downward spirals that bring changes unwittingly, unconsciously, or without planned efforts. These become their own kind of dilemmas for further and future action. The process is endless.

In this section, we try to reach for a broader context of some of the dilemmas that faced individuals at the several levels of the urban PAT program. It is one of our attempts to alert educators who may be considering adopting or adapting an early childhood program similar to PAT, that they need to think about a number of items within the broad domain of organizational structures and processes. The items have a potpourri quality about them, although we have striven for a bit of organization.

Minimal Resources, Poverty, and Innovative Programs

Anyone who has spent much time with innovative educational programs has some direct experiential knowledge of limited resources and the ever expanding dreams and agendas of innovators, reformers, and utopians (Smith & Dwyer, 1980; Smith & Keith, 1971; Smith & Klass, 1989; Smith et al., 1987, 1988). When utopians and their programs are situated in places like poor urban communities the complications increase. Sketching out these complexities is part of what we mean by a systemic analysis and interpretation. Such images and conceptualizations are a prelude for recommendations and altered programs—locally or disseminated elsewhere. Several illustrations, one regarding evaluation issues and one from an early parent education group meeting, convey much of our intent.

Reimbursement and Parent Educator Pay

When service programs are supported by tax dollars, interesting differences occur from business organizations that are supported by earnings and profits from selling products. We are not arguing "better or worse," rather that individuals and organizations entering a program like PAT need to have some clarity regarding their purposes, activities, and rewards. This introduces the tangle of reimbursement and parent educator pay, especially in the urban situation and especially with the subpopulation of difficult to reach and maintain families. The problem came up early in a conversation. The summary notes began our move toward understanding.

Another item we talked a bit about was the whole issue of reimbursement for the parent educators. I really need to get that down precisely. In essence, they have to recruit their own

*caseload, they have to work out their own schedule of visits,
and they get paid with some kind of a maximum, five visits per
year per family, three of those have to be home visits.*[1]

In a very real sense, an attempt is made to give the parent educator considerable responsibility for her activities within broad guidelines. It should be noted that visits over five are not paid for. A ceiling on possible program impact, at least for home visits, has been set.[2] The efficacy for families hard to reach, maintain, and help is open for question, so it would seem. The notes continued.

*The hassle in getting the people to the group meeting interlocks with these hard to reach families because it amounts to
more work on the part of the parent educators if their caseload has very many of these people. So in a sense the entire
reimbursement system ties into how all that goes. One of my
colleagues was struck with that because she had run into similar problems in another state with social workers. In effect, its
means more work for them with either less pay or no more pay.
That's a very difficult situation. But it's not unusual within the
social service, social welfare field if I understand what she is
saying. (2/25/88)*

The further stories are those of compromise and "making do" with difficult situations as coordinators and parent educators go about their jobs. The resolutions are far from optimal ones.

Organizational Structures as Constraints

When one takes a systemic view of educational programs, as we tend to do, the simple and the obvious one step patterns, if not causal chains, sometimes obscure more effective actions that might be taken. Some of those potentially more effective steps do have their unintended hazards for the linkages "go all the way round." We saw it this way in the early notes.

*In terms of suggestions, one of the things that's come out in
some of my suggestions is the "dos" and "don'ts" kind of list as
to how to get more people in and maintain them, of these difficult to reach families. On the other hand one of the things
that's struck me is that there are some structural characteristics
of the program which are perhaps more important.*

[1,2]In Missouri, the reimbursement procedures have been altered to include payment for single contacts, and now up to 25 home visits per year for selected families.

The paragraph continued with several particulars.

> *The fact that people have to recruit their clients on the one hand then they're paid according to the number of visits that they make and the number of meetings that the clients attend means that you'll be looking for people who are "good clients" rather than looking for the ones in the category I'm supposed to be researching because it cuts into your time, it cuts into your pay, and it generally would be considered a hassle I suppose to work with those people.*
>
> *Time, pay, and hassle, and those are all my words at this point, is a pretty formidable trio of reasons to stay away from difficult to reach and hard to maintain families. A related item would be the fact that the pay of the parent educators is pretty low. We'll need to compare that with other possibilities and alternatives that the people might have. But in effect this means that many of them are working a couple of jobs or, as well as, having primary care support for families, children, parents, related others. This interacts with the time hassle and general frustrations.*

The interconnected variables continue to appear.

> *The fact that the coordinators also carry a full-time caseload, or at least some caseload, suggests that they're in an overworked category as well. They are paid both better and don't get the spring vacation off because they're on 12-month appointments. But what that amounts to is that they're also very, very heavily busy doing the first line casework care and service. This then means that the time they spend coordinating is both less and that that presumably has to suffer to some degree.*

A specific illustration clarified the general issue.

> *One real implication of that, so it seems to me, is that if the group meeting phenomenon is to come off somebody has to spend a lot of time building those groups. Essentially that could be viewed as a coordinator role. Insofar as that is a major intervening variable in reaching and maintaining those people, and just on the surface watching the kind of free flow of give and take among the people at Hawthorne particularly, a lot of effort goes into that. Much of that is carried out by one of the parent educators.*

The train of thought continued to run.

> *To me at this point that group building part of the role it seems
> is a very important issue and one that deserves an important
> amount of personnel time, and probably personnel time from
> a little bit from everybody but most significantly from the coor-
> dinator. And the question exists as to whether they have the
> time or the inclination to actually do that.*

The causal chain, and some guesses at associated probabilities, ran back
a couple more links in the next thoughts of the observer.

> *How all that restructuring would go I don't know. Lurking even
> farther behind some of this is the whole financing of the pro-
> gram. In part the people in the central office are very much
> into a cost effectiveness mode ideologically, and also are very
> close with the dollar, and that seems then to create some
> additional influence or emphasis toward the way things go.
> Who has either the political power or the inclination to cut into
> all of that is another set of issues. (4/20/88)*

Our tentative heading "organizational structures as constraints" remains
significant in our view. When things in a "natural system" are operating
as they are, and even when one knows that what seem to be "natural"
procedures are negotiated regularities, it still remains difficult to engage
in some kind of critical second thinking. What are the reasons and what
is their legitimacy in the original thinking that put the program together
the way it is?

Mixed Authority

Early on, the notes were full of the problems of getting the project underway and working our way through the various organizational
structures and processes. Doing a research project often highlights issues
that are more general. One of these was the dual lines of authority in
PAT—that of the National Center and that of the local public school district. A relevant summary paragraph appeared in the notes.

> *There's a real interesting point about the relative autonomy
> and power of the public school district which supports and
> runs the program and the statewide office which organizes
> and runs the program and which has what kind of power over
> what kinds of things. That seems to be one of continual negoti-
> ation and renegotiation. So far, knock on wood, I think I have
> been lucky. The PAT people seem impressed. (2/25/88)*

That summary grew out of a conversation I had with people from the National Center regarding how the early stages of the inquiry were progressing. That conversation revealed the broader reaches of some of the issues in bringing an "outside" program to an institution such as a public school district.

> *The key item that she wanted to talk to me about was her question about how it was going. I indicated that I was moving along steadily but slowly or perhaps slowly but steadily. I'd told her that I'd met with each of the people and gone through the document to take up any concerns or problems that anybody had. I indicated that one of the supervisors had been a bit concerned that the final final version hadn't gone through her office. And I told her about the one item which she was contentious over and the fact that that came out of an earlier language that had already been approved and that it wasn't new language. The PAT administrator was very surprised, with an accent on the very, that I was able to work out an arrangement where I called the coordinators and at times and occasions to go to meetings such as the staff meetings. . . . In the course of all of that we got straightened out that I would call the coordinators whenever I went to a center or whenever I wanted to make arrangements with a parent educator. The PAT administrator again remained surprised that I was able to do that. Anytime she or other National Center personnel go to the city they have to call the supervisor and they can't contact the coordinators directly. I told her that that's at least what my understanding of our agreements were. (2/25/88)*

The moral of this short tale is that anytime an "outside" program such as PAT comes into a school district the possibility of mixed authority and conflict exist. Negotiation must continue throughout. The problems can be increased dramatically if key individuals either have special ego needs or if they don't "hit it off" at some simple basic level. Inquiry projects, even those initiated within the broader program per se, become part of that larger context. Smith's feeling his way along illustrates the more basic organizational realities.

The Functions and Dysfunctions of Record Keeping

Organizational dilemmas appeared everywhere, as the observer went about his task of coming to understand the urban PAT program. No item seemed to be simple and straightforward. Dilemmas, trade-offs, and choices appeared even in such an activity as "record keeping." The observer's latent values came to the fore in the summary observations and *interpretations*.

Another item is the record-keeping which seems to run all through everything and seems to put a quality of surveillance in the program that would drive me batty. But anyway it's there.

Interestingly, everybody's kind of checking on everybody and trying to make everybody accountable, from individuals on up through supervisors, etc. There are funny kinds of wrinkles where people ultimately get caught up even if they're falsifying records. Sheila was telling me that occasionally that happens. Occasionally, parents will call in to the program and ask about whether they are still in the program, because they are concerned about their child getting into the preschool center for there is some saving of places for preschool for people who have been in the PAT program. Then it will all of a sudden start unraveling where the parent educator who has been responsible for the family has been recording visits and the parent says that they haven't had any visits. Then it hits the fan. So in a sense the records don't work, yet in another sense they do become evidence for someone who has been cheating, when they find out where they've been signing in. In that sense they are legally caught, I presume.

But so much effort goes into all of these bureaucratic mechanisms that might well go into the program per se—if people could be trusted, if people were doing the work, and if people were bound by more general professional norms rather than more worker oriented accountability norms. There's an entire section that needs to be done on the dysfunctions of certain bureaucratic mechanisms. (2/23/88)

Falsification of visits was not a big problem in the program. Time spent on record keeping was the bane of everyone's existence, and most parent educators were busy always trying to keep up. The records had other functions, especially when turnover occurred among the parent educators, for replacements could be made with relatively little difficulty in maintaining continuity of the program. Similarly, year-to-year continuity was also maintained. That, too, was a large problem.

Evaluation Dilemmas: Locally and More Broadly[3]

Getting acquainted with program personnel is a continuous process during open-ended observational inquiry. The blend of initial observations and "tell me a bit about what you are up to in the program" brings considerable information, images, and ideas that then are processed through later observations and conversations. In time, patterns appear that are anchored in considerable later data, evidence, and inter-

---

[3]The evolving PAT evaluation addresses some of these issues.

pretation. But, as we have argued elsewhere, those first views have their own vividness and potency. One of these was with a program evaluator.

> *I had a long hour and a half talk yesterday with one of the National Center evaluators. He's in the throes of the multiple demands on an evaluation person. It's a real mixed bag of conflicting and difficult to integrate items. On the one hand, the administration apparently runs a pretty financially tight ship. A limited budget occurs in terms of doing all the variety of things that need to be done. That's a continuing hassle and restraint that somehow I find very, very difficult to live with. As it turns out the separate funding from the Foundation on my project seems to alleviate much of that. Don't know for sure though.*
>
> *In my perspective that sort of business relates to the kind of "fatal flaw" that exists in the main summative evaluation project. They don't have a control group that is developed out of some initial randomization of people. Politically that might not be possible. But the problem is that they went ahead and got lots of things going, and they are now trying to retrieve and salvage what could be argued as a nonsalvagable flaw in the design. Most of the alternatives of different kinds of comparison groups don't meet the arguments of parents who are trying to do things for their kids. Getting that kind of control is very difficult. There are horrendous sampling problems as we're finding in the variations within the city, the different sites within and between. There are also heavy limitations about testing in neighboring states and finding appropriate sites in neighboring states. Whether any of the schools will spend their money on that or whether the administration will be able to spend Missouri money in Kansas or Illinois is another question.*
>
> *And there are items related to a research advisory committee which is on the organizational charts but which has not been talked about or discussed with any clarity in meetings I have attended. . . . Again that's not totally clear to me. Who's to do what kind of work on that and related things again is not clear. Lots of ambiguity. (2/18/88)*

Large complicated issues interplayed with limited resources and with questions of priorities and central support. Beyond occasional conversations we chose not to get pulled into an even larger set of problems with our own difficulties with limited resources. That decision might well be second guessed.

Reconstruing Summative Evaluation

As first images of the urban PAT program began to accumulate, we had conversations with evaluators and other members of the PAT National Center staff. Many of these ideas developed along the distinction made by Scriven (1969) regarding summative and formative evaluation. Summative evaluation determines the effectiveness of a program with its clients, for example what changes have occurred in the children who participate. Formative evaluation refers to the kinds of observations and data that are fed back into the program toward its improvement (e.g., our attempt to look at aspects of improving the program for difficult families, "reaching, maintaining, and helping"). Although our effort was mainly formative, from time to time the conversations and the observations led to major conjectures about issues in summative evaluation and the assumptions in the earlier evaluation of PAT.

> *In addition I think there needs to be some continuing redoing of the original pilot kind of research, as the program has "softened," or in terms of what I perceived to be softened: the qualifications of the people who are running the program, the time commitments of parents in terms of much less than the one monthly group meeting and one individual meeting per month to something like the four or five or six overall meetings per year. That's a huge and drastic slippage. In the sense of the several group meetings I've been to where there have been somewhere between three and a half dozen or so parents out of groups of a possible 600 or 700 don't bode well for the clout of the program. Similarly, in the shift from parents who are first parents as the more powerful group a la Burton White et al., also has been softened to all kinds of parents. In addition, the people who are doing the parent education work, the run of the mill staff, are, so it seems to me very different than the Wilmas and the Sheilas and the Helenes who have been around for a long time and who have major experiential and training credentials. I don't see that in the average parent educator so far. Lots of variability among them with some very interesting and talented people. But at the same time there's much less commitment and true belief about the program in the newer people who are more like low paid functionaries rather than committed idealists, which is closer to the people running the program.*

Further conjectures lead back into the complexity of the kind of summative evaluation needed in programs like PAT.

All that suggests a timeline on the flow of the program from its initial enthusiastic collection of true believers to the more moderate in beliefs and more average in ability groups of people who then follow in the wake of the action and the rhetoric of the early group. The action and rhetoric of that early group becomes the standard by which all of the public information, the facades, the ideology and the public accounts are given. That reality doesn't exist in the day-to-day life of the program.

Smith then reflected back into an earlier as well as ongoing study of the Kensington School, an innovative attempt at school reform (Smith & Keith, 1971; Smith et al., 1986, 1987, 1988) in the Milford School District.

That's sort of an overall image or model coming out of the Kensington project which may well need to be tested in some detail in the Parents as Teachers' program. It seems to me that's a nice connection, a nice interplay between what we've done before and what exists now at that much larger level. (3/6/88)

Contrasts in facades and realities exist everywhere in the literature of new educational programs. Coming to terms with those issues is a very difficult problem in program evaluation. Our qualitative observational and interview study of the "mundane" day-to-day events in the program produces the kind of data that facilitates formative evaluation, the needed kind of rethinking and reconstrual of a program. The flow into measuring instruments, sampling strategies, quasi-experimental designs, and experiments per se are parts of a very difficult inquiry problem. Even considering the allocation of significant resources to such an effort is a major policy dilemma.

Conclusions

In any large public policy program such as PAT, negotiations and compromises produce an organizational structure and set of processes that seem best phrased as *dilemmas*. In another sense, these dilemmas become problems that never seem to go away and that never seem capable of some final solution. In our view, they are issues that one keeps working on. We have highlighted a few of those that arose as we observed, interviewed, and talked and reflected our way through the project with difficult families in an urban community.

Minimal resources for the magnitude of the parent–child problems never seemed to disappear although various creative solutions were being invented and continually being tried out. Innovative pro-

grams attract idealistic practitioners who seem to see infinite possibilities of things that need to be or might be done. Attempts to work out
reimbursement policies and practices that make sense often have "latent
dysfunctions" with families that are difficult to reach, maintain, and
help, for these families take more time and effort and often present the
parent educators with "hassles" and "frustrations" in the ordinary day-
to-day work of parent education. New programs, from the outside, pose
what we came to call dilemmas of mixed authority—who has the power
to decide which kinds of things? Finally, our involvement made us think
again and often of the distinction between formative and summative
evaluation. The former are attempts to gather data and ideas to help in
the reformulation of a program. We perceived that to be a major way of
casting our efforts. The more summative evaluation, with its concerns
for outcomes and differential effects of the program we saw as a quagmire of difficulties. These ranged from seemingly "slight" program
changes with major differences in day to day practice and delivery of
services to problems in population instability that makes it very difficult
to gather meaningful data in preset experimental designs for different
questions different audiences would like to see answered.

Dilemmas is not a nasty word, rather it is a difficult concept.

A SUMMARY VIEW

In the course of the study, the outside observer wrote a memo that summarized some of our discussion of the St. Louis PAT program as an
organization. We reproduce this with minor editing for it suggests the
overall kind of organizational issues residing in an attempt to implement a PAT program within an urban setting. We have extended our
charge as we presented our reconstrual to be an understanding of the
difficult to reach, maintain, and also the difficult to help families. The
organizational structures and procedures in the PAT program seem
important for understanding the issues in hard to reach and maintain
families. Once again, it is difficult to talk linearly about a systemic set of
relations. Figure 6.2 attempts to capture some of this interdependence of
PAT from the supervisory perspective.

One of our contentions states that any innovator of a new program needs to know "the lay of the land" of the school district in which
he or she is to work. One part of the territory is the groups and individuals who are "players" in the drama. Another point is the key element of
authority, who tells whom what to do and who reports to whom.
Hierarchies and chains of command do exist in most if not all urban
schools. The more tightly coupled the organization (Weick, 1976), the

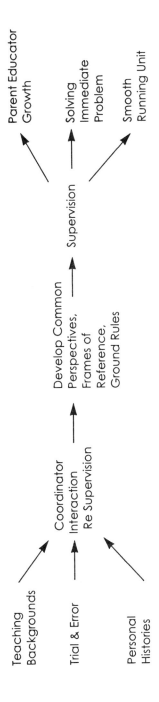

Figure 6.2. A miniature theory of PAT supervision

more one needs to attend to these structures and processes. In an early memo "Layers of Bureaucracy" (Memo 39), the outside observer raised a view of this hierarchy and the layers of organization involved.

> *Individuals who have not worked within a large urban school system often do not realize the organizational complexity, "layers of bureaucracy," if you will. To accomplish anything, such as installing or running a PAT program, attention must be paid to both the structure and the incumbents in the school district.*
>
> *In St. Louis, the layers look something like this:*
>
> > *1. Board of education*
> > *2. Superintendent of schools*
> > *3. Deputy superintendent*
> > *4. Associate superintendent*
> > *5. Executive director of state and federal programs*
> > *6. Unit director of early childhood education programs*
> > *7. Coordinators*
> > *8. Parent educators*
> > *9. Parents*
> > *10. Children*
>
> *Finding one's footing in and amongst levels and incumbents is no simple task. Although much is written into policy statements and formal rules of agreement, much remains uncodified and subject to informal understandings. Second, people at any one of the levels can be helpful and facilitative for a new program, or they can constrain, drag their heels, or directly block one's efforts. Third, individuals will have varying degrees of accuracy of self perception of their own roles, interpretations, and behavior in the events of the organization. Fourth, individuals will disagree on the nature of who is doing what, and even more importantly, why they are doing what they are doing. Fifth, these issues related to organizational structure, process, and incumbents often are very difficult to talk about openly and directly.*
>
> *Individuals who want to adopt a program such as PAT must look with care at the internal organization and the proposed PAT arrangements in their district. (Memo 39)*

With a slightly different emphasis, and one suggesting the move to processes, which we raise later and in detail in the chapter, Memo 19 raises further issues in organizational structure, chain of command, and other positions in the PAT scheme.

The formal organizational structure of the urban PAT program is quite simple. A director, "downtown," heads the program as one of several responsibilities. She reports to a higher level administrator, who, in turn, reports to an associate superintendent, and he to a deputy superintendent, and he to the superintendent. The superintendent reports to the board of education, and they are elected officials, that is, they "report" to the citizens of the community. Each board member stands for election every 3 years. For an outsider or someone beginning a new program in another city, it is important to realize that the PAT program is a part of the local public schools. It is not a social agency, nor is it an action unit of a university, nor an independent federal or state agency.

But the "director" is the key person in the overall administration of the program. The director has four "centers," each of which runs as a self contained unit of the PAT program. Each center has a "coordinator" who is responsible for the staff and activities of her center. The major category of staff members are the parent educators. These are, except for a few instances, women. They each have a "caseload" of approximately 60 families. Each family has a child between "zero" and 3 years of age.

Each center also has a secretary and an aide.

Overall, as formal organizations go, it is a fairly simple organization with a fairly simple structure. (Memo 19)

In the course of the study of St. Louis PAT, alternative ideas arose that suggest the kind of discussion we believe that needs to continue in any ongoing educational program. From our file, as illustrations of this kind of thinking about PAT as an organization, we report on one, a memo on "role differentiation in PAT."

Part of our agenda is to suggest alternative organizational arrangements that might prevail in the program. A memo on role differentiation led to further discussions and ideas. We present a glimpse of this kind of activity and thinking.

Formally, the two major service activities of the PAT program are home visits, a one-on-one relationship between a parent educator and a parent and child client and group meetings, once a month to four times a month sessions with a group of parents. Some of the centers run a "drop-in" program. Each of these activities breaks down into subactivities or tasks. And it is to these that this memo is addressed.

Many parent educators, especially new and relatively inexperienced ones, feel stressed by the recruiting process and the leading of group sessions. Different centers have begun to handle these tasks in locally differentiated ways. Coordinators, who have diverse responsibilities in administration and supervision, also tend to have more community awareness and recognition, and to have more extensive training and experience than the parent educators. And that is partly why they are coordinators.

But also within the staff, diversity in inclination, experience, and talents have led to the beginnings of role differentiation. Some individuals, often those with teacher training and classroom experience, enjoy the give and take of "teaching" the group sessions with a half dozen to 20 or more parents. Others, with little idea of lessons and lesson planning, are traumatized by the thought of "teaching" a group of parents. Others, who enjoy the one-on-one "counseling" or "tutoring" of individual parents do not like what is sometimes perceived as the "hassle" of recruiting. Part of the "reality" of the urban PAT program is that someone must recruit, for parents do not descend on the centers from a simple announcement in the newspaper or in the local school bulletins. Some of the parent educators like the outreach kind of role, visiting shelters, hospitals, and agencies and "selling" the program as one expressed it.

The question I want to raise is the degree to which the "natural" inclinations of individual parent educators should be allowed to prevail and the degree to which some specialization and differentiations of roles be allowed to occur. The dilemma then becomes one of equity—if I do such and such amount of this and you do such and such amount of that— what constitutes equivalence in our work loads? Or should there be special roles such as group leaders and recruiters? And people hired to do those tasks?

As things stand now, much of the differentiation seems to fall on the coordinators. The centers vary some in the inclinations, interests and special talents of the coordinators regarding these several tasks. They talk among themselves about the array of possibilities and how they might organize the work of their centers within the general guidelines of the program.

As we have observed and discussed these issues with staff members and among ourselves, several alternative interpretations and rationales have been espoused regarding the issue of role differentiation. From the perspective of the coordinators, every parent educator initially needs to learn and have some experience in implementing every aspect of the program in order to develop a global overview. This is a position that is shared by the National Center. Additionally, some coordinators speak of providing parent educators with growth experiences that will prepare them to assume coordinator positions should the number of program sites expand. Both parent educators and coordinators cite examples of parent educators who were initially hesitant to do on site recruitment and group meetings who eventually became quite skilled at these activities.

The special characteristics of the population being served must also be taken into consideration when making decisions such as role specialization among staff. We found that most parents, but especially those who fall into the difficult to reach and maintain category, wanted to see and interact with their own specific parent educator when they came to the center for group activities. This was especially true when parents first enrolled in the program. One solution to meeting the needs of parents and also considering the "natural" inclinations of parent educators is to have teams of parent educators plan and conduct group meetings. Within each team, parent educators exercised diversity as some parent educators more frequently facilitate parent discussions while others more frequently plan and supervise the children's activities.

The special characteristics of difficult to reach and maintain families also influence decisions regarding the recruitment process. First, as we discussed earlier, this group has been found to be most responsive to the individual face-to-face contact. In districts that serve large numbers of such families, it would be physically impossible for two or three people to make the individual contacts needed to reach a desirable number of families. Attempts to recruit during the summer months and build up a waiting list of families to be served in the fall are limited by a second characteristic of this group—their extreme mobility. Failure to immediately follow-up on a referral frequently results in loss of contact with the family. This foreshadows another major issue, the length of the program year. A seemingly simple solution to the problem of mobility would be to offer the program year round. But this carries a fiscal note and speaks to the larger issue of limited resources.

Thus, the method that seems to work best at the present time is to have a large cadre of recruiters working at the same time and also have the capability of providing timely follow up with parent education services. The question then becomes what strategies can programs adopt that will take advantage of the natural inclinations of parent educators and at the same time enhance their skills and self-confidence in areas of "low inclination." The St. Louis program has successfully used inservice training followed by teaming new parent educator/recruiters with skilled experienced parent educator/recruiters.

CONCLUDING A SYSTEMIC VIEW

This has become a long, but very important chapter. The PAT program is not only a set of curriculum issues and a set of teaching issues, it is also a large set of organizational issues. We would argue that adopters or adapters of the Missouri program, especially for the urban community and the subgroup of the population we have called "difficult families: hard to reach, maintain, and help" must look very closely to these problems.

Educational politics is not a bad word in our lexicon, rather it is an attempt to formulate policies and programs to meet community needs. Implementing these policies demands resources, often in short supply, which raises further difficult choices among many citizens and professional staff. We found the coordinator's position and role to be especially critical in the working of the program in St. Louis. The four women were fascinating professionals. The parent educators, some local and indigenous members of the community and some from "across town" and the suburbs brought different strengths and limitations. The selection, inservice training, and continuing development of this staff was a never ending and challenging part of organizational structure and process. Outside experts played in and out of the program. Dilemmas seemed an appropriate way to phrase the complexities of the "system" we observed and participated in. These varied from minimal resources to reimbursement procedures to mixed authority relationships. Evaluation was an ever present problem for multiple reasons. Finally, we made mention of the layers of organizational structures that exist in a large public school system and how the program flowed in an out of those structures and processes as alternative practices were created and tried out. Possibilities and constraints exist in partially open systems, so we found and worked in and around.

section
four

A Concluding Perspective

We were tempted to call this concluding section "a final perspective" but that seemed to belie both the intent and the substance of our inquiry efforts.

Reconstrual has appeared throughout our work. Essentially, we are trying for a new view, a problem redefinition, an alternative construction of the PAT program as it works its way through an urban community, in this instance the city of St. Louis. Furthermore, it is not just the PAT program that interests us. Rather, as in the title of our book, *Urban Parent Education: Dilemmas and Resolutions*, our goals are larger. The PAT program is a major particular and concrete instance for thinking through concerns for urban parent education in other forms and in other communities. "Dilemmas and Resolutions" extends our reconstrual into realms of politics and action. Our belief is that no simple set of rules or formulas will answer issues that are truly dilemmas where well intentioned individuals can disagree. Resolutions, as when choices are made and practices carried out by working professionals, are also never so clear-cut and universal as one might hope for in another kind of world. Reflection and thought are always front and center in those dialogues, decisions, choices, and actions. A tentativeness exists. Committed relativism is one individual's phrasing of the point of view (Perry, 1968) and the reflective practitioner is another's label (Schon, 1983, 1987).

This last chapter is more than a simple summary, conclusions, and implications. In its broader and farther reaches it is a reconstrual of program implementation and evaluation, best exemplified in Figure 7.1. In that, we attempt to combine the array of players in the Missouri urban parent education program, the settings and activities in which they are involved, and a model of practical reasoning in action. We believe this perspective grounds and buttresses the highly differentiated and quite specific set of recommendations we then raise. If a reader is to quarrel with or support any one of the recommendations, then he or she is led back into the larger context of the recommendation. Trade-offs immediately are apparent.

We believe that moves such as these extend our thinking—and that of the readers—well beyond the particular Parent as Teachers program in St. Louis, Missouri into a wide variety of social programs and their evaluation. "Manuals," at least in their more traditional forms are an endangered species, and legitimately so from our perspective.

chapter
seven

Summary, Conclusions, and Recommendations

A PERSPECTIVE

Brief summary or concluding statements to long research reports, practitioner manuals, or monographs and books seem an anomaly if not a contradiction. Our hopes continue to outrun our reach. Yet that is what we are about here. Ironies abound.

Our initial research focus on difficult to reach and maintain urban families in the PAT program has undergone a major revision and extension. Now we phrase our problem as "Families in Difficult Situations: Reaching, Maintaining, and Helping." Our data remain tied to one urban community, the city of St. Louis. However, as our report evolved, we found ourselves believing that our ideas and interpretations, and our recommendations as well, ran far beyond this one community.

We hold a particular, if not special, view of the relation of educational and social science to educational and social practice. The kind of educational and social science we do is "practice-based," that is, it grows directly out of programs in action, rather than out of disciplinary concerns, such as psychology or sociology. In this instance, the PAT program as it operates in the City of St. Louis is the program in action.

Furthermore, we believe that the qualitative field research stance we took in this study implies a set of methods and techniques useful for understanding educational and social programs. Participant observation and open-ended interviewing are two of these techniques. We have strong commitments to blending the best of experience near and experience distant theoretical conceptions, that is, the ideas of the people in the program and the ideas of outside commentators. In effect, we want to know how participants see the PAT world, and we want to bring our own broader ideas and perspectives into dialogue with the ideas of the program participants. That integration is no mean task as well.

One of the "practical" ways we have gone about our work lies in the very nature of the two of us as co-researchers and co-authors, our "inside–outside" relationship. One of us comes from the university with a variety of interests in education and social science and a long history of involvement in teaching teachers and doing research in the schools. The other comes from a career in teaching young children and adolescents and an involvement in the PAT program since its inception in the city of St. Louis. This brings a special form that others have called the necessary ingredients of detachment and involvement in field research. This interpersonal relationship complements our own individual abilities in moving back and forth on this important involvement–detachment continuum. Our relationship also helps to frame what we are doing as "action research," empirical and rational inquiry into one's own practices, programs, and institutions with the intent of improving those actions and socioeducational structures.

We need to voice a summary word about the premises underlying our work. We have strong commitments to the public schools, to the role of local, state, and national governments in providing leadership and resources to the public schools and, in turn, to the role of the schools in the development of infants and young children, as well as with children from 6 to 18 years, toward a society that is liberating, caring, and egalitarian.

Within this general position we take on a low key advocacy position and perspective. We believe that our hard to reach, maintain, and help families are a special group in our society that need special attention. The children in this group of families are at high risk for later problems in school and in society. We believe that the PAT program is one among a number that can make a difference in altering the probabilities of children's later success in school, and, still later, the children's development into independent, caring, and responsible citizens in the community. Much of this perspective is anchored in our general social idealism, in the array of educational research and practice literature, such as that described and argued in Schorr's (1988) book, *Within Our Reach: Breaking the Cycle of Disadvantage*, as well as our direct experience in the PAT program and this particular research project. Our findings grow explicitly out of the field research project. Our recommendations return always, even though circuitously and distally in some instances, to ways and means of solving the problems of the hard to reach, maintain, and help urban families. That is our central focus.

Finally, we believe all this comes together in a report that is descriptive yet analytical, that tells stories yet makes conceptual interpretations, and that accounts for what is, yet makes recommendations about what might or ought to be. "Principles in context and action" is our summary phrasing of our position. Such a product is the result of our deliberations over the last several years and might be seen as an instance of that form of thinking known as practical reasoning.

AUDIENCE, PROBLEM, AND METHOD

The Initial Perspective

When we began our investigation we had several guiding ideas in mind regarding what we were about. We wanted to produce a "manual" that would be useful to several audiences. Urban school administrators who might want to adopt or adapt the PAT program in their communities within Missouri or from other states were clearly one focus. During the actual time we were writing the initial proposal for this research project a telephone call came to the National Center from a school administrator in Naples, Florida about the adaptability of the PAT program for his community. "The man from Naples" became a guiding image. What could we say to him and his staff that would be helpful? Urban coordinators and parent educators who were working directly with clients and with the tangle of problems we called initially "difficult to reach and maintain families" were another audience. We wanted to be of help to them as they thought about their day-to-day activities. Furthermore, we wanted a manual that would enable evaluators and trainers of parent educators from the PAT National Center, and from institutions of higher education, to carry on with more insight and effectiveness their activities with hard to reach , maintain, and help urban families. Finally, we wanted a statement that would enhance the perceptions and thought of those individuals in the Missouri State Legislature and the Missouri State Department of Education, as well as those from other interested states, who had, or might have, a fundamental responsibility for the program at that level. Our audiences were multiple and varied. Multiple audiences create difficult reporting and writing problems, and they demand a kind of tolerance among individuals in any one audience subset for the needs of other practitioners in other subsets.

In what we called in the proposal, "an agenda of research questions and foreshadowed problems," we developed five categories of issues: recruitment, service delivery, attrition, characteristics of effective parent educators, and educational processes (Proposal, pp. 5-7). The overall report spoke to each of these categories of issues, and their subcategories as well, in considerable detail, approximately several hundred pages.

At one level, the importance of the overall research problem seems obvious. The proposal clarified our special view of the need for the study.

> Stress-producing environments associated with poverty, adolescent parenthood, single-parent households, and lack of parenting knowledge and skills due to limited education and/or ability can be found in every community, but are heavily concentrated in the inner cities. As the PAT program expands within Missouri and is replicated in other states, increasing numbers of families are being served who exhibit multiple characteristics that are assumed to result in risks for the child. There is a pressing need, therefore, to systematically observe, record, and document adaptations that are found to be successful in achieving program goals with such families. (Proposal, p. 5)

We still believe this to be true, but we believe also that our report represents a significant step toward understanding and meeting these informational needs.

The research methods we used need a word or two in this summary chapter. The methods are not the usual pre-set experimental design with control groups and pre and post measures nor were the methods those of the usual structured social survey questionnaire with random or stratified samples of participants that one finds in educational research and evaluation. Rather, we elected, as we said in the proposal:

> The basic thrust of the proposal is toward bringing a qualitative, ethnographic, participant observer perspective to the central issue of how the adaptation is working and what might be done additionally to enhance the program's success in future replications and extensions of the program to other communities. The product of the documentation effort would be a final report in the form of a "manual." The report would be a mix of (1) quite concrete narrative episodes of events, (2) an attempt to interrelate the particulars in a broader conceptual structure, and (3) a move to both particular and general suggestions and recommendations for strengthening the program. (Proposal, p. 2)

We believe we have a book that tells interesting and important stories of particular people in action, that brings these specific and particular episodes and events into an overall conceptual structure, a practical theory if you like, and culminates in an array of recommendations targeted to the many kinds of actors in the PAT program.

A word or two more on this kind of qualitative educational case study clarifies further what we were about as researchers and the kind of data we collected. Again, from the proposal, our initial statement was this:

> The kind of data to be collected is a "triangulated" set of field notes, summary observations and interpretations, interviews, and documents. These data come from the initial questions and the foreshadowed problems and "being around," that is attending meetings, visiting home and group sessions, talking to everyone involved, observing the "nitty-gritty" of the mundane in the day to day workings of the program. In a fundamental sense it is a "micro-analysis" of what people say and do, how they interact, what their sentiments, attitudes, and beliefs are. This gives multiple perspectives on the project and permits interpretation and suggestions to different audiences. (Proposal, p. 10)

As the project developed, one major alteration in methods occurred. In the course of initial observations and interviews, Smith found Wells to be one of the strongest advocates for the research project and one of the most analytical and articulate commentators on the PAT program. He also felt that they shared a perspective that would make working together fascinating, creative, and intellectually productive. He asked her to think about joining in the research and writing in an "inside–outside" relationship much as he had shared with a teacher, William Geoffrey, when he and Geoffrey studied Geoffrey's sixth-and-seventh grade classroom in a downtown school, two decades before. That relationship produced a book entitled The Complexities of an *Urban Classroom* (1968). Wells thought about the offer for several months and then accepted. The relationship broadened in several ways. She also sat in on Smith's seminar in Field Methods Research. Carol Klass, PAT's research coordinator, and Susan Treffeisen, PAT's coordinator of training, both from the National Center, also attended the seminar and did small qualitative studies of different aspects of the PAT program. This experience proved to be a very provocative and productive relationship for all four of us. The continuing conversations and discussions helped shape the data gathering, interpretations, and recommendations of this report.

Two "smaller" methodological events made a major difference in our work. Smith began writing "memos" based on his observations and conversations and Smith began intensive interviewing of Wells about her clients. The memos grew in number to about 50 and became further points of conversation between him and the multiple actors in the program. The interviews really became intensive analytical conversations between the two of us. The content wandered in and about all aspects of the PAT program. As we talked through the year, the conversations resulted in over 200 single-spaced typed pages of data.

As we constructed the book we drew heavily on these two sets of data and interpretations. For the reader, they represent a report of a further kind of "conversation" between Smith and Wells. In a sense, each of us "has our say" to each other in the play back and forth between the two sets of data. We believe that this is a very powerful way to talk to our multiple audiences of readers and to involve them in a more elaborated conversation about key issues in our topic—hard to reach, maintain, and help urban families.

One more aspect of the qualitative ethnographic case study research strategy and procedures needs mentioning. We follow the lead of those who want to "discover grounded theory," "construct new ways of looking at educational phenomena," "engage in problem redefinition," or "reconstrue meanings and interpretations of program events." We want a more powerful practical theory, one useful for those who deliberate at all levels within the PAT program. Two brief illustrations convey our meaning. We started with a concern for and focus on "difficult to reach and maintain families." We found another group of families that were important in the lives of parent educators working in the urban community. We called these "difficult to help" families. We reconstrued our problem then to be "difficult to reach, maintain, and help" families. That clarification enabled us to pinpoint interpretations and recommendations for practice more powerfully than before. As we argue in considerable detail in the body of the book, we believe that everyone connected with the PAT program would do well to think in these new categories. A second illustration concerns what we have called "reconstruing the parent educator role." We argue for thinking about the personal visits carried out by parent educators in terms such as *personal relationships, significant conversations*, and *informed decisions*. This is a different way of talking about the activities of the parent educator. We believe that such a reconstrual has implications for initial training of parent educators, for on-the-job supervision, and for the ways in which parent educators conceive their professional activities.

In this kind of research, the very nature of the problems under investigation change as the inquiry proceeds. We have tried to strike a balance in attending to the multiple problems identified in the initial proposal and the new issues and interpretations that arose during the study. Our book-as-"manual" is full of these ideas and the recommendations that follow on them. We summarized our overall research intent this way in the proposal:

> In short the Documentation Study will produce a readable, believable, data based account of the program in action in an urban community. It would be oriented toward the improvement of the program with suggestions for lay and professional individuals, school districts, and communities who are currently in the program or who might be making decisions about joining the program. (Proposal, p. 15)

We believe we have achieved both the letter and the spirit of that set of objectives.

A Later Perspective: A Structural Model for Findings and Recommendations

As we argued implicitly through much of this report, we have accepted the distinction between theoretical reasoning and knowledge on the one hand and practical reasoning and knowledge on the other. Furthermore, we opted for the latter. In our view, any report that makes suggestions or recommendations for improvement of existing social or educational practices or institutions falls within the category of practical thought. In effect, we are trying in a limited way on a specific program to combine our view of "what is" with "what ought to be." At the core, that is what a recommendation is all about. Also we believe that such thinking can be careful and rigorous, although different, from what is usually called scientific or theoretical reasoning.

Second, we have always liked the distinction regarding the multiple ways of representing reality. The enactive, the iconic, and the symbolic each carry their own flavor and set of advantages. Our "pictorial models" seem an approach to, if not an instance of iconic representation. One of the important advantages of a picture or figure lies in seeing the totality of a structure or process. With this in mind, in trying to think through a format for the presentation of a summary of findings and recommendations, we arrived at Figure 7.1.

The figure has three "facets." The first includes a list of the actors or players in the PAT drama. For example, the state legislature, the National Center, and the city schools (and the individuals within these organizations) are three of the key actors. The second facet contains the domains of activities and settings where the action takes place in the PAT program. The third facet is an outline of the intellectual processes in practical reasoning as these processes are tied to events in

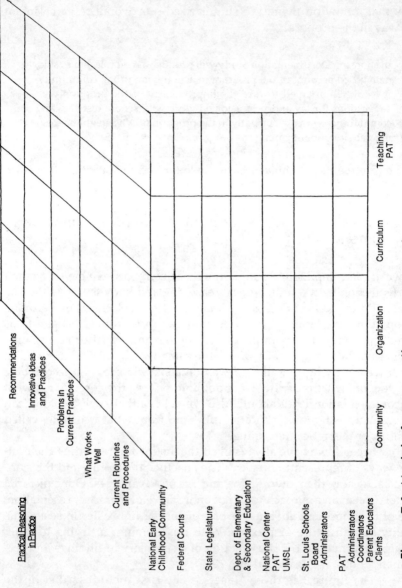

Figure 7.1. Model of an executive summary and recommendations

the program. This third dimension of the model has been the most troublesome. Overall, in our view, the model and the underlying conception is powerful, yet simple. It enables us to move away from general summaries of findings and recommendations for improvement of the program toward summaries and recommendations for an individual player in a particular place about a specific element or aspect of the program. The model enables us to suggest which individuals or groups might take responsibility for which kinds of improvements in which parts of the overall program. Finally, a systemic view is always at hand, so that any particular recommendation can be seen for its impact, directly or indirectly, on the rest of the system. Sociologists have a delightfully long and interesting label for this latter implication: They speak of "latent and unanticipated consequences of purposive social action."

Although we have not touched heavily on it, the national community of people interested in early childhood is both varied and important. Day care, early childhood programs, and urban education are in the center of national politics—presidents, senators, and congressmen speak out. Intellectual centers at many universities have similar concerns. For instance, the PAT program is one of five under study by the Harvard Family Research Project. The findings of our study are of interest to many agencies and political and professional incumbents who want to know more about PAT in general and in its workings in the urban community. The national media occasionally report on Missouri's PAT program.

In more detail, the actors at the state level include the legislature, the lobbies, the Department of Elementary and Secondary Education, the University of Missouri at St. Louis, the courts, and all the local school districts in the state. These are formidable and powerful agents that can and do make differences in education in Missouri. We assume every state will have similar actors.

At the PAT National Center the key actors are the program directors and administrators, the trainers, and the evaluators. But also, important have been the National Advisory Board, the several foundations that have supported the activities of the National Center, and individuals in the national early childhood community, some of whom have had close contact with the Missouri PAT. In a sense, other states, and their departments of education and their local school districts scattered across the country, are players as well. Our charge, in the very development of our research project, grew out of a concern for dissemination to other urban school districts in other states.

Within the St. Louis Public Schools, the Board of Education, the administrative staff, several committees, and the PAT incumbents themselves—directors, coordinators, and parent educators—have different roles and responsibilities. These are individual educators who are at the cutting edge of direct service. Their concerns have a different kind of "practicality " from those in other positions and locations in the system. The varied kinds of clients complete the dramatis personae.

We have summary views and recommendations regarding difficult to reach, maintain, and help urban families, for each of these positions and their incumbents. Within this kind of analysis, it is obvious that a recommendation to a parent educator will be very different from a recommendation to a member of a state department of education or a member of a state legislature. It should be equally obvious that the action taken by any one of the actors will influence directly or indirectly, and usually the latter, all of the other players in the system.

The second facet of the model raises the elements of the overall program in action. In general, we follow the outline of the book itself in suggesting several broad categories, each of which can be subdivided—communities and families, organizational structures and processes, and PAT curriculum and teaching. Here, too, in the ongoing program itself, everything is related systemically to everything else, yet it is possible to speak more analytically in the form of specific recommendations about each part of the program.

In regard to the third facet, practical reasoning in action, we have attended to the PAT program by analyzing it into several components:

1. Current practices and routines.
2. Those activities and processes that are going well.
3. The problems that exist in parts of the program.
4. The innovative ideas and practices we can cull from the views of the practitioners in the program, our own experience, and from the literature, that is, what people from other settings think, feel, and do in similar circumstances.
5. The recommendations that seem to follow. Organizing our observations and ideas in this form focuses and highlights the contrast between theoretical knowledge and practical knowledge.

Finally, we reiterate that our concerns always come back to those special urban families we have identified as difficult to reach, maintain, and help. That focus gives an integrity, we believe, to our intellectual efforts and to our educational idealism. Readers can then juxtapose their own situations, circumstances, agendas, and values to ours. We have great confidence in the resulting dialogue for the improvement of U.S. education as an institution, for the enlightenment of citizens in general, and to the enhancement of the PAT program in the urban community in particular.

SUMMARY OF FINDINGS

In the research proposal we stated five foreshadowed problems underlying our more general interest in hard to reach and maintain families: concerns for *recruitment, attrition, service delivery, effective parent educators,* and *educational processes* in parent education (Proposal, pp. 5-7). We were guided by a focus on "successful practices," actions, and activities that other communities might find helpful in working with populations similar to our difficult to reach and maintain urban families. As the study developed, as the analysis proceeded, and as the extended report evolved, other conceptualizations and phrasings of these issues occurred. Here we return briefly to the initial foreshadowed problems and questions as an outline for the findings.

Recruitment

Six specific items summarize our results regarding recruitment.

1. The St. Louis program successfully accents "outreach," going to centers frequented by young mothers with children. The centers included maternity hospitals, health clinics, WIC centers, offices of the division of family services, shelters for the homeless, and supermarkets. The report raises considerable detail in the subtleties in this kind of recruiting (e.g., not waiting to be approached by potential clients but engaging them in a friendly assertive manner and telling them of the program). If a child was present, the recruiter directly acknowledged him or her and noted and commented on something positive in the child's behavior.
2. The importance of personal contact and follow through is readily apparent. In a sense, the program is "sold" by the parent educator acting as recruiter. Interagency recruitment was most effective when parent educators were able to establish personal relationships with individual persons in the referring organization. The closer this person was to those who came into direct contact with parents and children the more effective the recruitment. In hospitals, this person was the head nurse on the maternity floor. At the WIC center, the WIC technician was the key person. At DFS the individual case worker was the vital link between the potential client and the PAT program.

3. Satisfied clients, those who perceive the program to be important to themselves tell and refer their sisters, cousins, and friends. This is a most important recruitment procedure. As parent educators establish themselves and their program, referrals of this kind increase. Careful follow-up is important.

4. The parent educator's display of enthusiasm for the program and her job as parent educator is a powerful dimension of recruitment. Many of the new clients learned about the program by "being around" during one or another of the personal visits, and observed the parent educator in action.

5. Effective recruitment of hard to reach families is more expensive than recruiting other families because of the time-consuming and labor-intensive character of the recruiting.

6. Assertive recruitment introduces major changes in the implementation and functioning of the program. One now has an increase in the number of difficult to maintain and help families. This takes more time, energy, and resources of the parent educator and of the PAT program. In effect, "success" in recruiting creates other problems.

Attrition

Combating attrition is a major problem. Several crucial items summarize our views.

1. Many urban families move frequently. Many are lost to the program during the summer months. Together, these two facts create the most difficult attrition and maintenance issue: the subset of problems in program continuity and in maintaining families in the long program hiatus, the 3 to 5 months during the summer time. Much of September and October is spent locating families, re-establishing contact, and reconstituting parent educator caseloads.

2. Communication with many urban families is often difficult. Many have erratic telephone service (no phone or loss of service for nonpayment of bills). Mail service often is ignored or difficult to integrate into clients' daily routines. Keeping an updated emergency contact name and telephone number of someone living in a different household as part of the record of all families was often helpful in reaching clients when contact was momentarily lost.

3. Direct personal contact, "stopping by," informally talking with relatives in extended families, becomes part of a parent

educator's repertory of techniques in keeping in touch with many hard to maintain families.

4. For those with phones, calling to reconfirm personal visits the night before or just as one is leaving the office is mandatory. Such practices increased the incidence of completed personal visit contacts. However even this does not always work. Alternatively, sending reminders of personal visits on post cards or in personal notes along with self-addressed stamped envelopes and response sheets for rescheduling visits was an effective strategy with some hard to maintain families.

5. Transportation to group meetings is a problem for many families. Public transportation is limited in St. Louis. Private automobiles are not available to many families. Paying cab fares for group meetings increases attendance significantly. Doing the phoning and arranging is quite time consuming for both parent educators and secretaries.

6. The process of trust building among hard to maintain families proceeds slowly in many instances. Many parent educators reported that they worked with some families for a full year before they felt that they and the parents were truly communicating.

7. Persistence, never giving up, on the part of a parent educator is a requisite as well. Not only does trust take a long time to establish for many "agency-hardened" clients, but every parent educator tells stories of clients who "returned" after long periods of time.

Service Delivery

Service delivery has been a major part of our descriptive and analytic inquiry.

1. The most important finding regarding service delivery, at the level of general perspectives, is the isolation of the category of "difficult to help" families. This group only partially overlaps the "difficult to reach and maintain" categories of families, our initial target group. This distinction helps in phrasing our later recommendations as well as our findings.

2. Our preliminary thinking continues by breaking the difficult to help group into subgroups. There are those families whose problems are mostly external (e.g., poverty, housing, shelter, jobs, etc.), those whose problems are mostly internal (e.g., self-oriented needs, dependency, anxiety, ambivalence to their

children, conflict with spouses and partners, etc.), and those who are a mix of the two. Recommendations for service delivery vary with the subgroups. Now we argue the need to think about the similarities and the differences among "difficult to reach," "difficult to maintain," and the several kinds of "difficult to help" families. Our monograph is replete with the details and complexity of these findings. We believe that this conceptualization adds power and specificity to thinking about and delivering of services.

3. The evolution of the Missouri PAT program from "third trimester of first time mothers" to any family with a child younger than 3 years and who might have older siblings has had massive effects on the current PAT program in St. Louis, and especially working with our targeted group of families. Information on "expectations of development," a major issue in the original framing of the PAT program is considerably less significant than in the original programs.

4. This different client population has led us, in turn, to a reconceptualization of the parent educator role. We found that some people talk about the Missouri PAT program as though it were still in the form as it was in during the pilot trials. Reconstruing the parent educators role in service delivery becomes especially critical in regard to families, living in difficult situations.

5. The reconceptualization of the parent educator role involves a view that accents concepts such as *personal relationships, significant conversations, idiosyncratic personal problems, informed decision making*, and *parent empowerment*. Although first and foremost a teacher, the parent educator's role is multifaceted. At times, the parent educator serves as a consultant, referral source, friend, source of support, social worker, counselor. By way of comparison, the relative dominance of these support roles rarely overshadowed the dominant teacher role when parent educators worked with "easy to reach, maintain, and help" families. Hypotheses on the potential causal relationships among the added concepts are equally important. Putting those ideas into day-to-day practice is a major issue in the education and supervision of parent educators. These ideas on reconstruing the parent educator role are developed further and at length in the report itself.

6. At the most practical and specific level in group meetings, we found such practices as introducing each parent and permitting them to relate an item or two about their child and the

child's development to be a powerful way to ease the parents into the discussion.

7. Group leaders varied enormously in their ability to bring parental participation into the discussions. Some parent educators are both more skilled in group activities, more interested in doing the activity, and drift into doing more of this kind of service delivery.

8. Coordinators juggled the trade-offs in continuing the parent educators' development as group leaders and in the quality of service being offered in the group meetings. Those dilemmas never seemed to end. The kind of thought processes required in resolving those dilemmas seemed not the simple application of rules.

9. In general, parent educators and other group leaders who were trained as teachers or social workers knew more about and did better at "teaching" a group lesson. Doing a more inductive, participatory kind of group discussion was the most difficult to organize and carry out by all group leaders.

10. Personal visits with families in which the parent educator had established a strong personal relationship were the most effective, as evidenced by the quality of the discussion, the vigor of participation by the parent, and the importance of the ideas and practices under discussion.

11. One part of establishing a workable relationship in the personal visit is the setting of ground rules, such as turning off the TV during the hour of the visit, for the conduct of the personal visit. Experienced teacher educators saw this in much the same vein as a teacher establishing control of her class at the beginning of the year. Once the ground rules were in place, and techniques varied in accomplishment of such an equilibrium, then "parent education" could proceed. Tactful reminders of these ground rules by parent educators occurred when parents "forgot."

12. Discussions of idiosyncratic problems of parents and children, supporting parents' attempts to "do more with their lives," and helping parents access needed community services were usually as important, and frequently appeared to be more important, than discussions of "expectations of development."

13. One of the most important simple gambits in the beginning of the personal visit was the question, "How are things going?" Parents varied as to whether they turned that into a discussion of the child's development or an account of their own lives. The more skilled parent educators wove their own planned

agenda in and out of the issues raised by the parent. Short-and long-term curriculum goals and activities were accomplished. Relevance was attained significantly.

Throughout the book, we raised a large number of additional findings. Also of considerable importance in our view are the interconnections among the findings, the seamless web of education, as one of our colleagues phrased it, and the trade-offs, the pros and the cons, among specific ideas and practices. We are a bit uncomfortable in presenting findings and recommendations for practice in this simple "listing" format. The continually changing context of each of our statements, that is, particular families and particular parent educators in a particular time and situation, makes considerable difference in the meaning of the findings. We urge our readers to consider the detail of the overall monograph.

Characteristics of Effective Parent Educators

The gradual evolution of our more social interactional perspective suggests some limits on what we called initially, the "characteristics" of parent educators. Each general statement has multiple exceptions.

1. Parent educators with backgrounds and degrees in teaching and social work brought a knowledge base that is very important for carrying out the multiple activities of being an urban parent educator.
2. Parent educators who have had children of their own or who have had extensive experience with children (e.g., classroom teaching) and who have developed an integrated workable view of those experiences have an additional formidable base of knowledge and practice skills that enable them to function well as parent educators. Most parent educators build this kind of knowledge and experience into their day-to-day personal visits. This kind of knowledge has not been well codified in the early childhood field, nor in schooling in general.
3. Individuals who are mentally healthy, that is, those who "have their acts together," and who have the knowledge and skills mentioned here made the best parent educators. These characteristics gave the parent educator a "presence" that is very important. Such parent educators represented attainable images, if not role models, for many of the young mothers.
4. Detecting these parent educator qualities in a group interview by experienced PAT coordinators seems to improve over time

and with increased interview experience. Careful selection is very important in the eyes of the coordinators who will later supervise the parent educators. Subsequent training cannot totally compensate for poor selection.

5. These personal qualities, some self-selection by clients and parent educators, and continuing supervision override general demographic variables of age, race, class, national origin, and gender in arranging caseloads and "matching" of clients and parent educators.

Educational Processes

"Findings" in the area of educational processes seem almost a misnomer. "Constructions" might be a better label.

1. Regarding evaluation and research in PAT, we believe that these inquiry activities are a form of learning for the various kinds of people involved with the program. We are concerned with what we need to know to better educate parents and children. We found that "having a significant conversation" was a better way to talk about what seemed to be happening in the personal visits than "teaching a lesson." Now we need to know more of the nature of significant conversations, of how one educates parent educators to build such a relationship. Additionally, the consequences of an hour or series of hours spent that way (i.e.) "What does a parent learn in such an experience or set of experiences?" introduces an array of educational issues.

2. We have reported many experiences of parent educators teaching mothers to observe and interpret their children's behaviors and actions. By way of example, we recall the mother who viewed her son as being "bad." This same mother, in a group meeting, observed other children acting no differently from hers and heard their mothers labeling their behavior as "normal child activity." What is it that these mothers have learned when they are able to do that? What has the aggressive child learned when he now can begin to share or to take turns? And how does this mother now view her child? And how has the parent educator "taught" all this? These are some of the teaching and learning perspectives that make up what we called in the proposal, *educational processes*. Our report contains many illustrations and ideas.

3. We have attempted to look at each of the positions in the total
    fabric of PAT, administrators, teacher educators, coordinators,
    and even action researchers such as ourselves, from the per-
    spective of teaching and learning.

Conclusion

A final part of our teaching and learning perspective takes on the special
flavor of human beings from a "systemic symbolic interactionist" perspective. The words are multisyllabic, the meanings are both simple and
powerful. By systemic we mean that each of the items we raised is connected with each of the other items. Mutual dependency exists. As we
teach and learn in one part of the system, changes occur in other parts of
the network of people and ideas. Abstracting particular items, out of
context, as we are doing here poses a number of risks in interpretation
and understanding. By symbolic interactionist we mean that human
beings and their ideas, feelings, and traits must be treated as important
in their own right and not as simple cogs in a machine or things that
someone does something to for "their own good." We have tried to look
at the world through the eyes and words of each of the participants and
categories of participants.

THE EVOLUTION OF PAT AND RECOMMENDATION

Making a recommendation is a complex social and intellectual process—
a mix of time, place, ideas, and values. The PAT program has many rep-
resentations and forms across the country and the state of Missouri. As
we have indicated it has been evolving continuously since White's early
work in New England. During the time since we began our work in St.
Louis, PAT—the National Center, the Missouri Program, and the St
Louis City Program—each have changed and grown in response to several of the issues and dilemmas highlighted in our book. For example,
The National Center has added training regarding teen parents, cultural
diversity, and environmental stress. These are major issues and major
foci for creativity in curriculum development and professional education of parent educators for urban communities and the special populations of families difficult to reach, maintain, and help. A kind of flexibility exists.

Administratively, the Missouri PAT implementation guidelines now
allow up to 25 contacts per year for families living in difficult situations.
They allow programs serving teen parents to be primarily through

group meetings. The St. Louis program has hired a small number of full-time parent educators, thereby increasing attention and commitment to the program. The difficulties and costs in recruiting have been acknowledged by making available small amounts of financial resources. Gradualism as a change strategy seems alive and well in the program.

Finally, within our recommendations and suggestions to educators locally and across the country, a lingering question remains: Is the program with its varied and multiple elements and its evolving nature strong enough for the tasks set by our special population, urban families with difficulties? Are the changes to the degree necessary? In these recommendations we speak also to the need for continuing inquiry and evaluation.

THE NATIONAL CENTER: RECOMMENDATIONS

At this point, we return to the model in Figure 7.1. From a combination of data on findings, perceived problems, alternative possibilities, and an explicit set of our values that are rooted in freedom, caring, and equity we offer explicit ideas for urban educators who might adopt and adapt the PAT program for difficult to reach, maintain, and help urban families. We have a number of recommendations to make.

The PAT National Center has several central functions—contributing to state policymaking, carrying out a diffuse kind of general statewide administration of PAT, contributing in a major way to parent educator training in the state and elsewhere, and through funding from outside foundations, originating and managing a program of research and evaluation. Each of these functions is shared with one or more of the other "actors" in the PAT drama. Because of the National Center's location within the structure of PAT in the state and within the framework of our general model, we make a series of recommendations to it regarding the hard to reach, maintain, and help urban families. In effect, many of these ideas and suggestions might be made more directly to the State Legislature or the Missouri Department of Elementary and Secondary Education.

Policy

Interestingly, as one works on a specific, but important problem (e.g., the hard to reach and maintain urban families) thoughts of a more general sort, policy issues, are implicated immediately. Throughout this book, we wrote of many of these. Here, we sketch some implications and recommendations that seem to follow from our descriptions, analyses, and value stance.

Recommendation 1—Continue policy of universal access.

The most general policy of PAT in Missouri is that of universal access. It has great appeal to multiple constituencies—rural, urban and suburban, Catholic and Protestant, White and Black, male and female. Additionally, no stigmas are attached to joining the program. Universal appeals can be made in recruitment. The program is not just for parents and children who "need" it, as defined by some group of legislators or educators.

Recommendation 2—Continue advocacy policy for our target population.

We argue and recommend that the National Center continue to advocate with the legislature for increased funds, especially for our targeted population. The biggest negative aspect of a universal access policy is cost. Universal programs by their very nature of servicing everyone cost more to implement. A second negative consequence is that the "difficult to reach, maintain, and help families," tend to require more resources in each of the categories of reaching, maintaining, and helping. This then makes for a "special" argument within universal access.

Recommendation 3—Reconstrue difficult families as families with difficulties: reaching, maintaining, and helping.

In thinking about families with difficulties, we believe that the more differentiated idea of "reaching, maintaining, and helping" allows all actors in PAT from legislators to direct service persons (i.e., parent educators) to think more carefully and analytically about the group of families that were thought to have special needs and who became the focus of this study. The distinctions allows one to see that solving one problem, for example successfully recruiting the hard to reach, creates attrition problems, that is, maintaining families in the program. The distinctions suggest different kinds of activities for resolving different and only partly related problems.

Recommendation 4—Reconstrue the parent educator role.

One of the most significant policy shifts from the initial Missouri pilot program to the development of the Missouri statewide program occurred in moving from a focus on first-time parents to an open program for any parent with a child younger than 3. This has extended services, but it has also dramatically affected the parent population in the PAT program, and, consequently, the nature of the parent educator role.

In effect, the parent educator has to "re-educate" parents rather than help establish an initial pattern of beliefs and practices regarding parenting. Our special population of difficult families accents further these changes. Rather than dealing primarily with "expectations about next stages" parent educators are faced with multiple and idiosyncratic "perceived problems." The reconstrual concerns a greater accent on the more in-depth "personal relationship" between parent and parent educator, with personal visits that take on the form of "significant conversations," and with outcomes of parental "informed choices."

Recommendation 5—Reimbursable activities should be expanded to include informal and attempted contacts.

Most of the families in our target group received an average of five reimbursable contacts. This number in no way represents the number of attempts that went into finalizing those contacts. Neither does it accurately reflect the number of informal contacts such as telephoning and "dropping by" to see how things are going and to set or confirm the next appointment. Thus it is more costly and time consuming to serve hard to maintain and help families. We believe that consideration should be given to including such activities in the reimbursement formula.

Recommendation 6—The National Center and its advisory board should continue to give high priority and attention to issues and practices regarding the hard to reach, maintain, and help families.

One of the most striking aspects of program policy is its continual growth with new ideas. Beginning with White's work at the core, the influx of national figures (e.g., Zigler and Brazleton) and their ideas have been a part of the continuing intellectual and practical evolution of the Missouri program. Arranging that, intellectually, politically and financially is both necessary and difficult. The benefits are obvious in program vitality, transformation, and growth. This has a further positive outcome, a contribution to the national political scene and debate in early childhood education.

Administration

Despite voices to the contrary, we believe that educational innovation is very much a political process, a process that takes a kind of leadership well beyond the technical (Selznick, 1957; Smith et al., 1988). Anyone adopting a program like PAT needs a leader who can work with the state legislature, foundations, the variety of local boards and superinten-

dents, as well as the scholars and academics in early childhood education and parent education. This is no small and simple task. School districts adopting and adapting the PAT program for urban schools must
look carefully to these considerations if they are to be as successful as
the Missouri program.

     *Recommendation 7—Increase the financial base of the National
Center.*

     In our view, these procedural differences in the above recom-
mendation occur not only because of stylistic differences but also from
the limited size and resources of the National Center. Time, energy, and
people are not available for follow up in planning, training, and evaluation to handle the large and necessary initiatives in these areas. As one
of the staff in the city commented, "collaboration takes time, and time
costs money." The most feasible source of the core support is state and
federal funding.

     The resource issue is not just a simple one of "more and more,"
but also one of a set of beliefs: how taut should a ship like PAT be run,
the limits in what one can convince legislators to spend, and strategies for
expanding the program. Obviously, special populations such as difficult
families magnify some of these concerns. Communities that begin urban
programs like PAT need to think through these issues very carefully.

Research and Evaluation

In PAT's current organization, the National Center is the locus of
research and evaluation activities of the PAT program. When we began
our work the revised Program Guide mentioned only three pieces of
research and evaluation, of which our study is one. Klass' January, 1989
proposed "Five Year Evaluation Plan" suggested a larger agenda of significant research and evaluation,some of which has been actively pursued. Two of the proposals "Hard core' impoverished communities"
and "teen families" bear directly on populations similar to the hard to
reach, maintain, and help families in the present study.

     *Recommendation 8—Involve the public and private universities as
research collaborators with PAT.*

     In the light of limited resources, of both a financial and trained
personnel sort, the various universities, and especially UM-St. Louis
where PAT was housed, should be invited to participate in the continuing study of PAT and its many facets. An invigorated program of doc-

toral students in early childhood education could increase the knowledge base of PAT significantly, at quite reasonable cost. A report such as ours could be one major document in giving an initial focus to such inquiry activities.

Recommendation 9—Extend "inside–outside" action research activities.

As a small prefatory point, we feel that the "inside-outside" kind of relationship, one from the university and one from the PAT program, that we have had as co-investigators of the inquiry project underlying this book is a very powerful way of studying ongoing educational programs. We do not believe it is idiosyncratic to us as individuals nor to the special relationship we have established. We would strongly recommend that other combinations of individuals be brought together on the various substantive problems within the program. In our view, it is a rare form of collaboration. Furthermore, it exemplifies some of the best possibilities of "action research" (Elliott, 1991), a much needed genre of research in schooling if programs are to be improved and if staff members are to be educated further and are to remain committed to the array of professional activities which is PAT.

Recommendation 10—Develop further focused experimental studies of issues and subpopulations within PAT.

In the course of carrying out our study, one of our most significant "findings" about the history of the evaluation of the PAT program is that the only in-depth quasi-experimental study involving a reasonably similar control group of parents and children occurred in the initial pilot project. At that time the parents were all first time parents, as in the White model. They received much more intensive services (approximately 12 contacts) than the minimum of five reimbursable visits per year (at least three of which must be home visits) as defined by the current law. In that first study, none of the families was from either of the two major urban areas in Missouri. And our targeted sample of difficult to reach, maintain, and help families did not receive special attention in the analysis. We feel experimentation should be continued. We feel that the need for this kind of data, on a sample of difficult urban families like ours, warrants special consideration. Initiating this process is one of our major recommendations regarding evaluation of difficult families.

Recommendation 11—Proceed with "basic" research on measurement issues with preschool children and parents.

In any program such as PAT, and particularly with families with difficulties, both parents and children, that we have observed, we believe the usual paper-and-pencil tests, survey questionnaires, and context free interviews have great weaknesses. We have strong commitments to a variety of measuring procedures: on-site time sampling observation techniques, Piagetian type interviews, and video camera and tape technology with parents, children, and parent educators and the interactions among these several groups. Although some might see this as diversion of funds into "basic research," our view is that some of the things one wants to know about project processes and project outcomes can be obtained validly only with these more sophisticated, time consuming, and expensive procedures.

Recommendation 12—Construct a Mosaic Model of Evaluation.

Each aspect of our description and analysis of families with difficulties — recruiting, supervision, personal visits, group meetings, inservice training, special populations (e.g., teen parents), and issues (e.g., discipline, social development, language development) — raises important practical issues about which all of us in PAT have considered opinions and beliefs, but that cry out for more definitive answers. A "mosaic model of evaluation" would create the tessare, the small empirical studies providing pieces of data and interpretation, that can be patterned into an overall picture, a perspective of the empirical, theoretical, and practical meaning of the program. We believe this meaning will be most significant if it continues to blend both qualitative and quantitative approaches, as in the current efforts now under way. One of our larger commitments within educational research, theory, and practice is to such rallying points as "reforms as experiments" (Campbell, 1959), "scholar teachers" (Schaefer, 1967), "schools as centers of inquiry" (Schaefer, 1967), and "action research" (Corey, 1953; and Elliott, 1991). We recommend that the PAT program of research and evaluation move in those directions.

Education and Training

Of all the parts of the PAT organization where we believe that our "manual" has important implications, the training unit and functions seem the most relevant. Our thinking cuts across the entire gamut from initial training to inservice activities. These implications follow on what we perceive to be one of our major "findings," the reconstrual of the parent educator's role. If our argument has merit, then the nature of personal relationships, of significant conversations, of informed decisions, and of parent–child relationships must be reconsidered as curriculum and teaching issues within the National Center's educational program for parent educators. Even the beginning of those discussions, and the deliberations that that entails, before curriculum development and writing begins, becomes a major task. If that takes on an empirical and theoretical quality, as well as a practical one, the kind of inquiry and evaluation demanded is large indeed.

Recommendation 13—Distinguish between training and education and accent the latter.

Along with Green (1965), Peters (1967) and others, we make a distinction between education and training. The former involves bringing the learner's intelligence into play as he or she perceives, thinks, and acts in the course of learning information, ideas, skills, and attitudes. The latter connotes learning of information, habits, and skills in more routine, rote, or indoctrinizational ways. Our report accents an attempt to move from a training to a teaching or educational perspective. As parent educators confront the variety of new situations and problems we have detailed in our report, education, beyond training and toward professional judgment, seems essential. These changes from training to education seem important for both preservice and inservice work with parent educators.

Recommendation 14—Convert the illustrations, vignettes, and interview protocols of this report into preservice and inservice teaching and learning materials.

Converting the ideas and descriptive data into learning experiences, "curricula" and "lessons" for preservice and inservice programs for parent educators is a major next step, we would hope, on the agenda of the National Center. We believe our interview excerpts and the dilemmas explicit in the memos would make excellent teaching materials. The underlying educational theory and practice, be it exemplified by David Ausubel, Jerome Bruner, Carl Rogers, or other contemporary figures, singly or in concert, abstractly and concretely, but always tied to practice, needs to be articulated.

Recommendation 15—Increase the variety of learning experiences in the continuing education of parent educators.

Modern teacher education programs (Cohn et al., 1987; Shulman, 1987a , 1987b; Sockett, 1987, and Zeichner & Liston, 1987) accent skills, reflection, and creativity in teaching. In our view, exercises in the observation of experienced parent educators, small group discussions, simulation, micro-teaching, role-playing, videotaping of teaching with attendant critique sessions, and the development of the novice parent educators' own lesson plans and curriculum units in the education of parent educators would increase their repertory of judgment, understandings, skills, and abilities. The "tutorial" one on one relationship of the parent and parent educator personal visits and the small group instruction of the PAT programs group meetings demand an array of knowledges and skills.

URBAN PAT PROGRAMS: RECOMMENDATIONS

Recruitment of Hard to Reach and Its Consequences

As we have indicated, one of the most interesting phenomena in the PAT program in the St. Louis urban community is the recruitment process. As one successfully recruits individuals who are hard to reach, then significant changes occur in the maintaining and presenting of services to the families. And this is no small change in the lives of parent educators and, consequently, in the overall program.

Recommendation 1—Recruit the hard to reach with an outreach strategy.

The city's recruitment efforts are quite varied and quite successful for those families who tend not to respond to general public announcements. The overall strategy is "outreach," going to maternity hospitals, social service agencies, shopping centers wherever pregnant women or women with young children are apt to be. The program is presented and explained. Questions are answered. Enrollment forms are passed out. Telephone numbers are exchanged. Out-of-state adopters of the program need to look very carefully at their own communities for comparable entry points. More fundamentally, the commitment to "outreach" is the major point.

Recommendation 2—Implement some degree of role specialization into parent educator roles.

Outreach recruitment activities are difficult for some parent educators; others enjoy and are very good at this kind of contact work. We believe that some specialization should occur and that some parent educators should have more recruitment responsibilities built into their workload than others.

Recommendation 3—Facilitate the complex skills in recruiting in most of the parent educators.

The skills in recruiting any parent to the PAT program, and especially the outreach recruiting of the hard to reach, are many and varied. Throughout our report we raised some of those. Observing a parent educator's work with a group of women in a shelter was one of the most provocative observations in the entire project. Her "simple, direct, honest, interested," approach, before the meeting began, proved irresistible to the mothers present. In addition, the preparation of long contact with the agency and the relationship she had with the staff are not conditions that occur without considerable time and effort. In our view, time spent this way is well spent for long-term recruiting efforts.

Recommendation 4—Recognize the costs and additional resources in successfully recruiting the hard to reach.

As one is more successful in recruiting the hard to reach then the numbers of hard to maintain also increase. There are multiple costs to such success. Those who make program policy and the local administrative staff have begun and must continue to recognize such costs. Eventually this means more time and financial resources for serving these families.

Maintaining Hard to Reach Families in the Program

The interdependency of hard to reach, maintain, and help families is both the focus of this report and one of the findings. Several large and small but important practical suggestions arose as we observed and talked about the program as it related to these difficult to maintain families. Attrition is a continuing set of issues.

Recommendation 5—Develop PAT into a 12-month program.

Problems of maintaining families in the program has many antecedents, one of the most important of which is the long summer lay-off. Transiency of several kinds is everywhere in the urban setting. The3, and sometimes 4-or 5-month, summer gap in program service creates great difficulty in finding parents in the autumn. Much of September is spent locating families who were enrolled in the prior year. One of our strongest recommendations is that the PAT program should become a 12-month program. Such a change then has other consequences and demands in an organization such as the public schools, for example increased resources and incongruency with usual organizational procedures. As one argues for changes in one spot, changes occur elsewhere. Costs must be played off against one's seriousness in wanting to improve the development of children from difficult to maintain families. Research into how much "improvement" occurs with such added service with these families is a difficult but important inquiry problem.

Recommendation 6—Realize and continue to accent the importance of persistence in working with difficult to maintain families.

In interviews, offhand conversations, and observations parent educators repeatedly told us that persistence is one of the major aspects of the parent educator's role, especially with difficult to maintain urban families. Families frequently move more than once in a year. Keeping track of the families is a major effort. Similarly, many families miss appointments. Encouraging parent educator persistence, not giving up, is the challenge.

Recommendation 7—Establish early and carefully the ground rules of the parent educator relationship to the parent.

We have had a number of things to say about the importance of the initial personal visit with our hard to maintain families. Getting the "ground rules" established on times of visits (when convenient for the parent and when unlikely to be interrupted) and conditions of visits (when TV can be turned off) is essential for a livable and workable relationship to be established. Part of being a skilled and successful parent educator is being able to set up these routines easily, reasonably, and with parental understanding and acceptance.

Recommendation 8—Use lesson plans flexibly and creatively.

With the difficult to maintain families, lesson plans become flexible gyroscopes that guide you where you want to go as you improvise and flexibly try to work with and involve the parent, respecting their immediate problems and concerns of the moment. Coordinators speak of "seasoned parent educators," those with the experience and skill to continue working easily and with success with difficult families. One does not have to be a Rogerian counselor to realize the importance of listening as a parent educator. The "How're-you-doing gambit?" (and a "How is your child doing?") at the beginning of a personal visit is powerful when it is a serious overture. It often provokes significant conversations when the parent educator listens carefully and empathetically. The conversation then flows in and out of the intended lesson. This seems important generally, but especially with the difficult to maintain families. Facilitating this is a major recommendation.

Difficult to Help Families

In the substantive part of our description and interpretation, one of the most significant "findings" involved the creation and differentiation of a category of families as "difficult to help." This then broke into subgroups, those mostly with external problems, those mostly with internal problems, and those with a complex combination of both. Although these ideas need considerable further clarification, both empirically and conceptually, our recommendations follow on our beginning analysis.

Recommendation 9—Reconstrue the parent educator role.

The most central recommendation for difficult to help families lies in the needed and observed change in the parent educator role and relationship. As important as it is, information about anticipated child development stages is not sufficient. We believe that the policy change from serving families who are first-time parents to serving parents with two or three children, and now, a change in bringing into the program the harder to reach, maintain, and help families, the job of the parent educator has become different in degree if not kind. In our longer description and analysis we spoke of more intense "personal relationships" between the parent educator and the parent and the shift in the personal visit from more of a "lesson" to more of a "significant conversation." While each is "education," and each appears in the PAT Program as constituted, a change in emphasis appears. We recommend that program staff at all levels begin thinking in these terms. As we have indicated elsewhere, we believe that this change in emphasis has major consequences for selection, training, and supervision of parent educators. Further related specific recommendations appear at several points in this summary and conclusion.

Recommendation 10—Identify and develop the skills and understandings necessary in working with extended families.

The complexity of extended families pose a variant of family context from most of the families discussed in the manuals and earlier statements about the program. Our recommendations here focus mostly on having parent educators realize some of the dilemmas they as parent educators often, but again not always, face. For instance, grandmothers of the child (the mother's mother) often exert considerable control and authority, because the parent and the child are living in her home. When parent educators intervene and "empower" the parent, antagonism may well arise with the parent's mother. Furthermore, when the program "advice" runs counter to the grandmother's beliefs about child-rearing, further complications set in. Realizing this, talking about it, and seeking support from the grandmother, we feel, becomes part of the parent educator's job. This can take considerable time. When the triangular relationship with the grandmother works, it adds a substantial resource for the young parent.

Recommendation 11—Build a "difficult to help" category into the thinking of parent educators.

As we saw unique events and patterns we created and borrowed labels for ideas that seemed important to us. One set of these involved such phenomena as "not enjoying the child's development," "affective distance between the mother and the child," and "too many problems with which to cope." Figuring out how to deal with these aspects of "difficult to help" families is a major long run agenda for the parent education program in general and for parent educators in particular. Building trust, doing referrals, and continuing the PAT home visits were some of our initial thoughts. The theory and practice implications spin out well beyond into selecting, teaching and educating parent educators, doing curriculum development, and carrying out program evaluation. We keep seeing, and trying to convince others, of this fuller agenda for PAT.

Recommendation 12—Know and use referrals and the available (even if shrinking) services of other agencies.

For those adopting a PAT program knowing when to seek outside help is one of the most important skills that a parent educator must have in working with the targeted families who are the focus of our report. Throughout our observations, we have been struck by a growing awareness of the shrinking base of available social service resources for families who cannot afford to pay even the lowest amount on a sliding fee scale. It appears that all of the agencies that are designed to serve our target group are victims of inadequate budgets. Clearly the watch phrase of the future is "interagency collaboration."

Recommendation 13 — Base programs in local elementary schools.

Only one of the centers that we observed approached being a neighborhood center where parents walked to the center and regularly participated in the "stay and play" times. As consideration is given to expanding funding in Missouri in order to offer the program to increasingly larger percentages, and with both the pros and cons of arguments regarding desegregation efforts and local schools, we recommend that thought also be given to basing the program in each local elementary school. With particular reference to our target population of hard to reach families, we believe that the goal of forging a strong and early partnership between school and home is facilitated when the family relates not to "a" school or school system but to "the" school that their children will eventually attend. Principals and school personnel would know parents and children before they entered the formal school setting. By coming to the local school for group meetings parents would become accustomed to the school setting in a nonthreatening way. At the other extreme, young middle class families who are returning to the city from the suburbs frequently choose to send their school aged children to private or parochial schools. Often they harbor negative stereotypes of urban schools. We believe that positive early involvement and control of their local schools through the PAT program may go a long way towards encouraging these parents to send their school aged children to public schools.

Parent Educator Activities and Relationships

Recommendation 14—Continue to utilize critical moments in the personal visits with parents.

For a long time we have been enamored with the concept of critical moments in teaching and learning. The move away from a clientele of first-time parents in the third trimester of a pregnancy seems a real loss in terms of having impact on parenting skills, concepts, and attitudes. Rather than helping shape the initial parental view of the parent–child relationship, the parent educators' job often is changing and rebuilding an already established set of beliefs and practices. That is a different and often more difficult task.

In the course of our inquiry, another variant of the term, *critical moment*, arose. A number of illustrations occurred of critical moments for joining and staying with the PAT program. These occasions tempered the meaning of hard to reach, maintain, and help. Parents, single mothers especially, in the midst of small and large crises seemed particularly susceptible to program influence. Instances of recent divorce, of recent moves to the community, of being isolated from the mother's parents and family or being in conflict with the child's grandparents for any number of reasons, all suggest critical moments or perhaps "critical situations." The core meaning seems to be times and occasions when parents need and recognize the need for special help. Programs and parent educators attuned and responsive to such conditions seem more likely to succeed in their objectives. Time and energy on such matters would seem to be well spent.

Recommendation 15—Develop skill in using impromptu contacts.

Phrasing critical moments and situations from the perspective of the parent educator raises a pattern we have called "impromptu contact." We have been impressed with the frequency and importance of the informal telephone contact between many parents and parent educators. It is one of those "uncounted for reimbursement" activities that takes an enormous amount of time and which contributes substantially to the program. Calls are initiated both ways: from parent educator to client and from parent to the parent educator. They occur at odd times during the day and evening. They involve difficulties with the children or aspects of the personal lives of the parents that impinge on the children. Parent educators who foster these contacts are more influential in the lives of their parents and hence are more successful in reaching program goals. Some parent educators fall more easily into such activities and relationships than others. Encouraging and helping with this is an important supervisory activity.

Recommendation 16—Experiment with and investigate the use of male parent educators.

One of the more striking characteristics of educational institutions in general and the PAT program more specifically is the dearth of male practitioners. Within the St. Louis Public Schools' program there are only three male parent educators. Much has been written elsewhere about the negative consequences of such staffing patterns, particularly for children from female-headed single-parent households. Within this family group, males, especially young Black males, appear to be at the greatest risk. Given that a significant majority of the families that fall into the hard to reach, maintain, and help categories are female-headed single-parent households and coupled with what we know about the potency of role modeling, we believe that a concerted effort should be made to include more males among the ranks of parent educators. Our feelings regarding this arose late in our discussions. For several reasons we did not gather extended data on these parent educators.

Recommendation 17—Move toward full-time parent educators.

We are not so naive as to think that a move to male parent educators is a simple undertaking. It involves revising some of our major belief systems regarding gender identification and the values society places on certain roles. This inevitably leads into discussions of full-time versus part-time, benefits versus no benefits, livable wage versus supplementary wage. To paraphrase a male teacher at an alternative high school who was very attuned to the need for a male perspective in working with teen parents, he responded to a query as to what it would take to convince him to become a parent educator: "You've got to pay a livable wage." He was not particularly interested in working part time. The three male parent educators all worked multiple jobs. Many single mother parent educators face the same problem.

We are fiscal realists who are well aware of the budget constraints that confront educational and social service communities. We also realize that for many the present part-time structure of the parent educator position is ideal. But we would also argue strongly for some full-time positions to continue to attract the special classes of parent educators that will be needed to work effectively with at-risk families.

Curricular Issues

Recommendation 17—Have a clear perspective on program goals, such as success in school.

For those considering adopting a PAT, one important emphasis program, and one that we would support, is the need to keep one eye on the long-term potential consequences of the program, helping the child toward later school development. Although not the only legitimate long-

term goal, it is one that unites many stakeholders in the PAT program. It
supports an interest in the quality of the child's life at the moment.
Helping parents and helping parents relate to their children right now
we assume is related to the child's long-term success in school, but
these, too, are also important. Working with the dilemma continually in
mind is a major recommendation.

*Recommendation 18—Attend to idiosyncratic personal problems as a
major goal with difficult families.*

For us, "idiosyncratic personal problems" of parents and children loomed large as a complex set of goals and activities within the
program. For instance, in one interview, the parent educator reported a
mother's comment, "I'm not doing enough with my life," as she was
burdened with the problems of a young child. For another, the child's
temper tantrums filled most of the mother's thinking time about her
child. For hard to reach, maintain, and help families these idiosyncratic
personal views and problems seemed even larger and more important
as agenda items for discussion among program leaders, curriculum
developers, and for future inservice training of parent educators. In this
volume we have barely begun the kind of thinking needed to see the
implications for curriculum, not to mention the kind of research on practice suggested by the phenomenon.

*Recommendation 19—Include more than child development informa-
tion as part of the curricular offering.*

In off hand moments, parents and parent educators reflected on
broader goals of the program—helping parents obtain school credentials
and get jobs on the one hand, and helping parents and children live in a
more equitable and integrated society on the other. Dependency,
empowerment, and raising one's children better became intertwined.
PAT has many meanings in the day-to-day lives of staff and clients.
These meanings enter into their actions and interactions. We believe that
this creates a continuing and important agenda for PAT at each organizational level.

*Recommendation 20—Teach parents "ways of thinking" as well as
information.*

One of the most successful curricular tactics of several of the
parent educators is what we have labeled as *ways of thinking.* We were
struck with phrases such as "listing your alternatives" and "And so,

what do we do now?" used by parent educators. In the personal visits they tried to move parents to a consideration of the very concrete alternatives available to the parent in her immediate situation with these particular problems. "Realistic-problem-solving-into-action-now" might be another way of phrasing their intent. Many of the parent educators worked very hard at these skills, even with the most difficult to help clients. Educationists argue a good bit about the desirability and feasibility of teaching children of all ages thinking skills. Here we are arguing that improving thinking skills is an appropriate curricular objective with difficult to reach, maintain, and help parents. As we read the program guidelines, (e.g., pp. 29-33) the labels *intellectual skills* in parenting, or *intuitive and analytical thinking* in parenting, or *cognitive processes* in parenting, or *problem-solving skills* in parenting do not appear. With some of our most successful parent educators working with difficult families, these were major curricular items.

Teaching Issues

In the body of the report we have had much to say about the parent educator as teacher. Here we highlight and re-emphasize a few of the points made earlier. Many of these recommendations overlap those we raised in the education of parent educators. Here we shift the focus to parent educators working with parents and children.

Recommendation 21—Increase one's repertory of lesson types and activities as a parent educator.

As our observations of personal visits and group meetings cumulated we came to a point of view that argued for a wider domain of types of "lessons." We illustrated this with the continuum that might range from a Carl Rogers or a Jerome Bruner "inductive approach" on the one end to a more Robert Gagne or David Ausubel "expository approach" on the other end. Engaging in significant conversations with parents is part of this variety. This has implications for early "training" or "teaching" of parent "educators," and for the way in which the parent educators then construe and carry out their activities. It is not the "rightness" or "wrongness" of any one position in general, but rather the variety of possibilities available in the repertory of parent educators and the educators of parent educators as they find themselves in the varied and complex teaching and learning situations in the urban community. As indicated elsewhere these are the ideas and skills taught in good preservice and inservice teacher education programs.

Recommendation 22—Clarify both conceptually and concretely "where a parent is."

An old principle of teaching suggests that the teacher find out what the student knows, and begin teaching him or her at that point. Much of our concern about teaching parents with multiple kinds of difficulties is finding out the idiosyncratic nature of them and their situations and beginning there. Again the principle is simple, the doing it with a particular client takes on subtle shades of meaning. It demands the best of one's teaching skills.

Organizational Issues

Whenever an educational program of any magnitude is implemented within a school district, organizational issues come to the fore. As organizational formats are created, someone is called on to administer them, for ties to the larger permanent organization must be made. Responsibility and coordination become part of the fabric of the innovative program. A number of recommendations concerning the adoption and adaptation of the PAT program follow from these observations and conclusions.

Recommendation 23—Recognize and work creatively within the specific organizational context of the local district.

The PAT program in St. Louis exists in a context of several organizations—the state department of education, the federal courts, the National Center and several advisory bodies. Each of these, as we have indicated, plays an important part in the way the PAT program in the city functions. The families living in difficult situations are a particular instance of this. For anyone who will adopt or adapt such a program achieving clarity in the nature and number of these organizations and how PAT will relate to them is mandatory. The organizational context is a major kind of reality for any new program.

Recommendation 24—Build in monitoring procedures.

Administrators, supervisors, and coordinators need to develop simple procedures that monitor the activities of program personnel such as parent educators with a minimum of excess paper work and loss of trust, and yet keep the PAT organization functioning smoothly in the interests of parents and children. The occasional, periodic call to parents regarding their participation in the program works well in St. Louis as a continuing check on parent educators and the reporting and recording of "phantom visits."

Recommendation 25—Build in a first-line supervisory staff.

In the St. Louis PAT program, the coordinators were the key immediate administrators and supervisors. They continued to carry a parent educator client load, although reduced in numbers. Overall that kind of first line supervisory responsibility seemed to work quite well in this large urban school system.

Recommendation 26—Deal clearly and directly with safety of PAT personnel.

Personal safety of parent educators is an organizational and community issue requiring discussion early in the institutionalization of a PAT program. With care and prudence, parent educators move easily throughout the St. Louis community. Little of the program is offered at night. Calling parents immediately beforehand and having them waiting or watching for the parent educator is helpful for entering and getting acquainted within apartments, housing projects, and neighborhoods. Discussions at staff meetings were helpful here. In some instances, experienced parent educators accompanied newer ones into new neighborhoods. These seemed to be successful procedures.

Recommendation 27—Acquaint oneself with and enjoy the diversity of the urban community.

As always, "insights" depend more than a bit on where one sits or where one has been or toward where one is moving. We have been struck with the diversity of the St. Louis community. Parent educators need to know and experience this early. A mix of "walking the streets" and reading seems a feasible recommendation. Those of us from St. Louis have an advantage in the work of sociologists such as Sandy Schoenberg and her colleagues. They have published booklets on St. Louis neighborhoods, *Soulard, Carondelet, The Ville,* and *The Hill,* as well a more general book, *Neighborhoods that Work* (Schoenberg & Rosenbaum, 1980). Presumably other cities will have similar resources. Community identity becomes a resource for parent educators.

In summary, we have collated a number of recommendations with a focus on "the urban school district." The ideas grow out of the experience with one district, St. Louis. We believe that much of this is generalizable to other districts and school personnel. We urge that such individuals consider carefully our suggestions.

THE FARTHER REACH OF PAT:
FROM ST. LOUIS TO OTHER COMMUNITIES

Conclusion and Recommendation

Doing this kind of action research in the collaborative, inside–outside kind of style left us with several summary views, conclusions, and recommendations that seemed to run much farther out from the program per se, yet that seemed of too much significance to leave unsaid. As individuals growing up within several miles of each other in the City of St. Louis, but separated by the personal–social differences of age, gender, social class, and race, we found a number of our experiences in this research project raised broad and general findings and recommendations. Although we have focused more on immediate issues of families in difficult circumstances, reaching and bringing them into the program, and once in, maintaining them in the program, and finally helping them, the hard to help, these other more distal findings and suggestions for other communities we speak of these items as "the longer reach of PAT."

Broader Perspectives and Context

Recommendation 1—Continue to battle simplistic stereotypes, prejudice, and discrimination.

One of our shared observations is the overriding importance of doing battle with stereotypes. Over the long run, stereotypes are among the most difficult problems in making the PAT more successful with the hard to reach, maintain, and help urban families. Both of us has encountered Whites who feel everything "east of Skinker Blvd.," that is, in the City of St. Louis, is "poor, Black, and bad." We have found Blacks who seem paranoid to the point of finding evil intent in the actions of any White individual. Taking individuals and events, one by one, on their own terms, and in their relationship to PAT goals and program is both difficult and necessary. The interplay of averages and variability in social and educational phenomena is a difficult path to find and even more difficult to walk. In part, we are advocating—with this family, in this situation, at this time, what can we do to move toward a more egalitarian, caring, and integrated community of professionals and citizens. Another large issue concerns what we call *realism*. In and amongst the individual perceptions, stereotypes, and evaluations of programmatic events and practices, we believe that some aspects can be viewed with considerable agreement among observers both inside and outside the program. Others will see our perception and interpretation of these same events as rose-tinted-glass optimism, and still others will see our views of the events as negativism on our part. Neither is our intention. Continued working toward common perceptions of events and clear labeling of those events should be a major priority for innovators in other communities. Continually phrasing one's value stances and perspectives within this intellectual process is mandatory if one is to move toward the kind of deliberation and thinking that results in recommendations.

Recommendation 2—Bring people and specific events, a kind of normative symbolic interactionism, into manuals and discussions of PAT.

We believe discussions of programs like PAT profit from quite concrete descriptions of specific events with their situations, and actors and action, their interaction, and their personal and interpersonal sentiments. The "big" words of social science and education must be grounded in the day-to-day views of the men, women, and children in the program. We have tried to present this detail throughout, perhaps to a fault. We believe this is essential toward improving the quality of thought about families hard to reach, maintain, and help. Value-laden concepts, ideas, and theories grounded in stories and narratives of children, parents, and parent educators are part of our larger, long-term views of PAT program needs.

Recommendation 3—Enhance open dialogue throughout the program about the issues in difficult families.

Long before either of us became involved in this PAT project we were committed to the importance of "dialogue," talking frankly but empathically about the issues of urban education, as the best way of coming to grips with stereotypes and realism, optimism, and pessimism. Although this will not solve all contested issues, we feel that that is where a large portion of hope lies. Both of us found ourselves tested regarding our commitment to this principle of dialogue, nearly beyond our patience at different times, with different individuals, in and out of the program. We anticipate that innovators with urban PAT programs as their agenda will find the same experience. Many of the most difficult, broader issues, often cliched as "race, class, and gender" as they relate to parent education are difficult for many people to talk about. Our experience in St. Louis suggests that other communities adopting or adapting PAT programs need to open dialogue on these issues.

After PAT—What?

Some of our recommendations run ahead of our data and conceptualizations, but seem logical consequences of our web of empirical hypotheses and priorities among values. We speculated some about what happens to children after they leave the PAT program.

Recommendation 4—Extend follow-up programs to PAT within the public schools.

We believe that early intervention can have its effects, but other later events, relationships, and programs intervene and continue to influence importantly the way in which a child develops. One shot interventions, such as an isolated PAT program, without later supporting efforts and programs, will find, we expect, considerable regression in the child's development. We believe that this is likely to be especially true of our group of difficult to reach, maintain, and help families. We argue strongly for multiple preschool and day-care programs for ages 3 to 5 between PAT and kindergarten. Perhaps because we are educationists, we believe one strong strand of these programs should reside in the public schools. This raises important political, social, economic, and educational issues. What kind of individuals, families, schools, and communities do we want to have?

Recommendation 5—Continue involvement of parents in post PAT years.

One of the central tenets of PAT is the involvement and empowerment of parents as first teachers. We believe that one part of the programming subsequent to PAT is the continued partnership with parents. School districts beginning a PAT program should look toward those post PAT years with creative strategies for later and continuing parent involvement. Obviously, ideas and resources of several kinds will be needed.

OVERALL SUMMARY AND CONCLUSIONS

We have focused and refocused on the problems of difficult to reach, maintain, and help urban families in the PAT Program.

We observed the program in detail, interviewed people at all levels of the program, and read multiple program documents over a period of several years. This kind of qualitative field study, although different from the experiment and the social survey, has its own kind of power as an inquiry method.

The PAT program in St. Louis is alive and well. The successful recruiting of hard to reach parents has led to more families who are hard to maintain in the program. We observed and related the many ways in which attrition is being battled. We initiated discussions regarding urban families whom we called "hard to help." This idea was latent in the talk and thought of program personnel. In isolating it, bringing it to the attention of ourselves and others in the program, we have begun what we feel is an important line of thought. Along the way, we began major discussion of reconstruing the parent educator's role.

Our recommendations varied as widely as urging aggressive, personal recruiting for reaching the hard to reach. We urged increased telephone contacts for the hard to maintain, even while noting that phone services are often problematic for this subgroup. Furthermore, we recommended that the St. Louis Schools and other districts around the country make the program a full 12 months rather than 9, for our special population of families in difficulty. Finally, the ideas and resources for helping the hard to help constituted another large set of recommendations. For our targeted urban families we raised a series of important issues in reconstruing the parent educator's role. Continued inquiry, including a strong strand of action research toward long-term improvement of the program, became another of our recommendations. All this seems important for decision makers in St. Louis, in Missouri, and in other urban locales that want to adopt or adapt important educational programs like PAT.

References

Allen, F. H. (1942). *Psychotherapy with children*. New York: Norton.

Atkin, J. M. (1973). Practice oriented inquiry: A third approach to research in education. *Educational Researcher, 2*, 3–4.

Ausubel, D. (1963). *The psychology of meaningful verbal learning*. New York: Grune & Stratton.

Ausubel, D. (1968). *Educational psychology*. New York: Holt, Rinehart & Winston.

Berlak, A., & Berlak, H. (1981). *Dilemmas of schooling*. London: Methuen.

Bernstein, B. (1971). *Class, codes, and control* (Vol. I). London: Routledge & Kegan Paul.

Bestor, A. (1970). *Backwoods utopias* (2nd ed.). Philadelphia: University of Pennsylvania Press.

Brazelton, T. B. (1981). *On becoming a family: The growth of attachment*. New York: Dell.

Bronfenbrenner, U. (1979). *The ecology of human development*. Cambridge, MA: Harvard University Press.

Bruner, J. (1960). *The process of education*. Cambridge, MA.: Harvard University Press.

Bruner, J. (1966). *Toward a theory of instruction*. Cambridge, MA: Harvard University Press.

Bruner, J. S. (1986). *Actual minds, possible worlds*. Cambridge, MA: Harvard University Press.

Campbell, D. T. (1969). Reforms as experiments. *American Psychologist,* 24, 409-429.

Carmichael, L. (Ed.). (1946). *Manual of child psychology.* New York: Wiley.

Cohn, M., Kottkamp, R., & Provenzo, E., Jr. (1987). *To be a teacher: Cases, concepts, and classroom observations.* New York: Random House.

Corey, S. M. (1953). *Action research to improve school practices.* New York: Teachers College, Columbia University.

Eliot, T. E. (1959). Toward an understanding of public school politics. *American Political Science Review, 53,* 1032-1051.

Elliott, J. (July 1978) *What is action research?* Paper presented to CARN Conference, Cambridge, England.

Elliott, J. (1991). *Action research for educational change.* Milton Keynes: Open University Press.

Etzioni, A. (1961). *A comparative analysis of complex organizations.* New York: The Free Press.

Etzioni, A. (1966). *Studies in social change.* New York: Holt, Rinehart & Winston.

Flanders, N. A. (1964). Some relationships among teacher influence, pupil attitudes, and achievement. In B. Biddle, & W. Ellena (Eds.), *Contemporary research on teacher effectiveness.* New York: Holt Rinehart & Winston.

Gagné, R. M. (1977). *The conditions of learning* (3rd ed.). New York: Holt, Rinehart & Winston.

Gilligan, C. (1983). *In a different voice: Psychological theory and women's development.* Cambridge, MA: Harvard University Press.

Glaser, B., & Strauss, A. (1967). *The discovery of grounded theory.* Chicago: Aldine.

Goodenough, F., & Rynkiewicz, L. M. (1956). *Exceptional children.* New York: Appleton-Century-Crofts.

Gould, R. (1978). *Transformations: Growth and change in adult life.* New York: Simon & Schuster.

Gould, R. L. (1992). The phases of adult life: A study in developmental psychology. *American Journal of Psychiatry, 129,* 521-531.

Hamilton, D., Jenkins, D., King, C. MacDonald, B., & Parlett, M. (Eds.). (1977). *Beyond the numbers game.* London: MacMillan.

Hexter, J. (1971). *The history primer.* New York: Basic Books.

Hunter, M. (1967). *Reinforcement.* El Segundo, CA:TIP Publications.

Hunter, M. (1971). *Teach for transfer.* El Segundo, CA:TIP Publications.

Jacobs, J. (1961). *The death and life of great American cities.* New York: Random House.

Kanner, L. (1949). *Child psychiatry.* Springfield, IL:Thomas.

Larner, M., Halpern, R., & Harkavy, O. (Eds.). (1992). *Fair start for children. Lessons learned from seven demonstration projects.* New Haven, CT: Yale University Press.

Lewin, K. (1948). *Action research and minority problems*. In K. Lewin (Ed.), *Resolving social conflicts* (pp. 201-216). New York: Harper & Brothers.

Lewis, O. (1951). *Life in a Mexican village: Tepoztlan restudied*. Urbana: University of Illinois Press.

Lewis, O. (1959). *Five families*. New York: Basic Books.

Lewis, O. (1961). *The children of Sanchez*. New York: Random House.

Maier, N. R. F. (1963). *Problem solving discussions and conferences: Leadership methods and skills*. New York: McGraw-Hill.

Malinowski, B. (1922). *The argonants of the western Pacific*. London: Routledge.

Missouri Department of Elementary and Secondary Education. (1986). *Parents as teachers program planning and implementation guide*. Jefferson City, MO: Dept. of Education and Secondary Education.

Noddings, N. (1984). *Caring*. Berkeley: University of California Press.

Ojemann, R. H. (1958). The human relations program at S.U.I. *Personnel and Guidance Journal, 37*, 199-206.

Ojemann, R. (1967). *A teaching program on human behavior and mental health: Books I-VI*. Iowa City: State University of Iowa.

Parents as Teachers, National Center. (1989). *Program Planning and Implementation Guide*. St. Louis: Author.

Perry, N. G. (1970). *Forms of intellectual and ethical development in the college years*. New York: Holt, Rinehart & Winston.

Pfannenstiel, J. C., & Seltzer, D. A. (1985). *Evaluation report: New Parents as Teachers Project*. Jefferson City, Missouri: Missouri Department of Elementary and Secondary Education.

Prescott, D. (1938). *Emotion and the educative process*. Washington, DC: ACE.

Prescott, D. (1957). *The child in the educative process*. New York: McGraw Hill.

Rogers, C. (1942). *Counseling and psychotherapy*. Boston: Houghton-Mifflin.

Rogers, C. R. (1951). *Client centered therapy*. Boston: Houghton-Mifflin.

Rogers, C. R. (1972). Learning to be free. In R. Biehler (Ed.), *Psychology applied to teaching: Selected readings*. New York: Houghton-Mifflin.

Schaefer, R. J. (1967). *The school as a center of inquiry*. New York: Harper & Row.

Schoenberg, S., & Rosenbaum, P. (1980) *Neighborhoods that work: Sources for viability in the inner city*. New Brunswick, NJ: Rutgers University Press.

Schon, D. (1983). *The reflective practitioner*. New York: Basic Books.

Schon, D. (Ed.). (1987). *Teaching the reflective practitioner*. San Francisco: Jossey-Bass

Schorr, L. (1988). *Within our reach, Breaking the cycle of disadvantage.* New York: Doubleday.

Selznick, P. (1957). *Leadership in administration.* New York: Row, Peterson.

Selznick, P. (1966). *TVA and the grass roots. A study in the sociology of formal organization.* New York: Harper & Row. (Original work published 1949)

Sheviakov, G. V., Redl, F., & Richardson, S. K. (1956). *Discipline for today's children and youth* (rev. ed.). Washington, DC: National Educational Association.

Shulman, L. (1987a). Knowledge and teaching: Foundations of the new reform. *Harvard Educational Review, 57,* 1-22.

Shulman, L. (1987b). Sounding an alarm: A reply to Socket. *Harvard Educational Review,* 473-487.

Smilansky, S. (1968). *The effects of sociodramatic play on disadvantaged preschool children.* New York: Wiley.

Smith, L. M. (1987). *Adaptation of the Parents As Teachers Program for Difficult to Reach and Maintain Urban Families: A grant proposal.* Jefferson City: Missouri Department of Elementary and Secondary Education.

Smith, L. M., & Carpenter, P. (1972). *General reinforcement package project: Qualitative observation and interpretation.* St. Ann, MO: CEMREL.

Smith, L. M., & Dwyer, D.C. (1980). *Federal policy in action: A case study of an urban education project.* Washington DC: NIE.

Smith, L. M., Dwyer, D. C., Prunty, J. J., & Kleine, P. F. (1988). *Innovation and change in schooling: History, politics, and agency.* London: The Falmer Press.

Smith, L. M., & Geoffrey, W. (1968). *The complexities of an urban classroom.* New York: Holt.

Smith, L. M., & Keith, P. (1971). *Anatomy of educational innovation.* New York: Wiley.

Smith, L. M., & Klass, C. S. (1989). Assessing the whole child. In H. Simons & J. Elliott, (Eds.) *The relationship of naturalistic inquiry to assessment and appraisal.* Milton Keynes: Open University Press.

Smith, L. M., Kleine, P. F., Prunty, J. J., & Dwyer, D. C. (1986). *Educational innovators: Then and now.* London: Falmer Press.

Smith, L. M., Prunty, J. J., Dwyer, D. C., & Kleine, P. F. (1987). *The fate of an innovative school: The history and present status of the Kensington School.* London: Falmer Press.

Smith, L. M., & Wells, W. M. (1990). *"Difficult to reach, maintain, and help" urban families in PAT: Issues, dilemmas, strategies, and resolutions in parent education.* St. Louis, MO: Final Report to Smith-Richardson Foundation.

Sockett, H. (1987). Has Shulman got the strategy right? *Harvard Educational Review, 57*, 208-219.

Taft, J. (1933). *The dynamics of therapy in a controlled relationship.* New York: MacMillan.

Torrance, E. P. (1965). *Rewarding creative behavior.* Englewood Cliffs, NJ: Prentice-Hall.

Weick, K. E. (1976). Educational organizations as loosely coupled systems. *Administrative Science Quarterly, 21*, 1-19.

White, B. (1985). *The first three years of life* (rev. ed.). New York: Prentice-Hall.

Whyte, W. E. (1955). *Street corner society.* Chicago: University of Chicago Press.

Wilson, W. J. (1987). *The truly disadvantaged.* Chicago: University of Chicago Press.

Zeichner, K., & Liston, D. (1987). Teaching teachers to reflect. *Harvard Educational Review, 57*, 23-48.

Zigler, E. (1987). Formal schooling for four-year-olds? No. *American Psychologist, 42*, 254-260.

Zigler, E., & Lang, M. (1991). *Child care choices. Balancing the needs of children, families, and society.* New York: The Free Press.

Author Index

Subject Index